The Mission Chinese Food Cookbook

The Mission Chinese Food Cookbook

DANNY BOWIEN
and CHRIS YING

An Anthony Bourdain Book

ecco

An Imprint of HarperCollinsPublishers

HarperCollins books may be purchased for educational, business, or sales promotional use. For information please e-mail the Special Markets Department at SPsales@ harpercollins.com.

FIRST EDITION

Designed by Walter Green
Photography by Andrew Rowat, Alanna Hale, Gabriele Stabile, Todd Selby, and Chris Ying

Library of Congress Cataloging-in-Publication Data has been applied for.

ISBN 978-0-06-224341-6

15 16 17 18 19   OV/QGT   10 9 8 7 6 5 4 3 2 1

For Youngmi, my strength, and Mino, my inspiration

and

For Mom, Dad, and Jami

Contents

Foreword

by Anthony Bourdain

Nothing else matters.

Only deliciousness.

There was a time when "authenticity" was a serious factor in assessing the meal you were about to have—or the one you had just had. Was this pasta sauced the way the nonnas would do it, back in Modena or Naples? Is this a "real" taco—or an American's idea of a taco?

And "cultural appropriation": this, too, was a factor.

Were those Chinese or Koreans preparing that sushi? Weren't they historical antagonists? Should I feel queasy at the prospect of a white guy serving Thai food?

All such questions became instantly quaint with the emergence of Mission Chinese.

The mutant offspring of a taco cart, a charitable pop-up, a loose gathering of chefs, it ended up metastasizing from a two-nights-a-week experiment inside Lung Shan, an existing Chinese restaurant in San Francisco's Mission District, to the hottest, hardest-to-get-into, most influential restaurant in New York.

On any given night, Mission Chinese in its original iteration, a crummy, half-assed tenement building on the Lower East Side of Manhattan, would be clogged with pleasure-seekers—many of them chefs—greedily scarfing up everything on the menu. It was a hallowed ground, with crowds spilling out into the street, forming a line of the food-obsessed who would cheerfully wait for hours. Food writers would be stacked in holding, like planes circling over O'Hare in bad weather. At every table, drunk, happy people Instagrammed their food between bites. Meanwhile, Danny Bowien, improbable King of New York, improbable host, toastmaster general, and Korean American kid from Oklahoma City, popped in and out of the kitchen, dropping teapots of mai tais (as I remember dimly, anyway) and one plate after another of sizzling, searingly delicious food in front of his deliriously happy guests.

"Oh, NO! It's *too* hot!" said chef Eric Ripert, standing suddenly bolt upright, a look of genuine alarm on his face.

He'd just had his first bite of Mission Chinese's notorious Chongqing Chicken Wings—a dish with a somewhat higher "burn quotient" than my Michelin-starred friend was used to.

He ran urgently to the bathroom, returning later with the news that the music from *Twin Peaks* was playing in there.

Eric went on to thoroughly enjoy his first Mission Chinese experience, the Salt-Cod Fried Rice being a particular highlight for him. He wouldn't return to the chicken wings that night, but the next morning my phone rang early.

It was Eric. In his French accent, still thick with sleep, he said, "We have to go back for that chicken. I've been thinking about it all night. I don't know why. I don't understand. But I think I need more."

Without knowing it, Ripert had, I believe, put his finger on one of the more important, revolutionary aspects of what Mission Chinese is doing.

Great restaurants teach us something—not just about food or hospitality, but about ourselves and our desires—that we didn't know before.

When Mario Batali's Babbo opened in 1998, it taught us that, yes, we want, maybe even *need*, beef cheeks and calves' brains and lambs' tongues in our food.

Ten years later, Dave Chang's Momofuku Ko taught us that, given the opportunity, we'd rather enjoy fine dining at a counter, dispensing with the bullshit.

And now Mission Chinese has taught us that we are, in fact, capable of experiencing much more pain while eating than we might previously have thought possible. That we can enjoy food just as spicy—maybe even spicier—than our fellow food enthusiasts in Chengdu and that, like them, we can sit there, sweating and pink-faced, mopping our necks, heads aflame, growing only more gloriously and deliriously happy. That we not only "get" what is going on in a scorching ma po tofu, but we now crave it. Have to have it.

It's like you live your whole life pretty damn sure that you don't like pain of any kind. It could be a trio of oiled-up supermodels waving that bullwhip or nipple clamp, but you ain't having any of it. Then something happens. Life changes. You learn some very dark shit about yourself. And Mission Chinese shows it to you.

But it's not just about the heat, or the fact that the food is so maddeningly, addictively flavorful. What makes Mission Chinese a game-changing enterprise (I know, it's a hideously overused term, but stay with me) is not just the democratic everybody-waits-on-line, first-come-first-served ethic, or the fact that the menu reflects, to an unusual degree, what *chefs* in particular want to eat. It's not even the whole DIY, over-the-top, supercharged, pleasure-dome-in-a-shithole thing.

It's the fact that Danny Bowien, and a few others like him—mostly first-generation immigrants from Asia—are changing, redefining, and defining *forever* what "American cuisine" really is.

America, after all, is a young country. We are still, after all these years, struggling to define in any meaningful way what it is to *be* American. We are, almost all of us, from somewhere else. Or our parents were. Or our grandparents. We don't have a national cuisine like the French. Or an imperial one like the Chinese. Our "old school" is mostly from the South—itself a reflection of African culinary traditions and ingredients, Native American foodways, French aspirations, Scots Irish appetites, and cooks who were, by and large, slaves.

The driving engine of gastronomy in America now, and the restaurants determining those things we, as consumers, diners, restaurant goers, and cookbook buyers want, crave, and will soon *demand*, are places like Mission Chinese and people like Danny Bowien. They are boiling down the Asian immigrant experience into newer, ever more reckless, ever more delicious adventures. They are taking us further and further away from the antiquated notions, long meaningless, of "the way things should be."

Cuisines—*all* cuisines—are always changing, constantly in flux. As Chinese culture moved down the China Straits into what are now Singapore and Malaysia, it changed, mutated, taking on the spices of India, the ingredients and traditions of the Malay. With Genghis Khan's conquests in the West came the spices and flavors of the Middle East and Africa.

Change is good.

So what follows is not just a cookbook. Yes, there are recipes here for some of the tastiest, most insanely flavor-packed, dangerously addictive dishes you are ever likely to find. They are the signature Mission Chinese dishes that set San Francisco, and then New York, afire.

But it's also a story—a uniquely American one—of how to do everything wrong and have it end up brilliantly, gloriously right.

Foreword
by David Chang

Danny Bowien is a chef in conflict. Since moving to New York, he's been cooking under the microscope of public interest and his story shows you just how intense that microscope can be.

But let's be clear: The attention and the scrutiny are there because Danny makes really good fucking food. It sounds like a throwaway line, "Oh, you make really good food," but no, it's a remarkable skill. You have to acquire it, learn it, practice it. It's not something that many people can do—with Danny, it's innate. He simply knows how to make things taste really good.

I had tried his food in San Francisco before he came out to New York. And, to be honest, I remember being upset that this motherfucker was doing something I've wanted to do forever. Chinese food is far and away the number one thing I eat in my life, and I love the idea of updating it. *If I weren't doing Momofuku, this is what I'd be doing*, I thought. But I got over my anger relatively quickly when I saw how well he was executing it. Danny is genuinely innovative in how he thinks about Chinese cooking. He uses his food to tell a story. In a weird way, unless you were Asian you might not have fully gotten the joke—but you still loved it. (Danny's upbringing as an Asian kid with white parents has always fascinated me. He's got some built-in Korean self-loathing, but without the overbearing tiger-parent upbringing to feed it.)

He uses his experience to make Chinese food in a way that nobody makes Chinese food. His cooking is this fantastic amalgamation of extremely thoughtful precision and totally carefree brushstrokes. When Mission Chinese NYC opened, it was a fucking

phenomenon. It was raw. It was weird. It was dirty. But if New York loves one thing more than building people up, it's tearing them down. This book is the story of a chef in our current era, about how easily you can get acclaim and fame when you have talent, which Danny has in abundance, and what happens when you fly too close to the sun.

This is a portrait of an artist that's still in progress. It is as important to people who want to learn how to make delicious Chinese food as it is for people who want to understand what makes creative people tick.

Introduction

When we started writing this cookbook, there was one Mission Chinese Food—a pop-up that had turned into a permanent resident of a no-frills Chinese restaurant in San Francisco. By the time we sent this book to press, almost three years later, we'd opened a second location in New York, closed it, reopened it, closed it again, and reopened it once more in a new location. Our publisher has been very understanding.

This is a strange cookbook, because it's not retrospective. We didn't reach the mountaintop and look back and start writing. If anything, it's a diary, written in real time as Mission Chinese has grown and changed, exploded and redefined itself. In the time it took us to produce this book, we've overhauled it completely at least twice, fretted over what we wanted to include, and revised the recipes countless times. The book is part of the fabric of the restaurant, perhaps more than any other cookbook has ever been.

We are constantly learning. I knew nothing about Chinese food when we first started—I wanted to figure out how to cook it, because I liked eating it. It's that simple. A good percentage of our signature dishes didn't result from us trying to be innovative—we just wandered our way into something new while trying to re-create something we'd eaten before. Our Salt-Cod Fried Rice is fluffy and light, because I learned how to make fried rice from Chinese cooks who've made it a million times. All I did was swap out the overwhelming funk of Chinese salt fish with milder salt cod and mackerel confit. (I still love the traditional version of salt fish fried rice, though.) Our menus have changed as we've become further steeped in the Chinese canon. In the beginning, I was addicted to the dizzying flavors of Sichuan—oily mapo tofu, tongue-numbing Chongqing chicken, fish poached in tart pickle juice—but since then my taste and experiences have expanded in a hundred directions.

I've absorbed so many unexpected lessons since we opened Mission Chinese Food in 2010, and they're all documented here. Early on in the writing process, we were hunkered down in a geodesic dome in Cazadero, California, near the Russian River, working on the book. I was writing about how proud I was that nobody from our staff in San Francisco had ever quit or been fired. The next morning I got a text message saying one of our cooks had punched another one and that I needed to come back to let him go.

This book is a record and a part of the brightest moments of my career as well as the darkest ones. A healthy portion of the advance money for this book went directly into the cost of building our first New York restaurant. And just as we thought we were getting close to finishing the book, Mission Chinese Food New York closed.

Later, when we sat down to work out the menu for the reincarnated New York restaurant, I realized I'd lost my entire recipe database. I called Chris Ying in a panic to ask if he had copies of all the recipes we were using for the cookbook. Thank god he did.

Chris is one of my best friends, the editor-in-chief of *Lucky Peach*, and the cowriter of this book. He's the one who planted the idea of a cookbook in my head. It was less than a year after we first opened in San Francisco, and he suggested we do a pop-up in China because it'd make good book material. If it seems cocky or silly that we started writing a cookbook so early in Mission Chinese Food's life, it's Chris's fault. But it also means that he's been there, in person, for all the crucial moments in the restaurant's life. He was there the day we opened (he jumped in and waited tables when he saw us drowning). He was in New York with me when I found our restaurant space and he was with me on my first trip to Sichuan Province. He's not just some writer I met and told my stories. He lived them with me.

We wrote this book in the form of a conversation, because that's how we tell stories when we're together. We interject to fill in details and press each other when we think the other guy is BS-ing. The third person in the conversation is Anthony Myint, my partner in Mission Chinese Food, the best man at my wedding, a talented chef himself, and the person who's probably done the most to help my career. If I'm the face of Mission Chinese, Anthony is the conscience.

Following each chapter of the story are recipes that were inspired by, or developed during, the period of time covered in the narrative. After the chapter set in Chengdu, for instance, you'll find recipes for Catfish à la Sichuan, Chongqing Chicken Wings, and Hot-and-Sour

Rib Tips. The back of the book contains all the recipes that don't have a specific context, along with a complete guide to the Mission Chinese Food pantry. If I had it my way, I'd just keep adding recipes to this book forever. But what this book represents is the body of work we've created to this point. Our dishes evolve every day as ingredients change and as we learn and improve our techniques, but everything in this book is presented as it's made—or was made recently—at the restaurants.

What this means is that not everything in this book is easy to cook. I didn't want to give you watered-down versions of anything. Everything can be done at home—and some things are actually pretty easy—but like I said, this is a true record of how we do things.

And finally, to those of you who have never eaten at the restaurants and are expecting a book of authentic Chinese recipes, let me just dispel that idea right now. To Chinese-food purists, the cooking at Mission Chinese Food is profane. We're not experts or historians. We're fans.

My cooking is a love-crazed ode to Chinese food. Chinese food is what I ate when I had no money, what I ate after work and on my days off. It's what my friends and I still crave above all else, what we talk about, what we get excited about. The recipes in this book are Chinese by way of Oklahoma, San Francisco, and New York. I'm so happy to share them with you.

—DANNY BOWIEN, 2015

The Miss
Chi
Fo
Cook

sion

nese

od

book

General Cooking Notes

Wok

Two pillars stand at either end of the spectrum of Chinese cooking techniques. The first is the long, slow cooking of dishes like lion's head meatballs, *dong po* pork, clay pots, and red braises. These are easily translated to the home kitchen.

The other pillar is *wok hay,* the fast-working, inimitable "breath" of a scorching-hot well-seasoned wok. *Wok hay* is everything to stir-fries, fried rice, beef chow fun, and Chinese greens. It's as much an intangible sensation of freshness and liveliness as it is a smoky, charred flavor. Employed properly, *wok hay* ensures that the various ingredients of a dish are all cooked to the proper doneness and caramelized appropriately, and that their various flavors are completely integrated.

There's no cheating this—*wok hay* is the x factor that separates Chinese restaurant cooking from home cooking. You need a jet engine for a stove, strong ventilation, a steel or iron wok, and some decent hand-eye coordination—no way around it. So what is the home cook to do? Short of rebuilding your kitchen into a Chinese restaurant, you'll never fully generate *wok hay* at home, but that's not to say you can't get close. Here are some tips for breathing some *wok hay* into your cooking:

Buy a wok and a wok ring. A good wok doesn't have to be expensive. It should be made of carbon steel or cast iron and feel comfortable in your hands. Our woks at the restaurant cost about $20. A wok ring fits around your gas burner, creating a nice, stable nest for the wok to sit on. Some specially designed versions—the WokMon, for instance—can concentrate and heighten the flames of your burner. If you've got an electric stove, you're going to have to stick to a traditional cast-iron or black steel pan. Sorry. But don't fret—so long as you give your pan plenty of time to heat up, you should still be fine executing the recipes in this book.

Season your wok. You'll find many different methods for seasoning a wok online. Our method is not for the faint of heart: First, wash the wok, scrubbing off any strange coatings it may have come with. Dry it, then fill the sink with cold water. Next, get the wok brutally hot, leaving it over medium-high heat for 8 to 10 minutes. Use an oven mitt to take it to the sink and, standing back, immerse it in the cold water. It will hiss and steam. Carefully dry it out and heat it up again, but not quite so hot this time, 3 or 4 minutes over high heat—you're going to add oil and you don't want a grease fire. Pull the wok off the heat and slick it with peanut oil. Use a paper towel to wipe out the excess oil. Now you're ready to cook.

When using your wok, heat it dry and add oil only once it is hot. At the restaurant, we use the swish-swirl-dump method of oiling a pan: Add more oil to the wok than you need, swish and swirl to coat the pan, and then dump the oil into a waiting heatproof receptacle. The oil that remains in the wok is all you need to cook with, and you can reuse the oil you dumped. (P.S. You can apply the same method with vermouth in a glass for a dry martini.)

Weak stove? Employ a mixing bowl. Stir-fry each component of the dish separately, letting the wok get very hot between each ingredient. As you finish cooking each component, dump it into the bowl. Once the individual ingredients are cooked, return everything to the wok and give the whole thing a final turn on the stove with the sauce to finish. By splitting up the ingredients initially, you'll avoid losing too much heat by overcrowding the wok.

Blanch first. At the restaurant, we always have multiple pots of boiling water at the ready. Some of the recipes in this book call for blanching before stir-frying, but you should use your judgment for other occasions when parcooking might come in handy. The point of a wok is to cook things quickly at a very high temperature. Anything you throw in the wok for a stir-fry shouldn't need more than a minute or two, tops, to be cooked perfectly.

When cooking with a wok, turn on the exhaust hood if you've got one. Otherwise, open any nearby windows. In case you haven't realized it yet, woks run hot and smoky.

Cook outdoors. While most home stoves don't have the firepower to generate real *wok hay,* an outdoor gas burner will. A roaring wood or coal fire also packs a punch, if that's within reason for you.

Spices

All spices in this book should be toasted whole, in a hot, dry pan, until fragrant before grinding. All salt is kosher.

Rice

People take rice for granted. I'm guilty of this too. We tend to think of rice as a plate on which you pile the real food. But we shouldn't. Rice has value, it has flavor. It can be cooked well, and it can be cooked poorly.

When I first started cooking Chinese food, the deeper I dove, the more I saw how many different functions rice has. I'd watch the cooks at Lung Shan wolf down an entire family-size crock of rice by themselves at lunch. For the working man, rice *is* the meal, and everything else is a bonus. But at dinner, when they were less concerned with fueling up for a long night of work, those same guys would eat only a small bowl of rice on the side of their meal. At Cantonese banquets, rice—usually fried rice or steamed sticky rice—doesn't arrive until the very end of the meal, as a follow-up to multiple delicate courses that stand up just fine without a starch component. Some dishes, like mapo tofu, need rice, but even then, it's not just about sopping up sauce. The flavor of rice is important—it's sweet, it's floral, it's a counterpoint to spice.

At the restaurant, we serve a basic run-of-the-mill jasmine rice. I'd use nicer rice, but it's too painful to watch people ask for three orders of rice and then leave most of it uneaten. I'll sometimes steam barley or peas or parcooked beans with the rice to emphasize that it's not just a pile of white fluff. Rice is important. Rice is food. Don't let its humble appearance fool you.

As far as cooking goes, rinse your rice a few times under cold water, agitating the grains with your fingers to loosen the starch from the grains. Drain, then cover with fresh cold water in a saucepan or rice cooker at a ratio of 1¼ parts water to 1 part rice. If you want to add an accoutrement like barley, add it at a ratio of 4 parts rice to 1 part barley/peas/beans/etc. Just remember that longer-cooking items like beans should be parcooked before mixing them with the rice.

Cover and simmer (or just press the Cook button) until the water is completely absorbed. You'll have to watch the rice more closely if you use a saucepan, to avoid burning the bottom of the rice. If you have the means to buy a rice cooker, I highly recommend picking one up. They're crazy simple, shut off automatically, double as steamers, and, if you measure correctly, they make perfect rice every time.

Pressure Cooker

I only recently discovered the usefulness of pressure cookers.
Like most people, I had been wary of them for years, scared off by
urban legends of kitchen explosions. But cooking in cramped kitchens
with tiny ovens obliged me to give them a shot. Rest assured, today's
pressure cookers are as safe as can be—at the restaurant, we use
one from Kuhn Rikon. We employ pressure cookers when we're testing
new braises at smaller-than-restaurant scale—meaning they're ideally
suited for home use.

The basic function of a pressure cooker is to raise the boiling point
of liquids. Under normal conditions, water can't get hotter than 212°F
without vaporizing into steam, but in a pressure cooker liquids can
reach up to 250°F, cutting down cooking times. Pressure cookers are a
straightforward, unfussy way to cook a large amount of tough protein—
beef cheeks, pork shoulder, shanks, feet, ears, etc. Pressure-
cooking is much easier and faster than braising and, in my opinion,
it intensifies flavors rather than muddling them. If you cook beans
with carrots in a pressure cooker, you can really taste the carrots. For
the home cook with limited time and space, pressure cookers are a
godsend. A couple of recipes in this book call for a pressure cooker
specifically, but you should feel free to employ one wherever you
come across a slow-cooked meat.

Mise en Place

With apologies to any professional cooks and chefs, I want to take a second to talk about *mise en place*. The term *mise en place* is French and translates as "put in place"; it refers to the gathered components of a dish, all prepped and ready to be tossed into the pan. But more important than the literal meaning is the concept—it represents planning, organization, and cleanliness. It's the foundation of all restaurant cooking, but especially Chinese cooking. When it comes to many of the stir-fried dishes in this book, the secret is having everything near at hand. Most of your effort will go into shopping and prep; the actual cooking of a dish goes by quickly. You don't want to be scanning your shelves for soy sauce or slicing greens while the other ingredients linger in your wok and burn.

New York,
Part I

When I was sixteen, I bought myself a slick new Dodge Stealth and wrecked it six days later, racing against a guy in his mom's Ford Taurus. For reasons beyond my understanding, my parents felt bad and fronted me the money for another Stealth. I was working at an optometrist's office, and I promised to pay them back.

Around the same time, my dad went through a midlife crisis and bought himself a completely impractical Trans Am with a T-top. He's a big guy, and he couldn't really fit into the car, so he had to give it up and buy a truck instead. I took over the payments on the Trans Am, and by the end of high school, I had not only paid off the second Dodge Stealth but the Trans Am as well. I also bought myself a Kawasaki Ninja.

When I was seventeen, I sold the Dodge Stealth for $6,000 and used the money to visit New York City for the first time. Six friends and I blew through the cash in eight days. In Oklahoma, they card you everywhere and it's illegal to sell beer on Sundays. They didn't card us at the bars in New York, and we lived like drunk kings for a week.

We stayed in Harlem with a friend who was really into food. She highlighted restaurants in a Zagat Guide for us and took me for my first falafel. I liked food—we passed the time in Oklahoma eating—but that week was transformative. Every meal was a new discovery for me. Even today, living in New York, I pass those same places all the time and reflect on those transcendent moments.

I decided to move to the city three years later, after finishing culinary school in San Francisco. A year and a half into my professional cooking career, I landed a job at a thirty-seat Japanese-French fine-dining place. My station was a flattop stove, sandwiched in the tiny kitchen between the chef and one of the sous chefs—both extraordinary cooks.

The chef, sous chef, and chef de cuisine were friends. When service began, the chef would always have a cold Pabst on his station. At nine p.m., their drug dealer would come by and they'd buy a bunch of cocaine, and when the kitchen got busy, they'd do some coke. The coke made them faster, and angry. I was twenty-one at the time, with long hair and tattoos. I was totally green, and they hated me. One night I was in the weeds, lagging behind. They looked at me and said, "What's your problem?"

I said, "Nothing. I'm trying to work, but you guys are yelling at me and I'm falling behind."

They walked me out to the bar and said to the bartender, "Eric, give him a double vodka and three PBRs." They stood there and watched me drink it all, then walked me back to the kitchen. It was summertime and hot as hell. I was sweating through my chef jacket, and now I was trying to cook while wasted. They were letting me fail, rooting for me to fall on my face. I didn't understand why then and I still don't.

The chef liked to do this thing where he'd soak a bar towel and tie a small knot on one end, then pop people with it. One night, in the middle of another manic service, I saw him winding up. As I reached for a pan, he snapped me in the tender spot between my forearm and bicep, and blood started trickling down my arm. I freaked out—when I see my own blood, I have a tendency to pass out. He started yelling at me to calm down, while another chef screamed from the protein station, "Stop bleeding!"

I answered back, "How?"

* * *

Chris Ying: Let's back up. You're a kid from Oklahoma who just finished culinary school in San Francisco. Other than an ill-advised $6,000 teenage bonanza, you've never been to New York. What brought you to the city? How'd you find work?

I moved to New York because if I had stayed in San Francisco, I never would have stopped partying. I wanted New York to beat me into shape. I was twenty years old and had developed a pretty good alcohol and drug habit, and I needed a change of scenery.

When I got to New York, I cold-called restaurants looking for a job. Nobody responded until I called Tribeca Grill, where, for some reason, the sous chef, Michael, actually took the call. He picked up and said, "Can you be here in twenty minutes?" I spent literally all the cash I had on a taxi and got there just in time. I gave Michael my résumé, and he showed me around and told me to come in the next day to trail—try out for the job, basically—and see how it went.

It went well enough that they hired me, and I ended up working there for a year and a half. The chef, Stephen Lewandowski, nicknamed me Loudness, because my hair reminded him of the dudes from a Japanese eighties metal band of the same name. The expediter was a Chinese guy named Jackie (as in Jackie Chan), who always called me Kimchi. I didn't know what I was doing, but I worked my ass off and was happy to be cooking for a living.

The restaurant was busy. On Mother's Day, we did something like fifteen hundred covers. The only thing I was required to do that day was

make a Cobb salad. The problem is that on Mother's Day, everyone orders the chicken Cobb. I swear to God, I must have made eight hundred salads that day. The prep cooks were handing me eight-quart containers of cherry tomatoes and buckets of chopped chicken. As I mixed each salad, I would flick my wrist behind me to shake off any dressing and cheese on my hands. I didn't realize that with each flick, I was sending a spatter of blue cheese onto the wall behind me. At the end of brunch service, the dinner cook came to take over the station and asked, "What the hell happened here?" I turned around and looked at the wall—a Jackson Pollock painting of cheese and dressing—and said, "I have no idea."

Tribeca Grill was my first cooking job. I didn't have any expectations; I just wanted to learn how to do everything. The trouble was, I'd come in and my whole station would already be set up. I never made anything. Someone prestuffed morel mushrooms with foie gras for me, and all I had to do was top the soup with them. The hot side would send over mashed potatoes and I would whip in some fat and send them back over.

I left when I saw an online listing for the position at the French-Japanese place and got the job.

Chris: You don't want to name the restaurant?

I don't want to call them out, because those guys are still cooking in restaurants, and maybe they've mellowed out. I hope they have.

Chris: Maybe they *should* be called out. But if you're nervous, fine—let's call it Bistro Teriyaki, or something fusion-y.

Anyway, I felt guilty leaving Tribeca Grill, because I'd only just grown into a cook who was of value to them, but I thought I was ready to make the jump to fine dining. I went in for the interview, and the guys were super nice and convinced me to leave my job and work for them for almost no money. I was twenty-one and had never seen the kind of food they were cooking.

The cooks there had renounced any utensils but spoons, and they made fun of me because I came from a place where we used tongs. I thought that was cool—I looked up to these guys and wanted to be part of their world. They were heroes. They had the sharpest knives and tried to be the fastest and most efficient line cooks and to execute the most difficult dishes possible. But the transition was too much, too soon. I was accustomed to making the same dishes every single day for a whole season. If I needed more *mise en place,* I could just ask someone and they would help me out. Here we cooked a constantly changing tasting menu, and it was every man for himself.

The chefs came in early, off the clock, and stayed late prepping for the next day. I'd been accustomed to getting in five minutes early, changing, and clocking in. They'd convinced me to work for $250 a week, but I was staying until three a.m., just so I didn't fall behind the next day.

Anthony Myint: You once told me a particularly heinous story about a pumpkin seed amuse-bouche. As a cook, it's always haunted me.

Holy hell, that was one of the worst nights of my life. One night a few months in, one of the chefs came up to me as I was cleaning up after service. He handed me a sauté pan, a container of grapeseed oil, and a bucket filled with pumpkin seeds. He told me to put a thin film of oil in the pan and toast the pumpkins seeds ten at a time until they ballooned up like footballs, always stirring in a clockwise direction. Then I was supposed to drain and cool them on a paper towel and finally cut each one in half with a paring knife and toss them in nori salt. "After that," he told me, "take apart the stove and scrub everything clean."

I stayed there the entire night but only managed to get the stove about 60 percent free of a year's worth of built-up carbon residue, and then I opened the restaurant in the morning. When the chef walked in, he didn't even look at the stove or ask if I'd cleaned it.

Chris: See, that sounds vindictive to me, but I'm sure some cooks would see it otherwise—like that's just the culture of the business. How much of your misery do you think was a result of them being special dickheads and how much was a matter of you being out of your element?

Looking back, I don't know if any of the dishes were as difficult as they seemed at the time, but I was young and I had no idea what I was doing. Service was a nightmare for me. The kitchen didn't use tickets to keep track of orders; they'd just call out dishes, and I wasn't able to remember them all. My palate wasn't developed yet, so I had the hardest time trying to season everything properly. Coming off my station was the "A + O + P": amuse, oyster, pudding. The pudding was an apple and olive oil gelée that I had to emulsify one tiny portion at a time with a baby whisk that was the size of a demitasse spoon. For every diner, I'd whisk a pudding, shuck oysters, and make the amuse, all while also plating salads with thirty different components and made-to-order dressing.

For a *chawanmushi* dish—a savory steamed Japanese custard—every time an order came in, we'd steam clams in white wine, then use the liquid to make dashi, cool it, whip in egg, mix in apple and duck confit, and steam the custard until it was set. I would have overcooked them constantly had the sous chef not been standing next to me, using his Jedi sense to detect when they were going to overcook, then lifting the hot lid with a spoon and throwing it at me to get my attention. I imagine if I had to work the same station with the same dishes now, I'd be fine. My complaints about the work are probably unfounded. But the abuse was legitimate.

As I was prepping, one or another of the chefs would often walk up to me, get a half inch from my face, breathe in my ear, and say, "You better not fuck anything up today." Sometimes they'd linger for a minute, standing there as I went on with my business. They hit me a few times, and sometimes threw things at me, but most of the time they were happy just to stare menacingly at me. At the end of every service, they would say things to me like, "Hey, Danny, do us a favor and hang yourself off the Williamsburg Bridge on the way home."

I'm not a religious person, but I would pray every day before work: *Please God, don't let me screw anything else up.* But things just kept deteriorating. The more I failed, the harder they pushed. Sometimes the chefs' friends would come in on their days off from their own restaurants, and they'd all stand at the pass and berate me mercilessly. One night, I lost it and blurted out, "One day, you guys will respect me," which was the least productive thing I could have done. It just gave them more ammunition to mock me.

Whenever I'd call my dad, he'd say, "I'm going to come out there and beat the chef's ass," so I stopped telling him what was going on with work. He hated the way I was living in New York—he wanted me to come home. I lived with two roommates in Williamsburg, in a neighborhood mostly populated with working-class Polish families. I was dirt poor and lived on eggs and potatoes, because they were cheap.

Chris: How'd you cook your eggs and potatoes? Fancy chef style?

Any low-budget way you can imagine. I would wrap raw potatoes in a wet paper towel and microwave them forever. Or I'd make mashed potatoes. I ate a lot of Spanish tortillas.

Anthony: If I knew the young, poor Danny, I would have told him that if you use mashed potatoes in place of raw potatoes in a tortilla, the exterior will crisp up really nicely.

Really? That's cool, but I wouldn't get too creative. Mostly I'd just boil potatoes and eat them. Sometimes I would splurge and buy ramen and make a baked potato and add it to the ramen. It was pretty gross.

Chris: Let's go back to the day you said, "You guys are going to respect me." That seems masochistic to me. Did you normally talk back like that?

No way. I never talked back. They just pushed me to a place I'd never been. When I said it, they made me do pushups right there on the line to entertain their friends, who were all drunk, laughing, after they'd just had this amazing meal at an expensive restaurant that I could never afford. I never did get to eat there.

Chris: I can't imagine standing there humiliating a cook who'd just made me dinner.

That's what I'm saying. The chefs were relentless, and they encouraged their friends to treat me like a zoo animal. On other days, they would send me on long trips to pick up food for them. An hour before service, when I was totally in the weeds, I'd have to take the train to Tribeca and get cheeseburgers and French fries from a restaurant they liked. I never got a burger of my own, and they made a point of telling me not to eat any of their fries on the way back. On my days off, if I had a little extra cash or found some change, I would pick up a White Castle burger. I'd buy one for fifty cents and nibble it in the smallest possible bites to make it last my whole walk home. When my dad eventually did come to visit, he took me to the store and bought me two 24-packs of Diet Pepsi, a big box of instant ramen, and a huge container of Utz Party Mix (the B-grade version of Doritos Munchies). I hid it all from my roommates under my bed and rationed it out to myself a little bit at a time. It hurt my dad to see how happy a little junk food made me. It hurt him to see the way I was living. But I loved being in New York, despite the difficulties. New York is electric. All things are within reach, and you can feel ten million people reaching out for something at once. Whatever my struggles in the kitchen, the minute I walked outside, everything was possible again.

I had a group of friends who were all around my age, working in different restaurants. They played in a band called Alabama Black

Snake or something like that. One guy, Brandon, worked in Manhattan at a Polish restaurant called Odessa. Boris, aka Bobbo, worked at Otto. Another guy worked for a local bar and would sell us super-cheap drinks. Bobbo eventually went on to open Uva Enoteca in San Francisco, and Brandon is now part-owner of Roberta's and Best Pizza in Brooklyn. It blows my mind to see how far those guys have come. Back then, we were just a group of underpaid, overworked kids who'd get together to have guacamole competitions and let off steam about our respective jobs.

Chris: So working at "Bistro Teriyaki" didn't kill your love for cooking.

Even while I was being clobbered at work, I was absorbing so much. Every dish was thrilling and unlike anything I'd ever tasted. There was a skate wing poached in duck fat, then pulled apart like pork shoulder. We made our own tofu and served it with *tonburi* (the seeds of an herb sometimes called field caviar). And it was the first place that I tasted *chawanmushi,* now one of my favorite dishes on earth. I became enamored of Japanese ingredients—*kanzuri* (yuzu-chili paste) and aged soybean pastes and other fermented foods that were practically impossible to find back then. Even now, if I'm cooking at home or improvising a dish, I'll probably cook something that's a combination of Japanese ingredients and French technique.

But I never set foot in the kitchen of another restaurant of that caliber again. My time there completely turned me off from working in fine dining. It wasn't the work or even the verbal abuse that turned me off, though. It was how inaccessible the food was. There was no way I could afford to eat there, and neither could anyone I cared to cook for. I don't think I could have put it into words then, as it didn't crystallize for me until much later, but what I was discovering was that if I was to going to be a cook—which was not a certainty—I wanted to cook food that my friends could eat.

Chris: So what was the tipping point? Why'd you finally leave?

About a year after I started, I was working the garde-manger (appetizer) station. There was a dish on the menu that required the hot-food side of the kitchen to slow-poach these beautiful Gulf shrimp and send them over to me to be plated. They would cook as few at a time as they could, because they didn't want anything left over at the end of the night. But sometimes people would order the dish à la carte and, combined with the tasting menus, that meant I'd have orders stacked up and not enough cooked shrimp. If I asked for more shrimp, the hot line would flip out at me. One night I called over, and the chef came barreling toward me with a ladle and said, "If you tell me you need shrimp, I'll black your eye with this ladle." I just said, "Okay, but I do need them. I have three orders." He looked me square in the face and said, "Go home."

The chefs were always telling me to go home or not come back to work. I'd ignore them and carry on with my business, and in a few minutes they'd act like it never happened. This time, the chef repeated, "No, really, go home." I looked up at him to confirm, then with tears welling up in my eyes, I walked downstairs to get changed. I figured I'd been fired. I packed my things and left. Of course, later that night the chef called and asked where the hell I'd gone. "You told me to go home! What did you want me to do?" He grumbled a bit and told me to come back the next day.

Exhausted and confused, I called my dad to talk to him about what had happened. When he picked up the phone, he told me that he'd meant to call me that night too. My brother was having a rough time. He's bipolar and had threatened to commit suicide. My dad asked me to come home to Oklahoma. Frankly, it came as a relief. I told my dad that if he bought me a ticket, I'd be there. The next morning, I called the chef and told him I was leaving. He didn't scream or yell, he only muttered that he'd have to find someone else to work the line that night. At work, those guys were complete animals, maniacs. But outside of work they were just really indifferent, unlikable people.

I left all my stuff in the apartment—my clothes, guitars, amp, everything. I arranged by phone for someone to sublet my apartment, and I asked my roommate to put my things in storage. I figured I'd be back soon. But I didn't return to New York for almost eight years. My roommate moved out and I lost touch with him. I miss those guitars.

But I didn't think twice about leaving. My family was more important to me than the job or the respect of people who thought I was a pussy. I was mentally and physically drained. I'd fallen out of love with cooking. It was a job I liked having, but at that moment, it wasn't something I could imagine doing for much longer.

Warm Egg Custard with Scallops and Ham Broth

SERVES 6 AS AN APPETIZER

Egg custards are prevalent throughout Asian cuisine.
They're all similar at heart—beaten eggs, a little broth, usually some form of seafood. Koreans like theirs fairly plain. Chinese home cooks steam whole clams in eggs. And the Japanese have *chawanmushi*.

Ours is more or less a *chawanmushi*: You mix eggs with dashi and tuck in a little surprise at the bottom of the custard—a piece of duck confit, a scallop, a mushroom. It's like the toy at the bottom of a Cracker Jack box. At the restaurant, we transform this dish with the seasons—in late summer we serve it cold, with uni and green apple.

My favorite way to eat this is when it's fresh out of the steamer, barely cooked and still wiggly. But it's easy for me to say that now, not being the one responsible for making it every day. When I was a young cook, I would catch so much flak for overcooking egg custards—don't mess it up.

1. Prepare the custard base: Whisk the eggs in a medium bowl, then add the dashi, mirin, and shoyu and whisk together well. Strain the mixture through a fine-mesh strainer or chinois into a large glass measuring cup or a pitcher with a spout. Set aside.

2. Prepare the ham broth: Combine the dashi, ham, and winter melon in a small saucepan and bring to a simmer over medium heat. Remove from the heat and allow the mixture to steep uncovered while you cook the custards.

3. Place a rack in a wide pot or roasting pan and add water to reach about 1 inch above the rack. Bring the water to a light simmer over medium heat.

Special equipment: Six 3½-inch ramekins or small heatproof glass or ceramic bowls

CUSTARD BASE
5 large eggs
2 cups Dashi (page 293)
2 tablespoons mirin
2 tablespoons shiro shoyu

HAM BROTH
1 cup Dashi (page 293)
2 ounces cured ham, such as prosciutto or country ham
½ winter melon (aka "hairy" gourd or mo gua), peeled, seeded, and thinly sliced

⅔ cup shredded cooked chicken thigh meat, such as meat from a rotisserie chicken
2 tablespoons very finely diced, peeled Granny Smith apple
3 sea scallops
2 tablespoons chopped fresh chives
1 tablespoon grated yuzu or lime zest

4.   Divide the chicken and apple evenly among the ramekins or bowls, then fill with the custard base, leaving about ¼ inch space at the top. Wrap each ramekin tightly in plastic wrap.

5.   Carefully place the ramekins on the rack in the simmering water. The water should come as high as the top of the custard base but no higher—add or remove water accordingly. Cover the pot or roasting pan with aluminum foil and simmer very gently for 8 to 10 minutes, until the edges of the custards have set but the very centers remain jiggly. Remove the ramekins and keep them wrapped until you're ready to serve; they'll continue to cook and set. Ideally, serve them within 10 minutes, but they'll keep warm for 20 minutes or so.

6.   Meanwhile, just before you're ready to serve the custards, use a slotted spoon to scoop out the ham from the broth, leaving the melon, and return the broth to a simmer. (If you like, you can slice the ham thin and use it as a garnish, but we usually discard it once it has given its flavor to the broth.)

7.   To serve, slice each scallop crosswise into 4 thin slices and place 2 slices on top of each warm custard. Top each with a tablespoon of the broth and a few slices of the poached winter melon. Finish with the chives and yuzu zest, and serve.

Chilled Egg Custard with Sea Urchin and Salmon Roe

SERVES 6 AS AN APPETIZER

Special equipment: Six 3½-inch ramekins or small heatproof glass or ceramic bowls

CUSTARD BASE
5 large eggs
2 cups Dashi (page 293)
2 tablespoons mirin
2 tablespoons shiro shoyu

¾ cup Tomato Water (recipe follows)
12 sea urchin tongues
6 tablespoons ikura (cured salmon roe)
3 tablespoons very finely diced, peeled Granny Smith apple
Extra-virgin olive oil, for drizzling

This is the refreshing summer remix of our warm egg custard (page 20).

1. Prepare the custard base: Whisk the eggs in a medium bowl, then add the dashi, mirin, and shoyu and whisk together well. Strain the mixture through a fine-mesh strainer or chinois into a large glass measuring cup or a pitcher with a spout. Set aside.

2. Place a rack in a wide pot or roasting pan and add water to reach about 1 inch above the rack. Bring the water to a light simmer over medium heat.

3. Divide the custard base evenly among the ramekins or bowls and wrap each ramekin tightly in plastic wrap.

4. Place the ramekins on the rack in the simmering water. The water should come as high as the top of the custard base but no higher—add or remove water accordingly. Cover the pan with aluminum foil and simmer very gently for 8 to 10 minutes, depending on the size of your ramekins, until the edges of the custards have set but the very centers remain jiggly. Remove the ramekins and keep them wrapped while they cool to room temperature.

5. Pop the custards in the fridge, still covered, and chill for at least 4 hours, or up to overnight.

6. To serve the custards, unwrap and top each one with 2 tablespoons of the tomato water, 2 sea urchin tongues, a tablespoon of ikura, a few pieces of apple, and a light drizzle of olive oil.

Tomato Water

MAKES ABOUT 1 CUP

¾ pound Roma (plum) tomatoes, coarsely chopped
1 garlic clove, minced
2 teaspoons kosher salt, plus more as needed
Fresh lemon juice (optional)

1. Pulse the tomatoes in a food processor until coarsely chopped into ¼-inch pieces—stop short of a puree.

2. Transfer the tomatoes to a fine-mesh strainer set over a deep bowl. (If you happen to have cheesecloth, line the strainer with it before adding the tomatoes, but it's not essential.) Stir the garlic and salt into the tomatoes—the salt will help draw out the water. Cover the entire apparatus with plastic wrap and refrigerate for at least 4 hours. If the tomato water is still draining off pretty steadily after 4 hours, let it keep going until it stops.

3. Save the tomato pulp for salsa or tomato sauce. Taste the tomato water and season to taste with more salt and/or a squeeze of lemon.

Oklahoma

I was born on May 2, 1982, in Seoul, South Korea, and adopted when I was three months old. A Christian agency that paired American parents with Korean kids sponsored my adoption. I have an older sister and a younger brother, both of whom were adopted too, but I'm the only Asian person in my family, and I was definitely the only Korean kid in my school in Oklahoma City. When my classmates saw my mom and dad, they would ask, "Are those your real parents?" and I would say, "Obviously they're not my birth parents, but they're my real parents."

When I was about seven, the adoption agency gathered a group of adopted Korean kids in Oklahoma around my age and took us to an international culture fair at the local convention center. They wanted to give us a little taste of our heritage. Inside, there were various booths representing different countries of the world, and they led us over to the Korean one. Some ladies were serving Korean sushi (*gimbap*), which I found gross. I didn't want anything to do with it. I just wanted to go home and put on my Rollerblades.

For all intents and purposes, I was raised a white kid in an Asian kid's body. I didn't read books about Korea or really concern myself with where I'd come from. I never felt uncomfortable about being adopted. Honestly, my dad was more sensitive about it than I was.

One day, when my dad came to pick me up from school, I climbed into his pickup truck and told him that two kids had called me a "chink" and put my head in the toilet and given me a swirly. (The other kids at school assumed that every Asian person was Chinese, so "chink" was a catchall slur.) My dad slammed on the brakes, spun his car around, and sped back to the school. He headed off the two kids as they were coming out. My dad's the nicest guy you'll ever meet, so I was shocked to watch him grab both kids by their collars and scream in their faces. When he got back in the car, I said, "Dad, that was insane." He sighed and looked at me and said, "Don't ever let anyone talk to you like that again."

Kids are mean, and being a kid sucks. I didn't really sweat it. And aside from the occasional bully, people in Oklahoma were friendly. Life was slow. It's the type of place where you sit out on the porch in the summer, drinking iced tea and trying not to move too much.

My dad worked for General Motors for most of his life. He never made a lot of money, but my mom knew how to stretch a dollar. She'd go grocery shopping every couple of weeks at the Buy For Less, knowing exactly what she needed. She'd fill up an entire shopping cart and have coupons for everything.

Most of our meals revolved around ground beef. Mom would buy tons of the stuff and then portion it into one-pound blocks and freeze them. Every night she'd pull out a block for Hamburger Helper, tacos, meatballs, stuffed cabbage. Occasionally she'd cook Chinese food. She would make egg rolls from a package or chop suey, which my dad liked, or she'd cook cabbage and carrots, thicken the sauce with a little bit of cornstarch, and then top it with crunchy fried lo mein noodles from a can.

Other than a stint on the wrestling team—I was recruited because the team needed someone for the seventy-five-pound weight class—my mom didn't really let me play sports, because I was so tiny. So I spent a lot of time after school with her, watching cooking shows on the small TV she usually had on in the kitchen while she cooked. She loved Justin Wilson's *Louisiana Cookin'*, and then Emeril, once he came around. When we got cable, I became fixated on Food Network and its stars. Emeril's shtick was taking things to the extreme. He could work the audience into a frenzy by "kicking it up a notch," wildly throwing extra ingredients into the pan, and shouting his catchphrase "BAM!" when in reality, he was just adding a very small amount of crushed garlic. I remember that *Molto Mario* was so informative; you couldn't stump Mario Batali with a question. And I vividly remember watching an early Bobby Flay show, where he went around with a barbecue expert to different restaurants. As much as I loved all the shows we watched, the food they were cooking was mostly just a fantasy for me. I had never tasted anything like what they were cooking, so I couldn't relate to them—Olive Garden was what I thought of when I thought about Italian food. But Bobby Flay hit home with me, because I had actually tasted barbecue.

Anthony: I don't usually think of Oklahoma as a barbecue destination. What's Oklahoma barbecue like? Is it distinctive?

Our place was called Buchanan's. They smoked meat in their parking lot. We'd get out of the car, walk up, and be immersed in barbecue smoke. A huge rack of ribs was twelve bucks. We'd get one or two for dinner, plus a loaf of white bread, barbecue sauce, and coleslaw. Oklahoma barbecue is sort of a bastard child of Kansas City– and Dallas- or Austin-style barbecue. In Texas, the big thing is brisket—just salt and pepper, no sauce. In Kansas City, it's about basting and sweet and saucy ribs. Oklahoma barbecue is in the middle. We don't have a definitive style, but we do have opinions. A properly smoked brisket is the Holy Grail to me. Smoking pork ribs is easy, but to nail a brisket, to have the fatty side cook evenly with the lean, takes skill.

Anthony: Would it be fair to say that you were the most adventurous—or dedicated—eater among your friends?

Definitely among my non-Asian friends.

Chris: I grew up in an almost entirely white part of California, and found myself gravitating toward the Asian kids. Did you do the same?

I found Asian friends, and we connected over food. My friend Chaffee's Vietnamese family would feed me things that they thought would freak me out, but I always loved it. Chaffee's mom is one of the best cooks I've ever known. And on days when Chaffee was busy, his dad and I would go out for lunch together. His dad spoke zero English, but he loved food, so we'd bond silently over dim sum at Grand House.

From time to time, I'd make my dad drive me to the Vietnamese market, so I could buy a whole cooked fish. The fishmonger would clean the fish, fry it, and douse it with fish sauce. It would smell up the car and drive my dad crazy. He'd say, "Danny, that's got the head on it still!" I'd roll my eyes and say, "Yeah, Dad, it's a fish."

In junior high, before we started drinking, my friends and I spent all our time eating. We'd hit all-you-can-eat Chinese buffets where we could get a meal, plus soda and ice cream, for five bucks. China Wok was our favorite, because of the way the manager answered the phone. We'd all gather around the phone, call him, and listen to him scream "CHINA WOK!" then repeat it louder and louder when we didn't respond. The food was delicious, though, and I always got a kick out of seeing the manager in person at the restaurant.

* * *

My mom got breast cancer when I was twelve. She fought it into remission and eventually had a double mastectomy. But then she was diagnosed with diabetes. A couple years later, on Christmas Eve, she had to have a heart transplant. She was in and out of the hospital for a lot of my childhood—so much so that it felt routine.

My mom was the cornerstone of my early years—she stayed home while my dad worked. I spent a lot of time at her side, cooking and helping out around the house. I was something of an outcast in school, never really part of any groups—my stint on the wrestling team was an exception—so I hung out with my mom. We went to church four times a week (my parents were devout Christians), and I always opted to sit with her rather than going to the kids' Bible study. But as she got sicker, it became harder for her to look after us. The less she could do, the more I took on.

During the periods when Mom was on a lot of medication for her various illnesses, she wasn't herself. I had a hard time coping with or understanding it, and I wasn't finding much support in church. Plus, I was a teenager and I wanted to get out of the house, to buy a car, to find a girlfriend, to party. My mom's sickness didn't drive me to rebel or to act out, but it did force me to fend for myself. I channeled my anxiety into work, and got my first job at thirteen, as a dishwasher at a Vietnamese restaurant. From that point on, I've always had at least one job.

My whole life, I'd been in the honors classes at school, a straight-A student. But as my mom got more and more sick and I started working, I lost interest in studying. My teachers started trotting out lines like "Danny has so much potential, if he would only apply himself. . . ." My grades turned to Cs, Ds, and Fs, but I got away with it because Dad was at work and Mom was sick. If I ditched class and the school called my house looking for me, I'd just go home and erase the message. Life outside school and church was more attractive to me. I joined a Christian band called The Stellas, and we landed a small indie record deal—nothing fancy, we had to pay for the recording sessions ourselves—and opened for some cool bands.

One afternoon, I was at the mall looking for colored contact lenses. The optometrist said, "You seem like a good kid, how old are you?" I told him I was sixteen. "What high school do you go to? Do you have a job?" He had gone to the same school, and he offered me an office job. I was working at a snow cone stand at the time, so I accepted the upgrade, started working six days a week, and stayed for three years. I really enjoyed it. I had no intention of pursuing a career in optometry, but the job gave me a safe answer when people would ask me what I wanted to do with my life. Where I'm from, most people had their whole lives figured out before they graduated from high school. So I would say, "Oh, I work at an optometrist's office and want to be an optometrist someday." Even now, I find having a safe answer to be helpful in deflecting people's questions when I don't necessarily have a real answer. From the day Mission Chinese Food opened, people have asked me what's next. I always have an answer in my back pocket—something about the various places where we might open new restaurants—but the real answer is, it could be anything.

I was working at the optometrist's office when my mom died. I was on my break, practicing wheelies on my motorcycle in the parking lot, when a sick feeling came over me. I went back to the office, and my dad called. He was crying as he told me my mom had had a heart attack and that I needed to come home. My house was about thirty minutes away from the office, but I was home in ten—I must've been going 130 miles per hour. I remember a lot of things about that day and have blocked or forgotten even more. I remember people coming over in a constant stream to try to comfort me. My youth pastor came over. I was in shock. I said to all of them, "It's okay. I'm not that upset about it." But after everyone left, I lay on my mom's bed and wept.

That night, my friend Tim picked me up to meet some friends about an hour away out in the country. We didn't talk on the drive out; we listened silently to the Smashing Pumpkins' "Mayonaise" on repeat, and when we got there, we drank in a field and listened to more music. No one but Tim knew my mom had died that day. On the drive back, both of us just looked out the windows in silence, and it was exactly what I needed—a break from people asking if I was okay and me telling them I was.

I woke up the next morning and for a moment thought that the previous day had been a dream. I stayed partly suspended in that fantasy until my dad told me that I didn't have to go to work or school, that I should take as much time as I needed. But I wanted to keep myself busy, so I went back to work immediately. I just tried to pull things together the best I could. Even though time has passed and the feelings aren't so raw anymore, they still catch me off guard from time to time.

It's a significant thing to lose a parent at a young age. It changes your worldview, like looking at a painting and someone whispering to you what they see; suddenly, you can't see it any other way. My mom was a devout Christian and would always tell us not to worry, everything would be fine, that it was all in God's hands. Losing her upended my faith. I stopped going to church. Religion doesn't have much pull for me now. On the other hand, what I lost in faith, I gained in strength. I watched my mom and dad go through so much together. My mom fought the illnesses physically, but my dad fought too. My dad's love for my mom was absolutely unconditional. There was never any question about his commitment, even when she got too sick to climb the stairs and had to sleep in a hospital bed downstairs. We'd almost finished building her a new, more comfortable house when she died. The irony was almost too much to take. Watching my dad's example of what a husband is supposed to be created a blueprint for my own life. I take so much power from my mom's death and how my dad dealt with it. Losing my mom was terrible; everything after is easier.

* * *

Our house turned into something of a boys' club after my mom died, even with my sister there. My dad got us a pool table that took up the entire living room. It was so big that you couldn't shoot from most angles without bumping into a wall. He hung a Budweiser lamp above it, like you'd find at a bar. It was nuts.

My dad spoiled us to take our minds off my mom's death. He knew that I liked going to parties and cooking for my friends, and he was scared that because I was young and dumb and had a really fast car, I'd kill myself driving drunk. So he made a deal with me that my friends could come over for cookouts and bring alcohol, as long as everyone stayed overnight. My friends would come over on Friday night, and in the morning, there would be thirty people lying on the floor. We'd make breakfast and do it all over again. Those were our weekends.

Dad did so much for the three of us, and we didn't make it easy on him. In the summer, he would wake up two hours early, load his truck up with two Jet Skis, and drive them out to the lake before he went to work. Then, when I got up, I'd drive out there with friends, ride the Jet Skis all day, drink beer, and then wait for him to come pick us up, so we wouldn't drive drunk. He'd take the other car and leave it at work, then drive all the way back and take us to Chili's.

Not long after my mom passed away, we took a family trip to Florida. My dream had been to eat at Emeril's at Universal Studios (which, in retrospect, was dumb—I should have asked to go to the one in New Orleans), and my dad obliged. I remember everything about that meal. We got crispy alligator tail with rémoulade, then gumbo, then a plate of seared beef medallions. They brought out a little copper pot of crawfish étouffée and poured it in the middle of the beef medallions, and I thought that was the coolest thing in the world. I loved that there were sliding glass doors to get into the kitchen, and that they let me take the menu home. I said to the waiter, "This is so cool. Is Emeril here right now?"

"No, man, he's not."

"Is he here usually?" my dad asked.

The guy sighed. "He's here sometimes, but he's pretty mean to the kitchen guys if they mess up."

I suppose I didn't expect them to be BAM-ing it up back there, but I was a little disappointed. My dad thanked the waiter for spoiling his son's experience.

* * *

Chris: Everyone I know who's ever met your dad has made a point of saying how nice he is. And he is—he's always treated me like we've known each other for years and years. But do you ever think he did you a disservice by cutting you so much slack?

My dad did the best he could for us. But with my mom gone and my dad trying to raise the three of us on his own, he couldn't stop my downward trajectory at school. I got expelled for mooning a guy who was on drum line with me. I had to start attending a remedial school, which consisted of kids who'd been caught selling drugs and beating up their teachers and me, the guy who had mooned someone. The teachers would give us our homework without explanation and instruct us to work silently. I was terrified I'd fail and have to spend another year in that hell, but just before graduation, half my high school was destroyed by a tornado. (It was Oklahoma, after all.) They let most of us graduate by default because so many people had lost everything.

After graduation, I went to community college for four months, then quit. I was comfortable at my job; I had a motorcycle and a car. College didn't appeal to me. I thought music might be my calling. I was still playing with The Stellas, and we were recording an album that I was funding because I was the guy with a steady job. But even though the band was technically a Christian band, the keyboardist was the only practicing Christian in the group. Then our drummer started dating the lead singer, and things began disintegrating. By the time we finished recording the album, I was out of the band.

My friend Chaffee called one day out of the blue. He'd moved to San Francisco to attend architecture school. "I heard your band's not doing so hot," he said. He reminded me how much I liked to cook and eat. "Why don't you come out to SF? There's a culinary school here."

When my mom first became sick, sometimes I'd try to comfort her by telling her that one day I'd open a restaurant with my brother and that we'd name it Gloria's, after her. I was twelve years old and I had no concept of what that really meant, but it made my mom happy. Now my mom was gone. Maybe being a chef had been an idle ambition, but without a college education, a band, or anything holding me back, there was no reason it couldn't be real. Culinary school would be my way out of Oklahoma.

I pooled together all the money I had and bought a plane ticket for San Francisco.

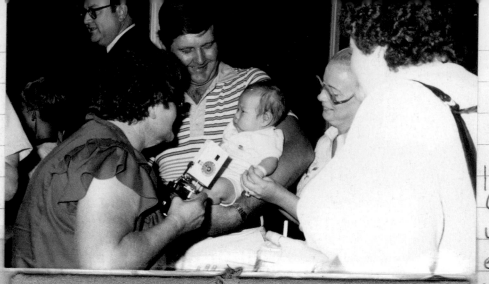

Picture of Dann
8/25/82 Will Rogers
airport, OKC. Jim's
Mom in blue, Jim
(DAD), Jeannie (mom)
white blouse with
embroided flower/
blond Hair/glasses.

To An Adopted Child

Not flesh of my flesh,

Nor bone of my bone,

But still miraculously my
own.

Never forget for a single minute

You didn't grow under my heart,

But in it.

James Daniel
Bowien

Authur unknown
to me; This was
above Danny's crib
when he arrived
from Souel, it
was always in his
bedroom until age
18.

Chris: I asked Danny's dad
to send me some photos
from Danny's upbringing
to include in the book, and
he sent me a thirty-page
scrapbook. Here's a sample.

Smoked Beef Brisket with Smoked Cola BBQ Sauce

SERVES 10

When I was growing up, Friday nights in the Bowien household were barbecue nights. It was a night off from cooking, which is magical for moms as well as professional chefs. We started serving barbecue at Mission Chinese in San Francisco for a similar reason. Barbecue's an easy pickup—once the meat is smoked, you just slice and serve.

As time went by, we went a little crazier with the dishes we based around the smoker and its output. We made smoked beef brisket noodle soup with sautéed mirepoix, thick rice noodles, and beef broth bolstered with smoker drippings. Topped off with a few thick slices of smoked brisket and some chopped cilantro and scallions, all of a sudden it's almost Chinese.

Now don't get me wrong; when I say barbecue is an easy pickup, I don't mean it's easy to make. Cooking a brisket evenly from the point through the flat is no small feat. It takes practice, attention, and adjustment. Smokers tend to have hot spots, and that's where you want the point (the fattier end) to sit. Usually the hot spot is in the back of the smoker, on the side where the vent is located. If you find that the fat isn't rendering from your brisket, you might run it at 220°F instead of at 215°F, as called for in this recipe. And smokers change as they're broken in. Briskets may take twelve hours on the first run but only ten as the smoker walls age and develop a layer of black soot.

Finally, if you're smoking a brisket for ten-plus hours, you might as well smoke other things while you're at it. Smoke some oyster sauce for Broccoli Beef (page 100), garlic for Beijing Vinegar Peanuts (page 203), and *menma* for Stir-Fried Corn (page 262). If you're planning on serving the brisket with the BBQ sauce, you'll need to smoke some cola too.

> **If you have room in your smoker, why not load it up with trotters and ribs too?**
>
> **For ribs:** Season spareribs with salt and pepper and smoke for about 4 hours.
>
> **For trotters:** Make a sun-tea brine (a big glass jar of water with a bunch of Lipton tea bags left out in the sun for a few hours, then sweetened with simple syrup and seasoned with 5 percent salt by weight). Soak the trotters in the brine overnight, then sprinkle them with pepper and smoke for 4 hours.

1. If there are big, unwieldy fat pockets or a thick fat cap (1 inch or so) on the brisket, trim these with a sharp boning knife. They won't render in the smoker, and they will prevent smoke from penetrating the meat. (Don't go too crazy, though—fat is vital for a tasty brisket.) Put the brisket on a wire rack set over a baking sheet and rub it all over with the yellow mustard.

2. Make the brisket rub: In a small bowl, combine all the rub ingredients, then coat the brisket with the mixture, gently patting the brisket to ensure that the rub adheres. Refrigerate the brisket, uncovered, for 24 hours.

3. The next day, heat your smoker to 215°F, then load it with the hickory and mesquite chips. Set the brisket out at room temperature while your smoker warms.

4. If you're using an electric smoker, place the brisket on the top rack, with the fat cap facing up and the point closest to the vent. For an offset smoker, just make sure that the point is closer than the flat to the heat source.

5. If you're making Smoked Cola BBQ Sauce, now's the time to smoke the cola. Smoke the brisket for 8 to 12 hours—don't peek before 8 hours. The brisket is done when it's soft, jiggly, and tender.

6. Remove the brisket from the smoker and wrap it tightly in aluminum foil or parchment paper. Let it rest for at least an hour before slicing. (Reserve the drippings for the Smoked Cola BBQ Sauce, if you're making it.)

7. To serve, cut thick slices of brisket against the grain and serve with BBQ sauce, pickles, and white bread. Or use it as a stand-in for braised meats, like the beef cheeks in our Broccoli Beef (page 100).

Special equipment: Smoker, 8 ounces hickory wood chips, and 2 ounces mesquite wood chips

1 (10- to 12-pound) beef brisket
½ cup yellow mustard

BRISKET RUB
¼ cup granulated garlic
¼ cup cayenne pepper
¼ cup freshly ground black pepper
¼ cup ground cumin
½ cup kosher salt
½ cup sugar
½ teaspoon celery seeds

FOR SERVING
Smoked Cola BBQ Sauce
  (page 236; optional)
Dill Pickles (page 196)
White bread

The sunlight is different in San Francisco. That's what I noticed first.

There's a crazy geography to the city. In Oklahoma, you'd have to drive a half hour to experience a different part of town, whereas in San Francisco you can walk fifteen minutes in any direction and be in a completely different place—the Castro, the Haight, the Mission, Golden Gate Park.

But the thing about the city that hypnotized me was the food: pizza that wasn't Pizza Hut, Mexican food that wasn't deep-fried and smothered in ranchero sauce. I love the huge plates of Tex-Mex you get in Oklahoma, but real Mexican food was entirely new to me.

I remember a meal at a restaurant called Globe on one of my first nights in town. Globe was hip in the early 2000s; it was a late-night cooks' hangout. It had a full bar and a wood-burning oven, and it was always a little too dark inside. I ordered mac and cheese, homemade sausage, and a whiskey, and I thought it was the most incredible thing in the world.

Back in Oklahoma, those nice adoption ladies had introduced me to *gimbap,* but my real Korean food baptism came in San Francisco. Chaffee and our friend Eric shared an apartment on the corner of Sixth Avenue and Balboa. My first night in town, I walked down the street from their place and popped my head into a Korean restaurant. The old ladies who ran the restaurant started speaking to me in Korean. When I just stared back blankly, they giggled, patted me on the back, and sat me down.

I told them I didn't have much money and I just wanted something cheap. They brought out spicy pork *bulgogi* and a dozen *banchan* and rice. I didn't recognize any of the little plates of pickles and dried fish and kimchi or understand why I was getting them, but before I could ask, they brought out a whole fish. After I finished eating, they told me I only had to pay for the pork—the rest was on them. The restaurant became a second home for me.

Chris: You're genetically predisposed to like Korean food.

I really believe it. When I eventually visited Korea, the food all made sense to me. And even though I'd never really tasted Korean food until that day in San Francisco, I instantly latched on to it. I'd stop into the restaurant whenever I passed by and try to order just rice and *banchan,* but they'd always make a big ordeal out of my visits and crush me with food. I took my Korean wife, Youngmi, there when we first started dating, and I finally got a translation of what they were saying to me.

(I guess they'd been trying to convince me to enter some kind of Korean *American Idol*.) Over the years, the ownership has changed hands, but some of the old ladies still work there. It's called Muguboka.

Chris: Is this the inflection point, when you became focused on exploring and cooking—sorry for this term—"ethnic" food?

Anthony: Come on.

No, I wouldn't say that. Those nice ladies fed me, and I loved them, but I wasn't thinking, *My goal in life is now to find and reconnect with my roots*. I think of my parents as my parents; my Oklahoma heritage is who I am. I didn't feel compelled to learn everything about Korean food. If it weren't for Youngmi, I probably still wouldn't know anything about Korean food. I don't crave Korean food as much as I do other cuisines—Japanese, Chinese, Mexican. When I started culinary school, I became focused on accumulating as many food experiences as possible.

I started school two weeks after arriving in San Francisco. At the orientation seminar, a PR guy stood up and spoke to us about how we'd been accepted into a very prestigious program and how proud we should be. He said something to the effect of, "In a few years, you will all be great chefs!" and the curmudgeonly French chef in charge of the program tried to interject and clarify that it would actually take at least ten years to become chefs, but the PR guy shot him a look that said, *Would you shut up? They just paid $54,000 to become chefs.* In my case, I'd just signed a loan for that amount, figuring I'd pay it back my first year or two on the job.

For six months, I was at the top of my class. I was the model student I'd been as a kid, coming straight home from school and studying. But I found myself in the same situation as I'd been in back in Oklahoma. A lot of my classmates had come to school for a specific reason. "I'm going to start a taco truck that serves Filipino fusion food." "I'm going to open a bakery in Los Gatos." Of course, there were plenty of people who had just gotten too stoned on their couches one night and decided they would become chefs—my own story probably fell closer to this side. But there were also guys who'd cooked for ten years in professional kitchens and wanted a degree to get ahead of the competition. When classmates asked me what I was going to do after graduation, I would say, "I really want to do well, open a few restaurants, and then come back and teach." That was my new safe answer, but again, I had no real plan for what I was going to do.

My lack of purpose wasn't the real problem, though. The problem was that I started partying. In Oklahoma, I hadn't been much of a pot smoker, but when I moved to California, it was almost unavoidable. And I started doing a lot of blow. A guy in my class was a dealer, and he'd just give it to me for free. In hindsight, it's almost ironic that right around the time we were beginning our Asian-food classes, I started going out to clubs until five or six in the morning, then taking the party back to someone's house, staying there till noon, and sleeping until seven or eight at night. If I even made it to class, I showed up completely burned out.

I was a pain in the ass to be around. All the money I got from student loans went to drugs and booze. If it weren't for Chaffee and Eric letting me stay at their apartment, I wouldn't have had a place to live. Eric had the bedroom, Chaffee the living room, and for a year, I slept in Eric's closet. When I came in at night, I'd have to tiptoe through his bedroom so I could curl up on the floor under the clothes hanging above me.

After a while, I stopped going to classes entirely. It's not as though I didn't see what was happening—I knew I was becoming someone I didn't want to be. The people around me weren't my real friends and I was failing cooking school. One night, I called my dad and told him I thought I was going to die—I'd been partying for a week without sleep. I can tell my dad anything. When my mom passed away, the one upside was that Dad and I established a much tighter line of communication; even if he wasn't proud of the things I told him, he would always listen. When I called to tell him I was partying myself to death, he said, "Come home, just come home. Come back and get your life together." I took a leave of absence and went home.

Anthony: I've always been amazed by your killer instinct—your willingness to fight and see things out. It's the reason I first liked working with you. I don't see you quitting something as big as culinary school. It's surprising.

Perseverance has only really been a part of my personality since we've known each other. For a long time, I had no idea what I was doing. I ran back to Oklahoma with my tail tucked between my legs.

Chris: How long were you in Oklahoma?

That's the worst part—I didn't go home, not right away. The school granted me a six-month leave, and I spent five of those months working at a clothing store in the Haight, continuing to party and waste time.

Anthony: Why aren't you just a burnout gutter punk in the Haight now?

Chris: Yeah, why am I not looking at you with disdain as you yell at me for being a prick when I won't give you any change?

I finally went home at a real low point, when I felt myself becoming that burnout. When I got back home, I could have ended up just staying in Oklahoma, maybe working in a restaurant there—I had learned enough in school to manage that. But I looked around and all my friends were doing the same things they had been doing when I left. Nobody had gone anywhere. At least I'd been to a different city, seen a little more of the world. I was failing my way back into my old life, and I had to get out. By some miracle, I don't get addicted to things—I will go really hard at something, then quit instantly; I smoked cigarettes for eight years, then went cold turkey without a problem. So I hitched a ride back out to San Francisco with a friend and stopped fooling around with drugs completely.

The director of my culinary school cut me a deal: finish one last class, and they'd let me graduate. You could say I'm lucky, but I think the reality is that if I didn't finish school, they couldn't collect the full balance of my student loan. My final exam was making a beef consommé. The instructor was practically begging me to finish it. All told, it was supposed to be a year-and-a-half-long program, but it took me almost three years to finish. I'm not sure I even graduated— I never received a certificate.

And I didn't pay back my student loan for almost ten years.

Chris: Tell them the truth.

The awkward truth is that I wasn't able to pay it off in full until we sold this cookbook. At one point, I was getting bills for $7,800 a month. There's just no way you can pay that on a line cook's salary. When the school discovered where I was working, they garnished my wages, taking 40 percent of every paycheck. But when I moved from San Francisco to New York and back to San Francisco, I lost track of the bills, and they lost track of me. So the loan went into default and interest ballooned the debt to more than $100,000.

I was nineteen when I moved to San Francisco and signed a contract for a $54,000 loan. Granted, I'm horrible with money, but I figured I was going to graduate from school and become a great chef, and so fifty-four grand was no big deal. The language in the advertisements is much different now, but back then it was incredibly misleading. I didn't realize how little a cook makes until I moved to New York and got my first job. When I met my wife, I had to confess about this enormous loan hanging over my head, and that my credit would be horrible for a long time.

From a strictly financial standpoint, I regret going to cooking school, but it's not so cut-and-dried. Maybe if I had really applied myself, I'd have gotten more out of it, or maybe if I had gone to a better school. My advice about whether or not to go to school is this: Know what you're getting into. Know that it will take you a long-ass time to pay back a student loan on a cook's salary. Know that there's plenty you can learn without going to school by getting a job in a restaurant kitchen, and that not everything you learn in school will serve a practical purpose later on.

Ideally, people who are considering attending culinary school should work in a restaurant first, then talk to the chef and discuss whether or not school is a good idea. Actually, I think that work experience in a kitchen should be a prerequisite for getting into culinary school.

I can say this because I learned the hard way. I wanted to be a cook, and I thought the thing that would get me in the door was cooking school. I didn't know what being a cook meant—financially or professionally. If I could do it again, I'd find that out first.

* * *

Chris: So then you moved to New York, got your first job at Tribeca Grill, then met those asshole chefs and got chased out of town. What next?

New York chewed me up and spit me back out. After two years of cooking at Tribeca Grill and the hell-on-earth French-Japanese place, I went back to Oklahoma to spend time with my family. I was questioning my career choice. I loved cooking, but did I love being a cook? This was my second time quitting. I wanted to be a chef, but did I want to be one of the chefs I'd worked for? The only thing I knew for certain was that I couldn't show my face in New York again.

I made my way back to San Francisco, where I loafed around for a few months, not doing much beyond working at a clothing store, until finally, Sara, the manager of the clothing store, who was a friend, sat me down and gave me a *Good Will Hunting*–style talk. You know: "The best part of my day is when I walk up to your door to pick you up for work and I think, *Maybe he won't be there*." She told me I had to get back in the kitchen. Sara's my patron saint. I have her name tattooed on my arm.

I responded to an ad on Craigslist for a job at Blowfish Sushi. Sushi had been the only thing that impressed those chefs in New York. They were jaded about most restaurants and talked trash about everybody, but they were entranced by sushi. I could never afford to eat it; on a couple of occasions, I sat with them and drank beer while they ate and waxed poetic at Blue Ribbon. I figured if I could learn to make sushi, I'd have the up on them in some way.

My experience in New York worked in my favor in getting the job at Blowfish, because the chef was a big food nerd. He'd eaten at El Bulli a few times and loved that sort of cuisine, and he was excited for me to show him some of the fancy stuff I'd learned in New York.

The kitchen had four stations: The first guy did sashimi and *nigiri,* the second guy just did *nigiri,* the third guy made rolls, and then the last guy, me, made all the rolls that no one wanted to make: dragon rolls, rainbow rolls, tempura rolls, all the fried stuff. By far the best cook was Jesse Koide. Jesse was good and generous enough that he would come over and teach me, even when the kitchen was slammed. I'd be rolling fifty rolls at once, and he'd come over to help and instruct me.

Chris: So even then, before you knew him at all—he later became sous chef and then chef de cuisine at Mission Chinese Food—you saw something special in Jesse?

I loved working with Jesse. He was a big brother and a mentor. He was open, warm, helpful, and excited about cooking: basically everything that my experience so far had convinced me didn't exist in a professional kitchen. But Jesse's time at Blowfish came to a ridiculous and abrupt end. The kitchen manager, a maniac with a speed problem, decided to pick a fight with Jesse one night and punched him in the face. This wasn't the first time the manager had

started trouble with Jesse, and the chef decided to wipe the slate clean. He fired both of them.

After Jesse left, management appointed me the new kitchen manager. Suddenly I was the twenty-three-year-old boss ordering around forty-five-year-old line cooks who had probably been cooking for longer than I'd been alive. My chefs in New York would have lost their minds if they'd found out I was in charge of people. I thought about them often. They were my model for the kind of manager I didn't want to be. I kept my head down and tried to earn the respect of the other cooks. I would come in on my day off to make staff meal. I just wanted to learn.

Jesse landed a job as sous chef at a restaurant up the street. I told him I wanted to join him so I could learn about California cuisine, but really I just wanted to work with him. The restaurant, Slow Club, hired me, and I started working there while holding my job at Blowfish. The diversity of the experiences was thrilling. I also began *staging*—interning, basically—at Bar Crudo, then Tsunami Sushi. At one point, I was working full-time at one place and part-time at three others. I was learning how to break down and slice fish from three different chefs at once. At night, I worked the sauté station with Jesse.

Anthony: Jesse was the lead line cook when I was cooking at Bar Tartine, the sister restaurant to Tartine Bakery. We only overlapped briefly, but Jesse was one of the first cooks I ever saw who was really in "the zone"—that caffeinated-yet-Zen state of spinning around doing five things at once without stopping to think.

So you can see why I wanted to cook with him, but I had to settle on one job. I finally did so when my friend Mercedes brought me in to become the chef de cuisine at a new Italian restaurant called Farina. Traditional Italian food was about as foreign to me as sushi had been, so it piqued my interest. Mercedes assured me that the chef, Paolo, was an amazing cook, but when I got there, the place was a mess. They had hired sixteen cooks: Three different people were squeezing lemon juice. One would cut the lemon and hand it to another person, who would squeeze it and then hand it to another person to pour through a strainer. And the food was horrible—Paolo didn't know how to teach anyone.

He *was* a good cook, though. He was from Genoa and knew everything there was to know about Ligurian food. Whenever he made something himself, it was spectacular. At the time, all these young star chef-butchers were getting press for working with whole animals.

Paolo would laugh, saying that any old grandmother in Liguria could break down a whole pig.

I gave Jesse the scoop and he came by one day to trail in the kitchen. The owners watched him cook and hired him on the spot as "sous chef to the sous chef." They truly didn't know what they were talking about, but I was happy to work with Jesse again. The only snag was that somehow I'd become Jesse's boss. Overnight, our roles were reversed. I was now in charge of the guy who had taught me everything. It was an uncomfortable situation.

Anthony: You once told me a story about a pretty serious confrontation you had.

Jesse internalizes a lot of stress, and when he gets stressed out, he drinks. At one of the other restaurants where we cooked together, when things got hectic, he would jump over the pass, run back to the office, take a four-second pull off a bottle of Cazadores, and then get back to cooking. It was really unhealthy behavior, and I watched it for years. When he started at Farina, I told him he couldn't let his cooks see him drinking like that. He was their boss, and I was his boss. And beyond that, the entire restaurant was wired with closed-circuit cameras that the managers monitored from upstairs.

One day I was in the office with the director of operations. I glanced over at one of the security screens and saw Jesse come around the corner, lean up against the walk-in, and start pounding the cooking cognac. I went downstairs, grabbed the bottle from Jesse, and started shouting at him. He had this guilty look on his face, like a little kid; I couldn't handle it. I threw the bottle against the walk-in door behind him, told him never to drink there again, and walked out.

He apologized, but the damage was done. I'd disrespected him and reacted in a way I didn't want to. He was like my big brother, and he put me in the horrible position of having to be the more mature person. What was I supposed to do? Our relationship started down a different path that day. I felt guilty, a feeling that was compounded as I grew closer to Paolo—working on recipes together, traveling, learning directly from him—while Jesse stayed in the kitchen, working the line.

* * *

The food was improving as we streamlined the kitchen, and Paolo began using me to translate his food for the other cooks. We worked well together. He trusted me, and I bought in to the whole program. Genovese food was the best—all other Italian food was bogus.

Farina is where I really honed myself as a cook, where I gained confidence in my cooking, and where I began to refine my palate and my point of view. Paolo took me on as a protégé. When the owners sent him to Genoa to compete in the second annual World Pesto Championship, he took me with him to see his hometown. After four layovers and twenty hours of travel, we arrived in Genoa completely drained, but we had to be up at six a.m. the next morning so Paolo could get to the Palazzo Ducale for the competition. As I was getting ready to crash on his mother-in-law's fold-out couch, someone handed me an itinerary. I couldn't really make out what it said, but I noticed that it was identical to Paolo's. I asked him, "Wait, I'm not competing, right?"

"Yeah, you are."

My stomach twisted and my pulse quickened. "Why didn't you tell me?!"

"I didn't want you to stress out."

"I'm stressing out!"

"Don't worry—we'll be right next to each other the whole time."

The next day, we got to the convention hall early and checked in at the registration table. Then we ran around the place as Paolo greeted everyone in sight. People kept asking him how California was and he'd tell them it was beautiful, and then they'd ask who the Asian guy was. "This is Danny; he's the best chef in San Francisco." They'd tilt their heads and look at me curiously, and I'd force a smile and say, "Hi." I was miserable—jet-lagged and terrified.

As the competition began, the competitors—a mix of grandmothers and professionals in chef jackets—took places on either side of a long single row of tables running the length of the hall. I settled in next to Paolo and looked at my ingredients. Everyone had the same kit: basil, olive oil, pine nuts, cheese, garlic, salt, and a mortar and pestle. I had never made pesto in a mortar and pestle before. At the restaurant, we made it in five-gallon batches. Before I could ask Paolo what the hell to do, an organizer walked over to tell me that I wasn't in my assigned station and sent me to the opposite side of the room from Paolo, next to an old woman who was as panicked as I was. A stream of curious journalists and photographers came up to get a look at the Asian guy who Paolo had been talking up to the whole room. I couldn't understand a word any of them said.

Fifteen minutes into our allotted hour, Paolo came over and said he was finished. I asked him how he thought he'd done. "I don't know,

I think I screwed it up. All the ingredients here are totally different." He was right. The basil was really moist, the pine nuts were really dry, the oil tasted different than ours, and they'd given us pecorino instead of Parmesan.

I was nervous to the point of shaking, so I started by tasting and smelling everything. I took the basil and squeezed it between my fingers and decided that I'd use more fat than usual to offset the additional water content. I put the pine nuts and salt in the mortar with just a sliver of garlic, because it tasted incredibly strong. I ground everything into a paste, and then scraped it out. *If you work it too much, it'll get too warm and develop a bitter taste,* was the theory I came up with in the moment.

I put the basil in the mortar and worked it clockwise. I wanted to break it down but not pound it. I got rid of some of the excess moisture, added back the nut-garlic paste, and started working them together gently, incorporating the oil as I went. The second the pesto emulsified, I stopped mixing and added the cheese.

I tasted it and thought it was actually pretty good. Paolo tasted it. He said, "Danny, I've been making this my whole life. You're going to win." But I have a lot of respect for cooks who have become great at one specialty, and I felt like an impostor. The judges walked through, tasting everyone's pesto, and we waited for an hour while they deliberated over who the ten finalists would be. Paolo didn't make the cut, but I did. He patted me on the back and kept saying that I was going to win, stressing me out again.

The organizers took down all the tables but one and set the ten finalists in front of all the other contestants and spectators. They gave us half an hour to re-create our pestos. I was one of the first to finish.

Unbelievably, I did win.

A man dressed like the pope of pesto presented me with a golden mortar and pestle. When we returned to San Francisco, the restaurant took the award. I didn't really mind—none of it felt quite real to me anyway. I did find it awkward that they began selling their pesto as "award-winning pesto" and that the price kept climbing.

Paolo was a great chef and I think we were making really impressive food, but the restaurant claiming my award was emblematic of more fundamental problems. They didn't like that the spotlight had been turned on me and Paolo, and tried to drive a wedge between us, poisoned the staff against us, and poisoned us against each other, spreading gossip and telling each of us that the other was talking trash. I quit six or so months after the competition.

The whole thing—winning the competition, battling management, leaving the restaurant—took a toll on my relationship with Jesse. From the time of that cognac incident, Jesse's and my relationship had been disintegrating in a slow burn. I admit there were a few times that I treated him unfairly because he was the closest person to me. You tend to take things out on people you love when you're upset, and I definitely did that to Jesse. Did he deserve it? No. I just didn't know how to handle myself. When I eventually left Farina, Jesse stayed on and took over for me. We didn't speak for a year and a half.

*   *   *

After Farina, I returned to my directionless ways for a while. I bounced around to a few different kitchens, just cooking without any desire to be a sous chef or chef again.

I started dating my wife, Youngmi, in 2007. I'd known her since my days at Bar Crudo. She came in one night for dinner, and I thought she was insanely beautiful, and I had to borrow twenty dollars from the chef so I could meet her for a drink after work. She met her boyfriend of a year and a half soon after that, but the minute they broke up, I jumped on the chance. We moved in together two weeks later. I wasn't sure about anything in my life except that I was going to marry her, and that certainty never faded.

I got a job at a restaurant where Youngmi was waiting tables so I could be closer to her. One Thursday during service, a cook-friend, David Cabello, started bending my ear about a line cook in the city who had sublet a Guatemalan food truck to serve his own fancy sandwiches. We'd never heard of anything like it. Roy Choi had just started his Kogi Korean taco truck in LA, but it hadn't become national news yet. The idea of a fine-dining cook renting a roach coach was brand-new to us.

"We're going to get a case of beer and wait in line. Do you want to go?"

I told him I was too tired. But that was the first time I heard about Mission Street Food, and the idea stuck with me.

A few weeks later, the truck had been shut down by a local dickhead who was nervous about his sidewalk getting dirty, so the operation had moved into a nearby Chinese restaurant. At this point, every cook in San Francisco was talking about Mission Street Food. You'd be in line for coffee and you'd hear people making plans to go to a run-down Chinese restaurant called Lung Shan for the pork belly and jicama (PB&J) sandwich. The cook who'd started it, Anthony, was becoming a local hero.

There were two-hour waits to get into Mission Street Food. It was incredible. During the day, you'd see a couple of local Chinese construction guys eating big plates of rice and noodles there, and most nights, the restaurant would do three or four delivery orders and that'd be it. But on Thursday nights, Lung Shan was packed. At first both menus were on offer. You could have Anthony's king trumpet mushrooms with burnt scallion crème fraîche, and a side order of potstickers.

From the time they moved Mission Street Food indoors, Anthony and his wife, Karen, decided that the restaurant would have a charitable component, so the restaurant donated a significant portion of its profits to a different charity each week. Anthony is the most giving person I've ever known. He spends almost nothing on himself. He's worn the same navy blue puffy vest and trucker hat forever. But he'll always figure out a way to give money away to help others. It's a trait I admire deeply, and it makes it easy for me to trust and love him.

After a week or two of being inside Lung Shan, Anthony started spreading his generosity to the cooking community by inviting guest chefs to come help develop menus and support the charity of their choice. This all took place before every chef on the planet was doing pop-up restaurants and opening food trucks, when most cooks didn't have an outlet to cook dishes that weren't in line with what they served at their restaurants. Anthony would let the guest chef—usually a line cook or chef who was off duty or between jobs—develop a theme for the menu and take over most of the kitchen. Anthony would help them navigate Lung Shan and fill in the menu with a few dishes of his own. Eventually, Mission Street Food added Saturday nights to the schedule and stopped offering the Lung Shan menu (but in-the-know diners could still get Chinese food if they wanted, and *shifu*—the Chinese term for a wok cook—still banged out the occasional delivery order from his station).

It took a resourceful kind of cook to be successful at Mission Street Food. You had to be able to walk into an unfamiliar kitchen and cook for three and a half turns of sixty people. And the kitchen you were walking into wasn't exactly a typical one. The chances that you'd ever used a wok before being in Lung Shan were probably slim. But that's what you had: a wok, two deep fryers, four burners, and an oven that couldn't fit a full baking sheet. There was no reach-in refrigerator. There was no walk-in refrigerator. The floor was lined

with flattened cardboard boxes that were swapped out when they became too stained with oil.

The Chinese restaurant staff would work around you, without much concern about you being there. *Shifu* sat on an overturned soy sauce bucket in the corner of the kitchen in front of his station waiting for an order to come in, ducking out for cigarettes now and then. Sue and Liang, the couple who own the restaurant, would be napping or watching Chinese soap operas or making deliveries. When he was called upon, Liang would repair a circuit breaker or a leaky faucet with a crazy DIY fix that none of us thought would work but always did. Anthony was usually the only Cantonese speaker around, so anything you wanted to communicate to the staff had to go through him or be said with waves of hands and nods, but if you put the effort in to get to know them, the Chinese staff was really friendly, and Liang was actually a bad-ass wok cook. If *shifu* called in sick, Liang could step in and bang out perfect beef chow fun.

I found out all this firsthand when I helped a friend with his guest-chef night and then did one of my own. It was August 2009, and I decided my theme would be Seoul Food. Living with Youngmi had been an education in Korean cooking. She made Korean food at home, and she'd taken me to Korea to see the family farm where her mom makes her own kimchi and soy sauce and fermented bean paste (*doenjang*) from soybeans they grow. It's amazing.

Chris: I think that that first trip to Korea is what prepared you to cook at Mission Street Food and eventually Mission Chinese Food. I also think it's representative of one of your strengths—being adaptable to unusual cooking situations.

On one of my first days in Korea, Youngmi's mom asked me to make dinner for the family. Of course I said, "Sure, what do you like?"

"Pork chops. Do you know how to make pork chops?"

"Sure, what else?"

"Mashed potatoes."

Okay, pork chops and mashed potatoes, I could handle that. We went to Costco and Youngmi's mom grabbed a sack of potatoes and a family pack of pork chops. I thought to myself, *There are only five of us, why is she buying so many pork chops? Does she want to freeze some?*

Back home, I was standing in a kitchen I'd never cooked in, looking for salt so I could season five pork chops, when Youngmi said, "No, Danny, just cook everything." Suddenly, I was surrounded by sixteen members of the extended family, buzzing around, speaking Korean. It dawned on me that I wasn't cooking dinner for five.

When they all sat down to eat—with chopsticks—I couldn't tell if they liked it. They ate quickly, and when they had finished, a whole second meal of kimchi and rice came out of nowhere and they all dove into that. I asked Youngmi if they'd enjoyed dinner, and she said they did. "Why are they eating all that kimchi and rice then?"

"That's just what happens."

Chris: I firmly believe that if every restaurant—fine dining, greasy spoons, whatever—offered all-you-can-eat rice and kimchi, or noodles, or baked potatoes at the end of every meal, diner satisfaction would go through the roof. No one would talk about being hungry after a tasting menu. And if a meal was bad, at least you'd have rice and kimchi to look forward to at the end.

It's true—and the same thing happened to me again a few days later at church with Youngmi's mom. Out of nowhere, her mom stood up to address the congregation and when I heard her say "Danny," I started waving, not realizing she had just volunteered me to cook for the entire church the next day. There were a hundred and fifty Koreans who wanted to eat spaghetti made by "a great Italian chef." We spent the afternoon looking for spaghetti and tomatoes, but the tomato sauce in Korea is all wonky, there was no Parmesan except for a powdery imitation, the olive oil tasted funny, and there was no basil. I did what I could, and they seemed to like it. But again, kimchi and rice came out to supplement my meal.

So it's true, my first night at Mission Street Food didn't feel completely foreign. If anything, I felt more comfortable in that hot, hectic Lung Shan kitchen than I'd felt in Korea. There was a three-hour

wait outside that night. It was crazy, but it still seemed like there was structure or at least meaning behind the chaos. More important, no matter what happened, no matter how bad my food might suck, the next week the restaurant would start over with a different guest chef and a different menu. There was no fear of the business collapsing under my mistakes. This was freedom. For my Seoul Food night, I made an aperitif of shiso and watermelon sorbet with iced soju; *doenjang jigae* (a pungent, savory stew) with clam dashi, golden enoki mushrooms, potato, kale, tofu, and green chile; cold summer noodles with fresh soy milk, sesame, cucumber, tomato, and radish sprouts; and braised pork belly, seared on a griddle and served with lettuce and herbs. Short of opening my own restaurant, I don't know when else I would have had the opportunity to serve Korean food like that. The fact is, most American chefs don't have the luxury of cooking whatever they want one week and something completely different the next. Granted, it can be dangerous bouncing from cuisine to cuisine without knowing what you're doing. But for me, it was an incredibly liberating experience.

Chris: I was still pretending to be a cook back then, moonlighting in the kitchen twice a week. Me cooking—that's how free and naïve Mission Street Food was.

Anthony: The real secret is that Ying has been in the thick of Mission Street Food and Mission Chinese Food since the beginning. People think he's a writer we hired for the book, but he's really just one of our line cooks.

Seriously, it took me months of knowing Chris and occasionally cooking with him to realize that he had a day job and wasn't a full-time cook. I'd started doing more guest-chef nights and helping Anthony on nights when other chefs were cooking. I saw a shimmering hope in that small Chinese restaurant—it dawned on me pretty soon after I started cooking there that it was the first time I was making food that I wanted to make. There was a trade-off, of course. If we wanted to use special equipment, for example, we were out of luck. Forget about Pacojets, we didn't even have reliable refrigeration at the time. But we improvised and made it work. We set up a charcoal grill inside a wok, poached *poularde en vessie** in a gas rice cooker, and turned a piece of slate into a griddle. I steamed *chawanmushi,* pureed it, emulsified it with browned butter, and charged it in a whipped-cream siphon as a sauce for a Hangtown fry. Anthony tried to make an immersion circulator out of the fish tank in the front window. We had nothing to lose, and no reason not to try anything. It was much more difficult than cooking in a nice, shiny, Western kitchen, but it was so damn rewarding, and we took a lot of pride in being able to conjure up quality food with no money, no equipment, and no space.

* * *

When I first started showing my face around Mission Street Food, I kept out of the way of the Chinese staff. I didn't speak a word of Cantonese or Mandarin, and while Sue and Liang could communicate in English, the extended family who made up the staff couldn't. I believe that being extra polite is the only way to succeed in a situation like that. You can't walk into someone else's restaurant—at any level—and act entitled or superior. There was a handful of chefs who came into Lung Shan—either as guest chefs or diners—and complained about how rundown and unsophisticated the restaurant was. Yes, it was a janky hole-in-the-wall Chinese restaurant, but the way I saw it, Sue and Liang and the staff had been kind enough to give us a chance to do whatever we wanted in their own home. You don't go to someone else's house and start talking about what a dump it is. I was honored to work side by side with them.

---

* I later had the great honor of eating the original version of this dish—Bresse chicken cooked in a pig's bladder with truffles—with its creator, chef Paul Bocuse. It was an unbelievably humbling experience, but to be honest, I remember our makeshift homage version more fondly. Maybe we put more love into ours, or maybe more truffle.

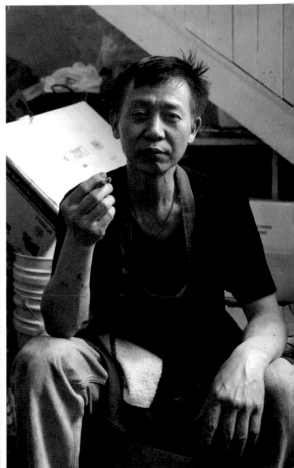

There was one line cook in particular who frequented Mission Street Food. He was always so miserable, I couldn't figure out why he kept coming. I guess he just wanted to be one of the cool kids but was too proud to admit it. He would hang around the kitchen and just go on and on about everything that he saw wrong with the place and all the things he would change until finally, one night when he was standing by the pass, sniggering and bad-mouthing the Chinese cook next to me, knowing that he couldn't understand him, I lost it.

"You're the best line cook in the world. Ever. Fine," I said. "But that guy has a different skill set, and when it comes to cooking Chinese food, he's definitely better than you. Actually, I bet he could walk into your restaurant and take over your station too. You could learn something if you paid attention."

Anthony: I know you feel this way in retrospect, but were you really so open then? For a while, when MSF was just getting started, I was pulling double-duty at MSF and Bar Tartine, where you were cooking. I remember you liked to stand around and talk trash about other restaurants as much as any of us.

You're right. But what I've realized is that the whole time we were railing against other restaurants, I was becoming an unhappy person. It's exhausting to be that negative. It's a teenager's mentality: No one wants to be the chump who admits to liking another restaurant or another style of cooking.

The truth is, I love watching other people cook. When I was working at Blowfish, I was so happy just to watch Jesse or the other sushi chefs perform the same task over and over again, absorbing their movements until it became something I could repeat, something almost natural. After my dustup with that trash-talking line cook, I decided to heed my own advice and learn something from Lung Shan. Sue and I worked out a deal where every day I would come in and give her five dollars, and she'd let me order anything I wanted. Then I'd watch the wok chef make my lunch. He didn't speak any English, so I'd just point to something on the menu and then I'd stand back and observe. Later on, when we decided to open Mission Chinese Food, my only education in using a wok or cooking Chinese food was from watching *shifu* at work.

As my relationship with the Chinese staff deepened, I found the respect and courtesy I showed them returning in equal proportions. One of my earliest memories of working at Mission Street Food is of a day when I was making chili vinegar. I hadn't secured the lid on the

blender tightly enough, and when I turned it on, hot vinegar and chiles exploded out of the top and all over the kitchen. I felt my stomach drop and began to panic a little bit. I scrambled to clean up, irrationally expecting a raging chef to turn the corner and freak out on me. One of the dishwashers, whom we called Auntie, was hanging around on a break. Without a word, she grabbed a bunch of towels and helped me clean up. Nobody was yelling at me for making a mess, nobody was laughing to themselves. Just Auntie, quietly helping out because she saw I needed it.

After service, sometimes we'd celebrate with a few beers, and Sue would politely wait for us to finish up before she started clearing all the chairs so she could sweep and mop the restaurant. It was sort of adorable. She'd sleep through Mission Street Food in her little hallway office, then wake up at eleven p.m., hang out with us for a little bit, and then see us off.

I was working full-time as a cook under Jason Fox at Bar Tartine throughout these early days at Mission Street Food. When Jason hired me, I told him just to throw whatever he wanted at me, to push me as hard as he wanted, and he humored me. He brought in a whole tuna so I could break it down and portion it, and we began executing a lot of ambitious dishes off a station the size of a small coffee table. I probably would have stuck around with Jason longer, but something special was happening at Mission Street Food. When Anthony offered me a more permanent position, I thanked Jason for the opportunity and moved down the street to Lung Shan full-time.

*   *   *

After a little more than a year's worth of Thursday and Saturday night services, the constant search for new chefs and new menus became hard to sustain. Some nights would suck. It was unavoidable—not every chef could come into a strange Chinese restaurant and make it work. We were having a hard time finding two guest chefs each week, and beyond that, having other people come in to set the menu was a crutch we didn't need anymore.

I never thought of myself as a chef at Mission Street Food, but in a sense we—Anthony, me, and another chef friend of ours, Ian Muntzert—had become our own chefs there. No one was telling us what to cook or how to cook it. We were pushing ourselves every week to be better. When we stopped bringing in outside help, the responsibility fell on us to come up with new themes for the menu every week. We landed on a series of homage dinners, where we'd try to re-create the dishes of chefs like René Redzepi, Massimo Bottura, Inaki Aizpitarte, Michel Bras, even Escoffier. We'd spend all week prepping for the homage dinner on Thursday. Half the time we had no idea what the dishes were supposed to taste like—we cooked from pictures and descriptions we found online. Then on Saturdays, we'd invite a guest chef or just cook whatever one of us wanted.

The Saturday after we paid tribute to Massimo, we decided on a whim to cook Chinese food. At that point, I was still more psyched about the homage dinners—Chinese food was just something to do—but on my days off I always craved Chinese food. Youngmi and I would rarely go to fine-dining restaurants. Even after eating at Lung Shan most days for lunch, I'd still go home and order Chinese takeout. Around this time, everyone in San Francisco was discovering Sichuan cuisine. Anthony and I and a couple of other guys would get together to go to Spices (I or II) in the Richmond or Z&Y in Chinatown, and we'd order all these dishes we'd never heard of before: water-cooked fish, twice-cooked pork, fire-popped spicy tofu skin, nomad-style cumin lamb, "saliva" chicken, and anything listed as "numbing spicy."

We were hooked on these textures and spices we'd never tasted before. Even if you cook in a wide variety of different restaurants, you get used to the way food tastes. That sounds reductive, but what I mean is, it's not often you come across an entirely new set of flavors.

The Sichuan peppercorn was the biggest revelation. Eating Sichuan peppercorn is a difficult sensation to describe if you've never had it—people call it "numbing" or "tingly," but it's got a little bit of cooling burn, too, like peppermint. Most Americans think Sichuan cooking is all about heat—tons of chiles and chili oil—but it's really about balancing numbing (*ma*) and spicy (*la*). The Sichuan peppercorn is supposed to offset the heat, which allows you to eat more chiles, and so on and so on.

But, of course, we didn't really understand this then. The restaurants we went to just played to the American craving for too-spicy food. So on Chinese night at Mission Street Food, we did the same. We made a few tamer things like salt-and-pepper sweetbreads and steamed halibut cheeks, but the dish I was chasing after was a burn-your-face-off bowl of mapo tofu.

To this day, whenever I go to a Chinese restaurant, I always order mapo tofu. I almost always like it too. Even when it's sweet and gloopy and not at all spicy, or has mushrooms and peas, I still like it. Over dinner one night at Spices with my friend Brandon Jew, one of us wondered out loud, "Why doesn't anyone cook mapo tofu like a ragù? Why don't they cook it down so you get a concentrated sauce with a ton of umami that you don't have to supplement with MSG?" So that's what I did at Mission Street Food. I built the sauce like a cross between ragù alla Bolognese and Texas chili and then finished it with spices that gave it a Chinese profile.

A lot of what we were cooking at Mission Street Food was both off the cuff and collaborative. We trusted each other to divvy up the components of a dish. Anthony was making a chili oil in the oven to finish the mapo tofu, but he forgot about it and let the chiles slow-roast in oil for something like twelve hours. The result was unbelievably hot. The sauce base I'd made was super hot, too. Together they were delicious, but so spicy it was ridiculous. And we didn't add enough Sichuan peppercorn, so it was just unobstructed heat.

Brandon came by and said, "It's close but it's not there yet." But Anthony thought it was the best he'd ever had. We've been chasing after that first taste like drug addicts ever since, but in reality, it was probably just that it was the first mapo tofu we'd ever had that didn't taste like other mapo tofu. We were really proud of it, especially how spicy it was. Ian drew a flaming butthole on the bottle of chili oil and dated it April 24, 2010.

Mapo Tofu

**SERVES 4 (OR 6 AS PART
OF A LARGER MEAL)**

Mapo tofu was my gateway into Sichuan food. It's a staple
of Chinese menus around the world, and there are infinite
variations. It can be spicy or sweet, oily or gloopy with
cornstarch, ruby red or light brown. It can be made with
pork or beef, and you're just as likely to find it studded with
mushrooms, peas, or carrots, and sometimes without meat
at all.

My friend Brandon Jew is responsible for giving me
my first taste of pure, uncut Sichuan mapo tofu. It was my
first real encounter with Sichuan peppercorns and their
otherworldly buzzing, numbing effect. The earth shifted
underneath me—there was an entirely new set of flavors I
could cook with. After that, I chased the dragon to every other
Sichuan place I could find. At Z&Y Restaurant, the mapo
tofu bordered on too intense. There was so much Sichuan
peppercorn, the flavor was almost medicinal. I later found
that mapo tofu in Sichuan Province in China isn't as spicy or
pungent as it is here. The flavor is clean—it's like something
you'd eat at Chez Panisse. Yu Bo, a superhuman Sichuan chef,
makes a transcendent version with nutty, gelatinous acorn
jelly instead of tofu.

Here are two of the dozens of versions of mapo tofu
we've made. They both start from the same base, but one
is vegetarian—vegan, actually—and the other is not. I
think they're the best iterations we've made, well balanced
and simplified tremendously from our early overly spiced
attempts, but I highly doubt they'll be our last. Serve either
version with steamed rice.

Note: Our mapo tofu is made like a ragù, so it's not easy
to make a small batch. However, you can refrigerate or
freeze the base and then make the braise in smaller batches
whenever you like. The base will keep for some time in
an airtight container in the fridge—at least two weeks, or
until you feel weird about how long you've kept it—and for
two months in the freezer.

1. Prepare the base: In a medium bowl, combine the shiitake mushrooms and hot water. Add the soy sauce and allow the mushrooms to soak for at least an hour, or until they are completely rehydrated and soft.

2. Drain the mushrooms through a sieve set over a bowl and reserve the liquid. In a food processor, pulse the mushrooms into small chunks. You should have about 1 cup of chopped mushrooms.

3. Combine the reserved mushroom liquid, doubanjiang, and tomato paste in a medium bowl. Whisk to combine, then add the chopped mushrooms. You will have about 3½ cups of the base—reserve 1¾ cups for this recipe and transfer the rest to an airtight container and refrigerate for later (see Note on page 62).

4. Prepare the braise: In a Dutch oven or large saucepan, heat the chili oil over medium heat. Add the garlic, fermented black beans, and chili crisp and cook, stirring occasionally, until the garlic softens and the mixture becomes spine-tinglingly aromatic.

5. Add the beer, mushroom powder, Sichuan pepper, and reserved 1¾ cups base to the pan and stir to combine. Bring the sauce to a simmer, then reduce the heat to low and simmer gently, uncovered, for about an hour. (At this point, you can cool and then refrigerate or freeze the sauce for up to 2 months.)

6. Bring a pot of well-salted water to a boil. Blanch the tofu cubes for 1 minute, then drain carefully and set aside.

7. If you want a thicker sauce, stir in the cornstarch slurry. Once the sauce thickens, fold in the tofu. Taste and season with soy sauce as needed.

8. There should be a thin puddle of shiny red oil on top of the sauce—if not, add a few more tablespoons of chili oil. Finish with a drizzle of Sichuan peppercorn oil, a sprinkling of ground Sichuan pepper, and a scattering of cilantro and scallions. Serve with steamed rice.

BASE

2 ounces dried whole shiitake mushrooms
3 cups very hot water
⅓ cup soy sauce
½ cup doubanjiang (spicy bean paste)
⅓ cup tomato paste

BRAISE

½ cup Chili Oil (page 290), or as needed
15 garlic cloves, minced
¼ cup fermented black beans
⅓ cup Chili Crisp (page 290)
1 (12-ounce) bottle cheap beer
2 teaspoons Mushroom Powder (page 299)
1 teaspoon toasted and ground Sichuan peppercorns
1 (15-ounce) package firm tofu, cut into 1-inch cubes
1 teaspoon cornstarch slurry (see page 292; optional)
Soy sauce

Sichuan peppercorn oil, for drizzling
Ground Sichuan pepper
Several sprigs fresh cilantro, chopped
1 or 2 scallions, trimmed and sliced
Steamed rice

Meat Variation

½ pound ground pork or a mix of ground pork
  and diced pork shoulder/belly
½ teaspoon fish sauce

1.   Make the vegetarian mapo tofu through step 4. Once the garlic softens and spine tingles occur, scoop out the aromatics as best you can and set them aside.

2.   Crank the heat up to high and get the chili oil almost smoking hot. Add the pork to the pan and brown it thoroughly, using a spoon to break up the meat. When you've got good color on the meat and you're teetering on burning things, crash the party with the bottle of beer. Use a wooden spoon to scrape up all the crispy bits from the bottom of the pan and stir them into the liquid. Add the aromatics back to the pan, along with the fish sauce, mushroom powder, Sichuan pepper, and 2 cups of the base and bring to a simmer. If the sauce looks thick, thin it with some more base or beer until it looks like a thin marinara sauce. Cover and braise over low heat for 2 hours. (At this point, you can cool and then refrigerate or freeze the sauce for up to 1 month.)

3.   If you want a thicker sauce, stir in the cornstarch slurry. Once the sauce thickens, fold in the tofu and slowly warm it through. Taste and season with soy sauce as needed, then finish as you would in steps 6 through 8 of the vegetarian version.

After about two years, Mission Street Food had run its course.
We'd grown out of the pop-up format and entered the strangest
moment of hope and uncertainty. We had no clue where we'd go
next. Although Chinese food night at Mission Street Food had been
a success, the next week we'd moved on to something else without
thinking twice. That was how Mission Street Food worked—one week's
success was just that week's success.

Anthony was already building out another restaurant two doors
down with Jason Fox and Ian, and in our spare time we'd started a
pop-up burger place a little farther up the block. Standing together
talking at the counter at Mission Burger is where the most obvious of
plans occurred to us. I knew for sure that I didn't want to return to fine
dining, so I suggested to Anthony that we should just use the Chinese
restaurant to cook Chinese food, and he agreed.

We walked over to Lung Shan, and Anthony told Sue about the
switch. He said we'd be open seven days instead of two, she agreed,
and that was basically it. We were Mission Chinese Food now. Later
that day Anthony sent me a draft of a possible menu: Old Ping's mapo
tofu; Mongolian beef cheek over chow fun noodles; Islamic lamb hot
pot with glass noodles; and a hybrid rice roll/burrito that he dubbed
"the Chinito."

Anthony: It should be said that Mission Chinese Food would be
nothing without Sue and Liang's unique blend of nonchalance
and faith in us. They're basically always up for whatever. When
we made the switch from Mission Street Food to Mission Chinese
Food, our business arrangement became more of a partnership, but
without any real hiccups.

Anthony and I got wrapped up in some crackpot fantasies about
how the restaurant would run, but we had no real plan. We made the
decision with Sue and Liang to return to offering the Lung Shan menu
alongside our own, so people would sit down and get two menus—a
classic one with potstickers, chow fun, egg drop soup, and orange
beef—and one with our weirdness. Anthony would work appetizers and
I would work the hot line. We'd wear earpieces and answer calls for
delivery while we cooked.

As for the dining room, we figured that since we were going to
be open seven days a week from lunch through dinner, we wouldn't
be very busy. Mission Street Food had been two days a week of
concentrated chaos that led us to believe we could handle anything.
We assumed the new, longer hours would spread business out over

the week, and we didn't need any servers—just us and whoever was around to help would be enough.

Youngmi and I got married in Korea on June 12, 2010, with Anthony as my best man. We flew back to San Francisco and opened Mission Chinese Food less than a month later, on July 5. Funny enough, Sue and Liang told Anthony that we opened MCF exactly eight years to the day after they had opened Lung Shan.

Meanwhile with Sue and Liang

Chris: What were your first impressions when Anthony walked in the door, looking to sublet your restaurant for one night a week?

Liang: He wanted to work in the kitchen, but I didn't think he was kitchen material. I thought he was a good-looking kid. I didn't believe he had the ability. But I was curious. My wife said that we'd get a couple hundred dollars a night, so I figured, let him have a gamble. When I first opened a restaurant, it was hard. Somebody had to help me. So I didn't mind helping him, giving him a chance to learn, so he could have his own restaurant.

Sue: This is the third restaurant we've owned. We were like Anthony at the beginning. We didn't have capital or know how to do it. Liang was a wok cook. His boss wanted to open a car wash but he didn't want to sell his restaurant. He asked Liang if he wanted to rent the restaurant. We worked for a year, and we made some money. We realized that we would make more money working for ourselves than working for someone.

L: My boss helped me, so I wanted to help Anthony.

C: But did you think Anthony's plan was strange?

S: I didn't think much of it. We didn't have much dine-in business, mostly takeout at night. I just thought, *It's $300 a week, let him have a try. We own the building—if it works, it works, if it doesn't work out, we don't lose anything. There's no risk.*

L: We mostly did takeout. Our English is not good, and we have trouble understanding customers.

Anthony: What did you think when I started redecorating, changing all the lights, and installed the giant dragon in the dining room? Did you think we were dumb?

L: At the time we didn't think it was a good idea.

S: The Chinese like bright lights. And you barbarians like dim lights, and more atmosphere. I'm not saying it's not good. You're not trying to attract Chinese customers, you're bringing in foreign customers. Chinese customers would come in and say, "It's so dark. How can we eat in this darkness? Go get us some candles. I can't see the dishes!" Also the music is so loud. The Chinese customers complained, "It's so noisy. It gives me a headache!" One summer, the circuit breaker shut off and the music went off, and the Chinese customers were very happy. The foreigners were less happy. But there aren't that many Chinese customers that come in by themselves now—mostly second generation kids who bring their parents.

C: Things immediately became really busy with Mission Street Food. What was your reaction to that?

S: It was unbelievable. It was strange. I kept thinking, *How come there are so many people standing in line?*

L: I've worked for twenty years in the restaurant business, and I've never seen anything like that.

C: What did you think when you met Danny?

S: He had a lot of things to say.

L: Lots of things to say. Danny's a very happy person.

C: How much of what he was saying did you understand?

L: About half. It was hard because I couldn't express my opinion.

C: Was he different than the other chefs who passed through?

S: Yes, yes. He's always smiling, and he had so much to say. Some of the chefs would come in and not make a sound.

C: What did you think when Anthony told you that he and Danny wanted to start cooking Chinese food here?

L: Business was so good when Anthony opened Mission Street Food, so we believed in his ability.

C: And what were your first impressions of the Chinese food they made?

L: At the beginning, I didn't know what to make of it.

S: It was too spicy. I didn't like it that much. What they were cooking was not traditional Chinese food.

L: We're used to traditional Chinese food. His food has influence from Japan and Korea.

S: We're used to it now. But I still don't like spicy food.

L: Sometimes it's too salty, because they use fish sauce, but I do eat it. I think it's very good now.

C: What's your favorite thing that Danny has cooked?

S: I like the bacon with the rice cakes.

L: I like the bacon too.

C: What's your least favorite?

S: Salad. The vegetables are raw. You don't worry about not washing the raw vegetables in salad?

A: It's already washed.

C: What about your kids? Do they like the food here?

S: My son eats here twice a day. The taste suits young Americans.

C: How do you describe this restaurant to your friends and family?

L: I describe this as American-style Chinese food.

S: I always tell my friends that my Chinese restaurant is different than any other Chinese restaurant. You can't get the same food at any other restaurant. It's still Chinese food but different than the usual. Most Chinese restaurants have fried rice, fried noodles, soup, and sweet and sour chicken. We don't have that. Other restaurants' mapo tofu is hot just by adding hot sauce. Our mapo tofu is really hot and really numbing. It's authentic. I always tell people that Danny is the number one chef in the United States.

C: When did you realize that Mission Chinese Food was becoming a big deal, or at least a restaurant that people all around the country knew about?

L: When they were ranked second [best new restaurant in the country by *Bon Appétit*].

S: Our friend told us that it was in the Chinese newspaper. "Your restaurant is number two!"

C: What have been the struggles of having Mission Chinese Food here?

L: It used to be that we each worked our separate halves of the restaurant. Now that we work together, I worry about making enough money. If we make money, everything's fine. If we don't, we worry, we still have to pay the mortgage. It's a big responsibility after we merged together.

C: Are there tensions between American cooks wanting to do things their way and how a Chinese restaurant is usually run?

S: Sometimes.

L: We fought with Danny a few times in the beginning.

A: I remember very clearly in the beginning, when business was not great yet, Danny wanted to use more expensive tomatoes. There was a big argument about whether or not we should even continue.

S: We are responsible for the cost of ingredients. We wanted to keep it low, and you guys wanted it higher. If there's no business, then we don't make money. And Danny would always invite people to eat, and we'd cover the cost, and it hurt me to give away the food for free.

L: At the very beginning, when business was not very good, Danny would comp people. That was the biggest argument.

C: What about now?

S: We've hired more people, and have more expenses. The business is more stable now, we don't worry as much.

L: But the more people, the more arguments. There's lots of pressure. I worry about people when we let them go, because our restaurant is famous, the lawyers seek them out and encourage them to sue us.

C: What would you be doing now if Mission Street Food had never started?

S: The same thing we were doing, until we couldn't work anymore. I was very content— we were making money, and I didn't have to go work for someone.

A: Are you still content?

S: There's more money than before. But it's harder now.

A: You could hire more people.

S: There's no reason for me to sit here and not work. We didn't make much money before, but there was not as much pressure.

C: So do you view Mission Chinese as a blessing? Are you happy that this happened?

L: It's a good thing. When I'm on the street, when I go out, people tell me my restaurant is very famous.

S: He likes that the most. "Ooohh, your restaurant is famous!"

C: What about the charitable aspect? Did you ever think twice about giving profits away to charity?

L + S: It's a good thing.

A: But if you did it your own way, lots of things would be much cheaper. As it is, we give a lot of money to charity.

S: Once you make money, you must repay society. Many Chinese people donate lots of money once they become wealthy.

C: What are you most proud of about this restaurant?

S: The food here is different. We would not be able to make it into this market alone. Before, we were limited to a very small population. Now we reach the broader society.

L: With this food, we're able to merge into the mainstream of American society.

C: How much longer do you want to be at Mission Chinese Food and what is your dream for this place?

S: I just want to work until I retire, but Liang still has ideas about franchising.

L: Business is going well. Me and Danny and Anthony can sit down and talk about branching out.

C: What role do you see yourself playing in this global Mission Chinese Food brand you're describing?

L: We sit in an office and advise other people how to open new branches. You don't have to work it yourself. Danny cannot make it by himself.

In the days leading up to the opening, I tried to pick up the thread on mapo tofu again. We were convinced that the one we'd made for Mission Street Food was the best version possible, and I began obsessively trying to remember how to make it. The first few attempts were bad. I kept adding and adding spices and seasonings and meat until there were thirty-three ingredients in the dish, all getting muddled together and lost. You couldn't taste the cardamom after a while, or the clove or even the meat. I also found that you don't want mapo tofu to be overwhelmingly meaty. I think of it like dressing pasta—a nice ragù isn't overloaded with meat, it has just enough to cling to the noodles and complement them. And a tofu dish is really about the tofu at least as much as it is about the meat. I went out and ate more mapo and tinkered until I was happy again.

The food was all I really thought about before we opened.

Chris: I visited you guys three times on that first day, and each time you were more underwater than the last. That very first order came in a minute after you opened, at 11:01 a.m., and Danny put it into a three-compartment plastic clamshell container. The two side compartments were empty and in the main compartment was a pile of rice drowning in mapo tofu. One of you looked at me and said, "Does this look right to you?" I stared at the container and said, "Have you guys never ordered Chinese food?" We each took a bite of that first order and then sent it on its way.

We probably never had more than twenty people in the restaurant at one time that first night, but I'd insisted on offering citywide delivery for lunch and dinner while somehow neglecting to create a system for deliveries, and employing Liang as our lone driver. We also had no table numbers, no servers, and no real system of communicating orders to the kitchen. Lung Shan didn't have any such infrastructure in place, because there was seldom more than one table of customers eating there at any given time. At one point, Sue opened the back door and all my order tickets flew off in a gust of wind. We were so deep in the weeds at that point it barely made a difference.

A lot of our food is eaten in people's homes. We sent takeout diners home with disposable cameras to follow it.

Anthony: What happened was that with Mission Street Food we were able to batch out orders of three or four of the same dish. But people eat Chinese food differently. They want options, and they want them all at once. Even though business was slower, we had to make one plate at a time and got caught doing three different things at once.

Chris: And you guys were still restricted to one wok? *Shifu* reserved the other one for Lung Shan orders?

Anthony: Yeah, but he got roped into helping us with fried rice.

No, I did the fried rice and it was messing me up all night. I kept thinking, *This is a lot harder than I imagined it would be.* I had watched it being made maybe a hundred times, but never made it myself.

Anthony: Remind me of how we divided the stations.

You were out front calling orders to me.

Anthony: Right, I was making the Chinito out front too. And we had a turnip cake on the menu that I was supposed to make. But I never figured out how to do it, and we 86'd it before we ever served one.

You were making Hainan chicken rice too.

Anthony: We didn't have that on the menu.

Or tea-smoked eel, I guess. There were two Chinitos: a vegetarian one and a roast duck one. I was making fried rice, lamb stew, chow fun, and Mongolian beef.

Anthony: Then I was probably running in and out, dropping chickens into the fryer.

At the end of the night, I felt punch-drunk. I didn't know what had happened, why we hadn't planned the restaurant better. It cracks me up to think back on it now. Did we really believe that I could wear a headset and take orders in the kitchen? How was I supposed to write down the address and phone number while cooking?

Sue came up to us and said, "You need to hire more people. Do you want me to call someone?" to which Anthony replied, "Can they be here tomorrow?"

She made a call to "the hotline"—the employment agency in Chinatown—and the next day, three people showed up at the restaurant for one job opening: a chubby Chinese guy, his mom, and his elderly aunt. They stood in a line and Sue said, "Choose!" (It's a totally barbaric system, but we pay everyone a good salary, so I don't feel too guilty about it.)

We chose the chubby guy, because his two relatives seemed too frail. He spoke almost zero English and had no real kitchen experience. I asked him what he liked to eat, and he said, "Huh?"

"Do you like steak?"

"Yes. Steak."

So I called him T-Bone, and he's referred to himself as T-Bone ever since.

Anthony: Actually there's a long-standing Chinese tradition of calling someone like T-Bone "fat guy" or "chubs." That's what Sue and Liang call him.

But in Asian culture it's a good thing, or at least a term of endearment.

Chris: They call me the same thing . . .

Once we'd selected T-Bone, Anthony told me he'd tossed and turned the previous night, thinking about all the obvious things we should fix. Mission Street Food had taught us not to languish in our mistakes, and maybe it's foolish to think this way, but we looked at every service like we were opening a new restaurant. Anthony came up with a simple ordering system to overcome the language barrier. We wrote each menu item on a whiteboard in the kitchen, and servers would tally how many orders they wanted of each item. For to-go orders, Sue would do the same, but she would circle her tally mark. As cooks completed the orders, they'd just wipe them off.

After that first night, I don't remember things being so bad.

Crunchy Tea-Smoked Eel Rolls

SERVES 6 (OR 8 AS PART OF A LARGER MEAL)

Smoking over tea, at least the way we do it, imparts a less aggressive flavor than wood smoking does, making it ideal for more delicate proteins like eel or chicken. That being said, some Chinese restaurants do tea-smoke the hell out of duck or chicken, ending up with something that tastes like cigarettes. We avoid that.

This dish has been on the menu in some form at Mission Chinese Food since day one. It began its life as what we called "the Chinito"—Anthony's pun (*Chinese + burrito =* Chinito), and a nod to our largely Mexican neighborhood in San Francisco. We'd buy *youtiao,* Chinese crullers, slice them open, and stuff them with duck confit and duck crackling.

For more textural variety, we wrapped the *youtiao* in rice noodles. Just up the street from Mission Chinese in San Francisco, a nondescript store grinds rice into flour and makes fresh sheets of rice noodles. Glazed with oil to prevent them from sticking, they were sold in stacks to Chinese folks in the know.

The problem with the dish was that *youtiao* are meant to be eaten fresh. They degrade quickly. The Chinitos were delicious at the beginning of the day and pretty stale by the end. I found a more reliable source of crunch in cornflakes and Chinese celery. If you've never had it, Chinese celery is more herbaceous and stronger than American celery. The stalks are thin, hollow, and crisp.

You can make your own rice noodle sheets, but if you're going through the trouble of smoking eel (and confiting ham hocks and roasting cornflakes), you'll be forgiven for cutting a few corners. That includes using packaged, precooked unagi.

1. Unwrap the eel and rinse off any sticky brown sauce.

2. Line a roasting pan with foil. Scatter the rice and tea over the foil and top with a rack that sits an inch or two above the bottom of the pan. (If necessary, prop up the rack with crumpled foil balls.) Set the pan over high heat. After a few minutes, the rice and tea will begin smoking. Lay the unagi on the rack and cover the pan tightly with aluminum foil and the lid, if you have one—you don't want the smoke to escape. Turn off the heat and allow the eel to bask in the smoke for 30 minutes.

3. Uncover the eel and sprinkle it with the sansho pepper. Set aside.

4. Now, on to the ham hock: Preheat the oven to 300°F.

5. Set an ovenproof saucepan over high heat and get it nice and hot. Coat the pan with 2 tablespoons of oil and sear the ham hock on all sides, about 2 minutes per side. Add enough stock to almost cover the ham hock, cover the pan tightly with foil, and slide it into the oven. Cook for 2 to 3 hours, until the meat is falling off the bone. Remove the pan from the oven and let the ham hock cool completely in the broth. Raise the oven temperature to 325°F.

6. While the ham hock cools, toss the cornflakes with the rest of the oil and spread them on a baking sheet. Toast in the oven until the cereal has darkened slightly, 5 to 7 minutes. Remove and let cool.

7. Shred the cooled ham hock; discard the bones.

8. Slice the smoked eel into strips about 3 inches long and ⅓ inch thick.

9. In a small bowl, mix together the hoisin, soy sauce, and cognac, if you're using it.

1 (11-ounce) package precooked unagi
1 cup uncooked jasmine rice
1 tablespoon loose Lapsang souchong tea
1 teaspoon ground sansho pepper
3 tablespoons vegetable or peanut oil
1 smoked ham hock
4 to 6 cups Rich Chicken Stock (page 301) or regular chicken or pork stock
1 cup cornflakes
½ cup hoisin sauce
1 tablespoon soy sauce
½ teaspoon cognac (optional)
6 fresh rice noodle sheets, homemade (see page 202) or store-bought
2 Chinese celery stalks, or 1 regular celery stalk, cut into ¼-inch-thick batons
½ cup micro shiso or other micro herbs

10. One at a time, lay out the rice noodle sheets on a cutting board or work surface. Place a few slices of eel in a row down the center of the sheet, then follow with a thin strip of shredded ham hock and celery batons. Spoon some of the hoisin mixture over the top. Gently roll the noodle sheet up into a cylinder about 1½ inches in diameter.

11. To serve, cut each roll into 3 or 4 segments and arrange them on a plate. Top with micro herbs and serve with any leftover hoisin mixture for dipping.

Salt-Cod Fried Rice

SERVES 4 AS PART OF A LARGER MEAL

The spirit animal of this dish is the fried rice with salt fish and chicken at R&G Lounge in San Francisco. What an umami power couple: the meatiness of chicken with the blue cheese–like pungency of salt-cured fish. Crazy.

I got a closer look at salt fish when I started cooking at Lung Shan. *Shifu* would bring in a red-and-yellow tin of it and use it to season steamed pork knuckles and peanuts for staff meal. It's an amazing ingredient, like fish sauce in solid form. I love the way it perfumes and seasons fried rice with a funky, fermented flavor. But I don't particularly love biting into a gnarly chunk of it. The aim of our Salt-Cod Fried Rice was to capture that pleasant fishiness without the stank.

Our first tack was to soak store-bought salt cod (from a specialty market or Italian grocery), shred it, fry it until golden, and then toss it with the rice. It works perfectly, but then a horde of customers complained that there was no visible fish in our Salt-Cod Fried Rice, so we gilded the lily with chunks of rich mackerel confit.

As for rice-frying technique, I owe everything I know to the hundreds of hours I spent watching the cooks at Lung Shan. Think of frying rice as like making a salad. You don't want to spend too long mixing and tossing it, or it will get soggy and flat. Go into a ripping-hot pan with the rice, then pull back on the heat, season, and toss. That's how you achieve fluffy fried rice. It's actually an ideal dish for a home cook, who probably isn't going to have a 125,000-BTU wok burner. Take the time to get your wok hot as heck, then use the residual heat to cook.

Fried rice is all about speed—at the restaurant, it takes us about 45 seconds from start to finish. The point isn't to rush, but to have all your ingredients prepped and near at hand, ready to go into the wok.

One last thing: I find the old maxim about day-old rice being best for fried rice to be nonsense. I don't believe in it. How could old rice be better?! Come on. Use fresh warm rice, not a hard puck of cold rice.

1. Start by making what we call a rice stack: Put the steamed rice in a medium bowl. Set the salt cod on top of the rice. Cap the cod off with the sausage. You want the ingredients to hit the wok in reverse order—sausage, fish, rice—and the stack facilitates this.

2. In a large bowl, combine the lettuce, scallions, and cilantro.

3. Heat a wok over the strongest heat your stove can muster. Add a few healthy glugs of the oil—about ⅓ cup—and heat until almost smoking. Pull the wok off the burner, add the eggs and mackerel confit, and stir briskly in one direction with a wok spatula, stopping well short of fully cooked eggs. With a hot wok, this will take only about 10 seconds. Dump the eggs and mackerel onto a plate.

4. Return the wok to the heat and get it smoking hot again. Slick with a couple more tablespoons of the oil, then dump in your rice stack. Gently break up the stack and use the spatula to press the rice against the bottom and sides of the hot wok. Wait 10 seconds, then flip and stir the rice. Flatten and press again, and wait 10 seconds. Flip and flatten a last time.

5. Season the rice with the salt, sugar, and fish sauce and give it a quick stir. Add the eggs and mackerel and give another quick stir to distribute them.

6. Scoop everything out of the wok and into the bowl holding the lettuce, scallions, and cilantro. Give everything a toss to mix, then dish out onto a serving platter.

3 cups warm freshly cooked jasmine rice (from about 1½ cups raw)

6 ounces store-bought salt cod, soaked and shallow-fried (see Note)

¾ cup lap cheong (Chinese sausage), thinly sliced

1 cup thinly sliced iceberg lettuce

½ cup thinly sliced scallions (greens and whites)

½ cup coarsely chopped fresh cilantro (leaves and stems)

About ½ cup vegetable or peanut oil

3 large eggs, beaten

½ cup Mackerel Confit (recipe follows)

1 to 2 teaspoons kosher salt, or to taste

1 to 2 teaspoons sugar, or to taste

1 to 2 teaspoons fish sauce

Note: Submerge the salt cod in cold water and refrigerate for 24 hours; change the water twice during the soaking. The next day, drain the cod, pat it dry, and break it into small pieces. Shallow-fry the fish in about ¼ inch of vegetable or peanut oil over medium heat until deep golden brown and thoroughly dried out—it should be almost jerky-like. This will take some time—be patient and expect to spend 10 to 15 minutes standing over the stove. Transfer the fish to a paper-towel-lined plate and let it cool to room temperature, then pulse the fish into thin shreds in a food processor.

Mackerel Confit

MAKES ABOUT ½ CUP

This is for all the people who insisted on seeing the fish in their salt-cod fried rice.

4 ounces boneless mackerel fillet (fresh or thawed from frozen)
About 1½ cups vegetable or peanut oil

1. Heat the oven to 300°F.

2. In a small saucepan, completely submerge the mackerel in the oil. Cover tightly with a lid or foil. Slide into the oven and cook for 25 minutes. Remove from the oven, and let cool completely in the oil. Flake the fish into small chunks and use immediately, or transfer to a container and store in the refrigerator for up to a week, still covered in oil.

We never talked about it, but at a certain point, I became the chef of Mission Chinese Food and Anthony moved into a managerial, front-of-house role. I'd never even thought about how our dynamic had changed until I heard him and his wife, Karen, giving a talk at Google, and he mentioned how he'd made a decision that the restaurant would be better if he left the cooking to me. He's always thinking a step ahead. And it's true that I had almost immediately begun agitating to make new dishes, to keep growing the menu bigger and bigger. But Anthony was always the judiciary and legislative to my executive branch—he kept me in balance. He'd suggest ways to improve a dish, or tell me when people in the dining room were leaving things uneaten.

Creatively, it was the best time of my life. I had no reputation to live up to, and really no one to please but myself and my friends. Almost everything on the menu was $10 or less, and the portions were massive. Business was shaky at the beginning—some days we'd only pull in $500.* It worried Sue and Liang that business wasn't booming like with Mission Street Food, but I was thrilled with the food and the freedom to do anything that came to mind.

For instance, we had a tiny table in the front window that was too small to accommodate more than two people sitting side by

---

* There was never any question that Mission Street Food's charitable model would carry over to Mission Chinese. From the beginning, we gave a portion of every entrée price to the San Francisco Food Bank. It was important to Anthony, and I thought it was a cool idea. It's only been over time that I've come to understand the real significance of it and the difference we've been able to make. Over four years, Mission Chinese San Francisco gave more than $310,000 to the food bank.

side, an order of rice, two dishes, and two beers. People were being made to feel silly for ordering a reasonable amount of food, because their table looked so overcrowded, so we scrapped it and installed a station where I could stand and make dumplings to order. Who doesn't love dumplings? The problem is that you can go to a place like Shanghai Dumpling King in San Francisco and get a big plate of really great pork and chive dumplings for $3. There's no reason to even try to compete with that, so I decided to make mine different, to use better ingredients and not try to beat the little old ladies folding dumplings in Chinatown at their own game. The first dumplings we offered were served with hot and sour pork broth, or filled with lamb, boiled peanuts, and dill.

The dumplings were amazing, but the problem was that nobody just wants one order of dumplings, and I was rolling and folding every one to order. I was marooned in the front of the restaurant, cut off from the rest of the kitchen, sweating and folding dumpling after dumpling. Chris would come in and ask for three orders of dumplings, and I'd just tell him we were out, because I didn't want to stand there and roll thirty dumplings for him to eat by himself. It was fun for a while, but I had to put a stop to it pretty quickly to preserve my sanity.

Chris: And then there was the period when you arbitrarily decided to do barbecue.

We thought it was funny that so many chefs were putting quotation marks around dishes on their menus to indicate that they were being

cheeky or ironic, so we thought we'd make fun of that and serve "barbecue" at our "Chinese" restaurant. We listed it on the menu with 'Chinese' in single quotes, and then double quotes around the whole thing: "'Chinese' Barbecue." The thing is, it wasn't Chinese in any way. Having grown up eating barbecue every week in Oklahoma, I just missed eating it and felt like trying to make it, and because our whole restaurant was founded on a whim, I could do it. So we secured an electric smoker from a friend and set it up in the basement. To vent the smoke, we ran 1-inch copper pipe up the stairs and over the front gate. When the smoker was running, there'd be a steady wisp of smoke leaking out above the sidewalk. It looked shady as hell, like we were cooking meth in the basement. We'd smoke beef briskets for twelve hours, plus pork trotters and hot links. Everything would come with smoked cola barbecue sauce, white bread, dill pickles, and onions, just like I had it growing up.

As it happened, there was actually a logistical benefit to doing barbecue too. With the restaurant running six days a week from morning till night, we were pushing up against our capacity and there was no fridge space—I was building Tetris towers just to get everything in.

Anthony: If you looked into the fridge, you'd see maybe 5 percent of open space in there. I don't think you're a unique organizational genius or anything, you just found a way because you had to. And for me that was always an inspiration. You had a clear vision and didn't let the finances handicap the business.

I think I saw the bigger picture. It's something I learned from Mission Street Food. You can't say something's impossible; there's always a way to do something. We only had one oven and it couldn't hold a full-size baking sheet. Barbecue was an easy pickup that we could just slice and serve. A lot of our early dishes were the results of necessity. The kung pao pastrami—which New Yorkers thought I'd created in honor of them when Mission Chinese eventually landed on their shores—was a dish I'd created to take advantage of the smoker. We'd smoke corned beef, then cut it into chunks and serve it with celery, peanuts, peppers, and onions. No need for the oven.

A few months in, Jesse joined us, essentially for the same reason—we needed him. He just showed up one day, and we picked up where we'd left off. We walked to Dolores Park and talked for a minute, but there was nothing to discuss really. He'd washed out of Farina for the same reasons I had, and now he was back, ready to start cooking together again. We realized we'd missed each other.

Day by day, we gave the restaurant a shape. We modified the dining room without veering too far from the original spirit. We wallpapered it, turned off the fluorescent overhead lights and put up Christmas lights and red lanterns, and we wove a gigantic paper dragon across the ceiling of the whole restaurant. But we didn't have any great ambitions; we just wanted to cover up the most noticeable blemishes without changing the place completely. I liked that it was still just a crappy Chinese restaurant, and that you could come in and get our Salt-Cod Fried Rice, Thrice-Cooked Bacon, and Mongolian Beef Cheek alongside the #62 from Lung Shan. Their potstickers and beef chow fun were the best.

I think back on this period often—late 2010, early 2011. I had more ideas than time to cook them. Almost all the dishes I came up with during those early months are still customer favorites, permanently locked on the menu. There are times when I worry if I'll ever come up with dishes as good, or if I'm still able to judge my own cooking with the clarity to recognize something great. I get sentimental about how Mission Chinese Food began, and it's the tiniest bit bittersweet to recall what happened next.

Kung Pao Pastrami

SERVES 4 (OR 6 AS PART OF A LARGER MEAL)

My love for kung pao chicken is boundless. From the great authentic Sichuan versions to the stuff you get at Panda Express, I like it all. Chicken, peppers, peanuts, and chiles— how can you go wrong?

When we opened Mission Chinese Food, I wanted to make kung pao bacon. Anthony was lukewarm about the idea, though—he thought it was a cop-out to use bacon. Bacon's a crutch. So, with my heart set on smoked meat, I turned to pastrami. Ideally, when you make this dish, you'll smoke your own pastrami (or have access to great pastrami). If not, you can substitute store-brought pastrami.

Our kung pao falls closer to the American side of the family tree—you know, with canned water chestnuts and celery—than the Sichuan one, though we replace the water chestnuts with al dente potatoes for the same vegetal crunch. The more I think about it, our dish is basically an homage to corned beef hash. It's absolutely inauthentic, as far as Chinese cooking goes. That's why we were flattered when we noticed that the Chinese restaurant down the street from us in San Francisco—not a fancy high-minded Chinese restaurant, just a regular takeout spot—had begun serving kung pao pastrami too. We'd made it!

Kosher salt

1 medium Yukon Gold potato, peeled, halved lengthwise, and cut into ⅛-inch-thick half-moons

About ¼ cup vegetable or peanut oil

¾ pound Pastrami (page 222), cut into ¾-inch cubes, or unsliced deli pastrami, cut into ½-inch cubes (deli pastrami meat will be saltier and less tender, hence the smaller size)

3 celery stalks, cut on an angle into ⅛-inch-thick pieces

1 red jalapeño, cut into ¼-inch-thick rounds

12 chiles de árbol

1 teaspoon Mushroom Powder (page 299)

2 to 3 tablespoons Chili Crisp (page 290), depending on how spicy you like it

2 tablespoons soy sauce

½ cup Fried Peanuts (page 294)

¼ cup Rich Chicken Stock (page 301) or store-bought chicken stock or broth

1 tablespoon Fried Garlic (page 294)

1 teaspoon ground Sichuan pepper

1 teaspoon toasted sesame seeds

2 tablespoons finely sliced jiu cai (Chinese garlic chives) or scallions

1. Bring a pot of well-salted water to a boil. Add the potato and blanch for 30 seconds. Drain and set aside.

2. Set a wok or large skillet over high heat and get it very hot. Add a thin coating of oil—it should be shimmering, almost smoking. Working in batches, if necessary, add the pastrami cubes in a single layer and don't touch them—allow some of the fat to render and the meat to caramelize for 30 seconds or so before stirring gently, so as not to break it up too much. Continue in this fashion until all the meat is browned on at

least a couple of sides, about 3 minutes. Transfer the pastrami to a plate or bowl.

3. Let the wok get scorching hot again. Coat with oil again, then add the celery, jalapeño, and dried chiles and stir-fry just until they begin to soften, about a minute. Add the blanched potatoes and continue to stir-fry for another minute or two, until all the vegetables are cooked but still have bite to them.

4. Add the mushroom powder, chili crisp, soy sauce, peanuts, and stock to the party, stir, and bring to a boil. Return the pastrami to the wok and toss to combine.

5. Scoop everything out onto a warm serving platter. Sprinkle with the fried garlic, Sichuan pepper, sesame seeds, and chives and serve immediately.

Thrice-Cooked Bacon

SERVES 4 (OR 6 AS PART OF A LARGER MEAL)

Twice-cooked pork (*hui guo rou*) is an emblematic Sichuan dish to which we've applied the Gillette rule. What's better than a two-bladed razor? Three blades! What's better than twice-cooked? Thrice-cooked, y'all.

Okay, that's not always true. But it works out well in this case. We start with Benton's bacon—the smokiest bacon known to man. Poaching the bacon tones down the smokiness a bit, and a quick fry renders out some of the fat. Finally, a turn in a hot wok gives the bacon a nice char along the edges.

But the real star of this dish is actually the *nian gao*, Chinese rice cakes made from glutinous rice flour, which are traditionally eaten at the Lunar New Year. The chew and heartiness of *nian gao* is difficult to describe. If you've ever had mochi, that's probably the best comparison. They're popular throughout China, especially in Shanghai, and you'll encounter them stir-fried, steamed, and, my favorite, in soups and stews. My first exposure to *nian gao* wasn't in China, though, but in Korea, in the form of *ddukbokki*, rice cakes cooked in red chili paste with fish cakes and tofu skins. Be sure not to overcook the rice cakes—they should retain a good amount of chew.

1. Put the bacon in a large saucepan and add enough water to cover it by about 2 inches. Bring the water to a very gentle simmer over medium heat and poach the bacon for 30 minutes, or until cooked through but still soft—you can cut into the bacon to check for doneness. Remove from the heat and allow the bacon to cool completely in the liquid, about 45 minutes.

2. Drain the bacon, pat it dry, wrap in plastic wrap, and freeze for 30 minutes. This will make the slicing part a breeze.

3. Meanwhile, bring a large pot of water to a boil and in a separate wok or deep pot; heat about 3 inches of vegetable or peanut oil to 350°F.

½ pound slab bacon (preferably from Benton's)

4 to 6 cups vegetable or peanut oil, for deep-frying

1½ cups fresh or frozen nian gao (Chinese rice cakes, available at Chinese markets; thawed in a bowl of water if frozen)

½ onion, cut into ⅛-inch-thick julienne

1 serrano pepper, cut into thin rounds

¼ pound bitter melon (available at Asian markets), stem end removed, halved lengthwise, seeded, and cut into ¼-inch-thick half-moons

1 tablespoon Chili Crisp (page 290)

1 tablespoon minced garlic

1 tablespoon fermented black beans

½ teaspoon whole Sichuan peppercorns

1 tablespoon sugar

¼ pound inari age (Japanese seasoned fried tofu; see page 297), cut into 1-inch squares

1 teaspoon Mushroom Powder (page 299)

1 tablespoon plus 1 teaspoon soy sauce

1 teaspoon ground Sichuan pepper

1 tablespoon Chili Oil (page 290)

¼ cup cilantro leaves

¼ cup chopped trimmed scallions (white and light green parts)

4. Cut the frozen bacon crosswise into slices a little under ¼ inch thick. Carefully lower the bacon into the hot oil and fry for 1 to 2 minutes, until it has taken on a little color and about a quarter of the fat has rendered out. Drain carefully, reserving a couple of tablespoons of the frying oil, and set the bacon aside.

5. You'll need to work pretty quickly from this point on. Return the wok to high heat and let it sit for a minute or so, until it's very hot. Meanwhile, drop the rice cakes into the boiling water to blanch them for a minute. Coat the hot wok with the reserved oil, add the onion, serrano, and bitter melon, and stir-fry for 20 seconds. Follow with the chili crisp, garlic, black beans, whole Sichuan peppercorns, and sugar and stir for about 30 seconds, then add the bacon.

6. Drain the rice cakes—they should be al dente—shake off as much water as you can, and dump them into the wok. Add the inari, mushroom powder, soy sauce, and 2 tablespoons water and toss to combine. Continue to stir-fry for another minute or so, until everything is heated through.

7. Scoop everything onto a serving plate. Sprinkle with the ground Sichuan pepper, drizzle on the chili oil, and top with the cilantro and scallions. Serve immediately.

Broccoli Beef

SERVES 4 (OR 6 AS PART OF A LARGER MEAL)

Pork belly, beef cheeks, lamb breast, chicken feet: These are the cheap but delicious secret weapons of cooks everywhere.

At the outset of Mission Chinese Food, we paid very little attention to food costs. I don't mean we were smearing thick layers of osetra caviar on everything, but we figured that so long as we were serving cheap cuts of meat, we could give you an unholy amount of food for your money. One of our first dishes was a sizzling platter of chow fun topped with an entire braised beef cheek. We're talking about a huge mess of noodles and a piece of meat the size of your dad's angry fist, *for nine dollars*. It was unbelievable. Chris would come in all the time, wolf down a plate of it, and be on his way.

Sadly, beef cheeks eventually went the way of flank steak—they were discovered by the hungry masses and started becoming more expensive. After a while, we couldn't afford for people to come in, order one item, and call it a day. We needed a dish that was better designed for sharing.

As was so often the case, inspiration came from watching the Chinese staff at Lung Shan. To their customers, they would serve your typical broccoli beef—flank steak stir-fried with American broccoli. But they didn't eat that. Instead, at lunch they would sit down to a piece of beef braised with oyster sauce or salted fish and a heaping side of stewed *gai lan*, Chinese broccoli. Our broccoli beef is modeled after their lunch: braised beef with a slightly funky oyster sauce, plus simply cooked vegetables. In a way, it's the closest thing to a truly Chinese dish we serve.

Also, if you're learned in the art of the pressure cooker, you can make this recipe in a third of the time.

Note: This recipe calls for smoked oyster sauce; you have four options here. (1) Mix some stored-up smoker drippings into bottled oyster sauce to taste. (2) Smoke oyster sauce from scratch as follows: Mix together 1 cup oyster sauce and ⅓ cup Rich Chicken Stock (page 301) in an ovenproof vessel, drizzle a thin layer of vegetable oil on top, and place it on the top shelf of your smoker. Smoke for at least 4 hours over your choice of wood. Stir

well before serving. (3) Substitute Smoked Beef Brisket (page 36) for beef cheeks; stick to regular oyster sauce. (4) Use regular unsmoked oyster sauce and just think smoky thoughts.

1. Prepare the beef: Trim the beef cheeks of any glaring connective tissue (silver skin) and any big pockets of fat, but don't get too fastidious about the fat. Rub the cheeks with the salt and sugar; put them on a wire rack set over a baking sheet and let them cure overnight in the fridge.

2. The next day, preheat the oven to 325°F.

3. Heat a Dutch oven or small roasting pan over high heat until smoking hot, then add the oil. Sprinkle the cheeks with the pepper and sear them, turning occasionally, until deep brown, 2 to 3 minutes per side. Remove the beef from the pot and set aside.

4. With the heat still on high, deglaze the pot with the red wine. Add the stock, soy sauce, fish sauce, bay leaves, and kombu and bring to a simmer.

5. Return the beef to the pot. Place a sheet of parchment paper against the surface of the braising liquid, then cover the pot with the lid or two layers of aluminum foil and transfer to the oven. Braise for 2 hours, or until the cheeks are tender and jiggly. Uncover the pot and allow the cheeks to cool completely in the liquid.

6. Cover the pot and refrigerate. (The cheeks will be easier to portion once cold, so it's best to chill them for at least a few hours or, preferably, overnight.)

7. When you're ready to assemble the dish, portion the cold beef cheeks into large bite-size pieces. Reheat them in a small saucepan with a little bit of the braising liquid and keep warm. (You can reserve the rest of the liquid for a future braise.)

8. Prepare the broccoli: Bring a pot of salted water to a boil. Have an ice bath ready. Blanch the broccoli in the boiling water for 30 seconds, then shock in the ice bath; drain.

BEEF

2 or 3 beef cheeks (about 2 pounds)
2 tablespoons kosher salt
1 tablespoon sugar
¼ cup vegetable or peanut oil
1 tablespoon freshly ground black pepper
½ cup red wine
8 cups beef stock or water
¼ cup soy sauce
1 tablespoon fish sauce
2 bay leaves
1 (4-inch) square dashi kombu, wiped with a damp cloth

BROCCOLI

½ teaspoon kosher salt, plus more as needed
12 ounces gai lan (Chinese broccoli), cut into 2-inch segments (4 cups)
2 tablespoons vegetable or peanut oil
1 tablespoon minced garlic
1 teaspoon Mushroom Powder (page 299)
2 tablespoons soy sauce
1 tablespoon sesame oil
2 teaspoons cornstarch slurry (see page 292)
2 tablespoons Smoked Oyster Sauce (see Note on page 100)

2 teaspoons sesame seeds, toasted
1 tablespoon olive oil
Steamed rice, for serving

9. Heat a wok over high heat. Once it's smoking hot, use a slotted spoon to transfer the beef cheeks to a warm serving platter. Add the oil to the wok and swirl to coat. Add the minced garlic and stir-fry until fragrant, about 10 seconds. Add the blanched broccoli, salt, mushroom powder, soy sauce, and sesame oil and give everything a few tosses to coat the broccoli. Add the slurry and bring to a boil, stirring continuously. Once the sauce thickens to a glaze consistency—this will take about 10 seconds—scoop the broccoli onto the waiting beef cheeks.

10. Spoon the smoked oyster sauce over the broccoli and garnish with the sesame seeds and a quick drizzle of olive oil. Serve with warm rice.

Dumplings

MAKES 40 TO 50 DUMPLINGS; SERVES 4 TO 6

Historically, dumplings and I don't get along. To wit: The best dumplings I've ever had were from a random street stall in Beijing—juicy pork and Chinese chives in thick wrappers. They also happened to bestow on me a month-long case of food poisoning. As I lay dying, I thought to myself, *Dumplings are so simple, why don't I just make my own?*

So I embarked on a three-pronged offensive: (1) improve the wrappers; (2) fill them with high-quality ingredients; and (3) make them to order. Nobody makes dumplings to order. In the best-case scenario, they're made in large batches ahead of time and refrigerated until an order comes in. At worst, they've been sitting in a freezer for who knows how long before they hit the water. That's why dumplings are usually so cheap.

My approach to the wrappers was to follow the path of fresh Italian pasta, minus the eggs—the operative logic being that Italians worship pasta with real chew and you want the same quality in a dumpling wrapper. So I started with high-gluten Italian "00" flour. I substituted Parmesan for salt, which brought a degree of umami to the dough. And I added a splash of white wine for a little acidity. As with Italian pasta sauces, the fillings are really secondary to the dough, and they are infinitely variable.

I learned how to roll and fold dumplings by hovering around dim sum and dumpling shops and watching their old ladies at work. At Vanessa's Dumpling House in New York, I learned that you can stack the dough discs on top of one another and roll out four at once. A little flour between the wrappers keeps them from sticking to one another. Had I learned that sooner, made-to-order dumplings might still be on the menu at Mission Chinese Food.

But, as I said, dumplings and I were just not meant to be. Turns out there's a reason people don't make them to order. Look at places like the international soup dumpling chain Din Tai Fung, where a legion of dumpling makers work nonstop at breakneck speed just to keep up with the demand for soup dumplings. It's insanely labor-intensive, and people always want to eat an ungodly number of dumplings. I couldn't keep up the pace. Now we use store-bought wrappers and I've given up the ghost on making dumplings to order.

The bright side is that you can carry the torch at home. And if you've got the time and inclination, fresh wrappers make all the difference in the world. Your homemade dumplings will be better than ours. Just don't invite too many people over.

1. Prepare the wrappers: Scoop the flour onto a clean work surface. Sprinkle the cheese on top and stir with a fork to combine. Form the flour and cheese into a little mound and use your fingers or a fork to dig a well in the center. Pour the wine and ½ cup water into the well and, using a fork, gradually work the dry ingredients into the liquid, pulling them in from the edges of the well until the dough has enough structure to work with your hands. Knead the dough, folding it over itself and massaging it, until all the flour is incorporated. If necessary, add just enough additional flour so that the dough is not sticking to your fingers but is still tacky. Then work the dough for 3 to 5 minutes, until it's smooth and firm—you're looking for Play-Doh texture.

2. Cover the dough with plastic wrap and allow it to rest for an hour at room temperature. The rest period is important, giving the dough the time it needs to relax and become malleable enough to roll out. You can make the filling in the meantime.

3. Unwrap the dough and knead it for 10 to 15 seconds to loosen it up. Divide it into four portions. Working with one portion at a time, roll each piece under your palms and fingers into a snake approximately ¾ inch in diameter. (Keep the other portions of dough covered with a kitchen towel until you get to them.) Cut the snake into 1-inch sections and liberally dust the pieces with flour. Use the palm of your hand to squash each dough piece into a fat disc. Use a dumpling dowel or a rolling pin to roll the discs into rounds about 3 inches in diameter: Roll back and forth across the top of the disc, rotate it a quarter turn, and repeat until you've got a flat circle that's slightly thicker in the center. Dust the finished wrappers with flour and set aside in a stack. (If you aren't going to fill them right away, cover the wrappers with a kitchen towel to prevent them from drying out.)

4. Working with one wrapper at a time, spoon 2 teaspoons of your filling of choice onto the center of the round. Dip your finger in water and run it over the outside edge of half of the wrapper, then fold the other half up over the filling to form a half-moon

WRAPPERS
3 cups "00" pasta flour, plus more as needed
½ cup grated Parmesan cheese (use a Microplane to grate it)
½ cup white wine

DUMPLING FILLING OF YOUR CHOICE
(recipes follow)

GARNISHES OF YOUR CHOICE
Chili Crisp (page 290)
Chili Oil (page 290)
Chinese black vinegar
XO Sauce (page 307)
Turbinado sugar
Fresh cilantro leaves
Toasted sesame seeds
Cucumbers, halved, lightly crushed with the broad side of a knife, and thinly sliced

shape. Press the edges to seal, squeezing out as much air as you can, then take the two corners of the half-moon and bring them together to form a tortellini shape, again using water to seal. Dust the finished dumplings with flour, stack them, and set them on a baking sheet. Cover and refrigerate until ready to cook. (The finished dumplings can also be frozen on the baking sheet. Once they're frozen solid, bag them, and keep them for up to a month. But really, they're best when fresh.)

5. To cook fresh dumplings, bring a large pot of water to a boil. Add the dumplings in batches of about 20, let the water return to a simmer, and cook for 3 to 4 minutes. Careful—a full boil can cause the dumplings to rupture. They will float to the surface when they're cooked through. (Frozen dumplings can be cooked according to the Chinese three-times-boiled method: Drop the frozen dumplings into a pot of boiling water, let the water return to a light boil, and add a cup of cold water. Let the water return to a boil once more, then drain.) Using a wire skimmer or a slotted spoon, lift the dumplings out of the water, draining them well, transfer them to a platter, and garnish as you see fit.

Pork Filling

MAKES ENOUGH TO FILL 40 TO 50 DUMPLINGS

6 ounces ground pork (preferably a 50:50 blend of shoulder and belly)
6 ounces ground chicken (preferably dark meat)
1 large egg, beaten
1½ tablespoons grated peeled fresh ginger
¼ cup finely chopped fresh cilantro
¼ cup finely chopped scallions or garlic chives
½ cup finely chopped Sichuan Pickled Vegetables (page 192) or napa cabbage
1½ teaspoons sugar
1½ teaspoons soy sauce
1½ teaspoons sesame oil
1 tablespoon fish sauce
1½ tablespoons hoisin sauce

Combine all the ingredients in a large bowl and mix thoroughly by hand. Poach or fry 1 tablespoon of the filling to check for seasoning, and adjust as necessary. The filling can be used immediately or stored, covered, in the fridge for a day or two.

Lamb and Sweetbread Filling

MAKES ENOUGH TO FILL 40 TO 50 DUMPLINGS

2 tablespoons salt

½ pound veal sweetbreads

¼ cup vegetable or peanut oil

½ pound ground lamb

2 teaspoons oyster sauce

2 teaspoons hoisin sauce

1½ teaspoons soy sauce

2 tablespoons finely chopped scallions or garlic chives

¼ cup finely chopped fresh dill

¼ cup finely chopped fresh cilantro

¾ teaspoon fish sauce

1 large egg, beaten

¾ teaspoon freshly ground black pepper

¾ teaspoon cumin seeds

¼ cup finely chopped unsalted roasted peanuts

1. Dissolve the salt in 8 cups water in a medium bowl to make a brine. Add the sweetbreads and let them soak overnight in the refrigerator. Drain the sweetbreads and pat dry with paper towels.

2. Heat the oil in a large skillet over high heat until it shimmers. Add the sweetbreads and sear them, leaving them undisturbed until they have developed a nice crust before flipping them over to brown the other side. Reduce the heat to medium and cook the sweetbreads to medium doneness, about 5 minutes more. Transfer the sweetbreads to a plate and allow them to cool to room temperature.

3. Dice the seared sweetbreads into ¼-inch pieces. Combine them, along with any juices that have collected on the plate, and all the remaining ingredients in a large bowl and mix thoroughly by hand. Fry or poach 1 tablespoon of the filling to check for seasoning, and adjust as necessary. Use the filling immediately or cover, refrigerate, and use within the day.

China

The *San Francisco Chronicle* reviewed Mission Chinese Food in March 2011, eight months after we opened. They gave us three stars out of four for our food and zero for ambiance. We all sat around a table with the paper and laughed about how crazy it was that we were even being reviewed to begin with. It was as though we'd infiltrated the mainstream and tricked everyone into thinking we were a real restaurant. I still think this way. I wonder if we deserve the awards and acclaim. There are restaurants with staffs that work just as hard or harder and never see any recognition.

But Mission Chinese Food was novel when we first opened. We were working with flavors that most people hadn't tasted before, and we were serving the food in a setting that was familiar to everyone—a low-rent Chinese dive—with a little bit of kitsch thrown in. The Communist propaganda and posters of otherworldly Chinese landscapes that had been on the walls when Anthony first walked into Lung Shan were still there. You walked through the kitchen to get to the bathroom. (You still do.)

First a small group of people with big opinions—a handful of chefs and food writers—said they loved what we were doing, and then it snowballed. You almost had to say you liked Mission Chinese because the guy next to you was going crazy for it. New York began to pay attention. *GQ* and *Bon Appétit* both declared us one of the best new restaurants in America. Mark Bittman wrote an article pimping us in the *New York Times*.

When my friends teased me about it, I made a point of downplaying the growing attention I personally was getting. I told them it was all ridiculous and meaningless, but the truth is that it all happened so fast, I didn't really know what to make of it. Even when tremendous things are happening to you, they're still just the facts of your life. Change is harder to grasp than immediate things—the prep work in front of you, the dinner rush, the dining room. And anyway, I chose to focus on the negatives. I was nervous and insecure—this was my first turn as a chef. In the past, reviews hadn't reflected on me, but now anything negative that anyone said was a direct attack on me—or that's how I felt about it. I couldn't stop myself from checking Yelp every morning when I woke up. San Franciscans are heavy Yelpers, and they all seemed to have an opinion about what we were doing. Most people were positive, but I zeroed in on the ones complaining that our food was inauthentic. "I've been to China, and this is not real Chinese food," was the chorus that burned in my ears all day. I never claimed to be cooking real Chinese food! But you can't just shout these things out to the Internet.

Anthony: I think what made it hurt was that what they were saying was actually true. We weren't making authentic food, and we weren't cooking perfect food. But that was never the point. If we wanted to, we could make an authentic, perfect Hainan chicken rice.

Anthony and I put Hainan chicken rice on the menu, specifically to avoid wasting the chicken we used to flavor the broth for our rice porridge. We'd pull the chicken out of the porridge, shred it, and serve it with steamed rice dressed in a gingery, tingly chicken-fat vinaigrette. Toss in some fried peanuts, cucumbers, cilantro, maybe some escabeche chicken hearts—another bonus of buying whole chickens—and that was it. The dish wasn't some idealized version of Hainan chicken rice. It was about making something really tasty out of a by-product—our version of something classic that we could sell for $6.

Anthony: I mean, I don't know how cheap we would have had to make it before people cut us some slack.

All the mounting attention and the people picking us apart were wearing us down. So the day the Bittman profile was slated to come out in the *Times,* with business going through the roof, we shut down the restaurant for a month. It wasn't just the overexposure that was getting to us. There were lines of people every night waiting for hours to get in. The cooks were working twelve-hour days without stopping to eat. Jesse was only doing prep all day, six days a week, and every time a new magazine feature would come out, he'd get buried trying to keep up. We needed a break to regroup.

Sue and Liang had been planning one of their regular trips to China. Over the year or so I'd been working with them (and Sue's mom, aka Grandma, who doubled as a prep cook and busser), we'd built the kind of tight bond you can only form when you see someone every single day, whether it's a good day or a bad day.

I wanted to get to know them better, to see where they'd come from, so I asked if we could tag along, and Liang immediately began talking up all the things he wanted to show us in his home village, and our restaurant's namesake—Lung Shan.

* * *

I want to make a quick digression to talk about the Lung Shan team. I don't want to get too sentimental and call us a family, but there were times when it felt that way. Sue and Liang's son's name is Tony, and he was maybe nineteen when we started MCF. He worked as a delivery driver for us, along with a squadron of his friends in tricked-out Hondas. We all knew that in his spare time he was smoking weed and drinking and partying like a nineteen-year-old does, but his parents were oblivious. One night at the end of service, Tony came in carrying an enormous speaker. I looked out onto the street and there were eight rice rockets parked in front of the restaurant. All of a sudden people start barreling through the dining room, out the back door, into the basement. I thought, *Okay, they're having a party*. The basement was a wasteland. It was full of old gear from Mission Street Food, piles of crap, a bench, some broken furniture, things generally forgotten forever. But over the course of the next week, we saw that Tony had started to trickle in DJ equipment, computer screens, speakers, TVs, and video game systems.

Chris: I was surprised it took him so long to realize he had this party pad at his disposal all these years.

By day seven, he was having full-on ragers in there at night. I would go into the basement and it would smell like vodka and like someone might have puked. I'd move a cupboard and there'd be twelve Coors tall boys, handles of vodka, all this hidden stuff. I didn't care, but his parents didn't know. He told me that some nights he'd have a hundred people in there.

Anthony: All the equipment he was using was plugged into extension cords running from the basement up to the restaurant, so during service, he would blow circuits all the time. We'd run down and say, "Can you shut off the TV?" They even had band practice sometimes.

One night after we closed, Liang came back to the restaurant to check on something, and Tony was down there smoking pot and having a rave. Liang lost it: "If you ever do this again, I'll kill you!" Tony had all this liquid courage and challenged his old man in front of his friends, "Then kill me right now!" His dad beat his ass in front of all his friends and kicked him out of the house.

A few days later, I was in the back getting together my mapo tofu ingredients and Liang came up to me looking distraught and said, "Danny, Tony's so stupid and crazy—maybe you can talk to him?" As it happens, Tony came in later that day, and I sat down with him and laid it out for him: "You gotta be smart. Your parents didn't grow up here. You might know that smoking pot once in a while won't kill you, but they don't think that way." I told him to apologize to them and to move his parties somewhere else where they wouldn't find him. He made up with his dad and moved back in, and everything was good again. Four days later, I was making barbecue up front and I looked out the window and saw Tony coming in with a pool table and a big sleeve of red cups, and I just thought, *Kids . . .*

Westlake Rice Porridge

SERVES 4

Early on at Mission Chinese, most of our recipes were direct references to the food of those cheap Chinese restaurants with laminated menus offering a hundred dishes from all over China. The primary reason was that Lung Shan—the restaurant in which Mission Chinese San Francisco resides—happens to be one of those restaurants.

Most afternoons, Sue and Liang, would offer a soup of the day—something from the standard Americanized Chinese canon: hot-and-sour, chicken and corn, sizzling rice, egg drop, West Lake beef. For whatever reason, West Lake beef soup stuck out for us. It's a pretty mild affair: egg whites, ground beef, and scallions suspended in a gloopy, cornstarch-thickened broth flavored with white pepper. I actually love it that way, but I also thought we could improve it, maybe restore some of the luster that I imagine the original version had.

The first step was finding a way to give the soup body without using cornstarch. Rice porridge (*jook*) is a bedrock of Chinese breakfast (and a favorite of many other Asian cultures). It's belly-warming, stick-to-your-ribs stuff. To make it, all you do is cook rice until the grains have exploded and yielded their starch to the soup. It's a way to stretch a dollar, and to turn a little bit of rice into a whole pot of food.

As simple as it is, rice porridge comes in a great many styles. Our method came from another local Asian business owner, Amanda, the proprietor of the Vietnamese grocery store on the corner. Amanda's porridge is clean and uncomplicated, using chicken broth as a base and fish sauce as seasoning. It tastes a bit like pho broth, without all the warm spices.

If you're already familiar with *jook*, feel free to adapt this recipe to your liking. I tend to like my porridge a little looser, more like a soup, with the grains of rice still discernible, but you can cook it into a smooth porridge if you want: Just keep adding water and cooking it down until it's as sticky and gruel-like as you want. You can also accessorize it however you like. Since ours is a riff on West Lake soup, we add braised beef, Dungeness crab, and egg, but you could also top it with shredded chicken, pickles, ground pork, or for a luxurious look, *ikura* and uni.

1. Give the chicken a good rubdown inside and out with the salt. Place it on a wire rack set over a baking sheet and refrigerate, uncovered, overnight.

2. The next day, in a large pot, toast the rice over medium heat, stirring continuously, until it's fragrant, 1 to 2 minutes, no more. Add 12 cups cold water to the pot, raise the heat to high, and bring to a boil.

3. Once the rice reaches a boil, lower in the chicken and let the water return to a boil. Reduce the heat to medium-low and vent the pot: Balance a wooden chopstick on either side of the rim of the pot and place the lid on top of the chopsticks, creating a gap between the lid and the pot. Simmer for 45 minutes.

4. Retrieve the chicken from the pot of rice, doing your best to scrape and shake off as much porridge as possible, and let the chicken cool on a plate. (When the chicken is cool, pull off the meat and reserve it for another use, or mix it into the porridge before serving. Discard the skin and bones.)

5. Meanwhile, raise the heat to medium and simmer the porridge until the rice grains have almost completely broken down and the liquid has thickened to the consistency of split pea soup, 10 to 15 minutes more. If the porridge gets thicker than that before the rice breaks down, add more water. Remove the porridge from the heat and season with the fish sauce.

6. To serve, ladle the porridge into individual bowls. Top each with an egg, some crabmeat, some of the diced beef cheeks, a tablespoon of the ginger-scallion sauce, and a scattering of cilantro and chives.

1 (3- to 4-pound) chicken
¼ cup salt
1 cup jasmine rice
1 tablespoon plus 1 teaspoon fish sauce, or more to taste
4 Soft-Cooked Eggs (page 306)
¼ pound lump Dungeness or other crabmeat, picked over for shells
1 cup small-dice braised beef cheeks (from Broccoli Beef, page 100)
¼ cup Ginger-Scallion Sauce (page 295)
½ cup chopped fresh cilantro
¼ cup chopped fresh chives

We flew into Beijing for an eight-hour layover and went straight to two back-to-back Peking duck dinners. The first was at Da Dong, a place that Heston Blumenthal had featured on British television as the best duck restaurant in the world—the "El Bulli of Peking duck." There was a sign outside the restaurant with a picture of "Dong's Famous Sea Cucumber." Inside it was even more ridiculous. It was like Disneyland.

Anthony: There was a hell of a lot of neon.

It was crazy busy and the room was packed with high rollers snacking on fruit platters set over smoking dry ice.

Anthony: It was less like Disneyland and more like Rainforest Café.

All the food was immaculately plated, where I had expected really simple dishes of duck cooked over open fire. It was a lot of smoke and mirrors, and pretty mediocre Peking duck. We'd elected to pay an additional fee to choose our own bird, so we walked into the back and avoided eye contact with the cooks who were looking at us like boobs for picking which duck we wanted them to cook for us.

The thing is, even if the duck had been spectacular, it wouldn't have mattered—I was ready to crap on anything and everything. My personal motive for coming to China had been to see what the Yelpers were fussing about. Our first meal in China was a bust, and that was it as far as I was concerned. I was right and everyone else was wrong. I felt entitled and superior—it was China's obligation to prove something to me, Mr. American Chef Man. I more or less ruined the trip for everyone.

At each meal, I'd wonder aloud what the big deal was. I got into an argument with Anthony at Lung King Heen—a Michelin three-star restaurant in Hong Kong—because I thought the chefs were using too much chicken powder and MSG. We went to a pop-up Sichuan dinner in the basement of an art gallery and I rolled my eyes through the whole thing, not considering that the chef was trying to do the exact same thing we were: serve her food wherever she could find a place to do it. I got food poisoning, and I snipped at everyone. I ranted about how much better Japan was than China. I was a huge baby. Youngmi; Anthony; his wife, Karen; Jesse; Chris; and Chris's mom suffered through all this.

Chris: My mom, in her official capacity as our translator and guide, was actually pretty amused by how strangely my friends interacted with one another.

I felt like your mom was the only one who understood me on that trip, because she was blasé about some of the restaurants too. I came up with the idea for a TV show where we'd ride around the Chinese countryside together on a motorcycle with a sidecar, telling it like it really is. Real talk. But we tabled that because we already had Chris's insane idea to execute.

* * *

Back in San Francisco, Chris had had the thought that we should do a Mission Chinese Food pop-up in China, to see what genuine Chinese people would think of our food. Chris's mom would act as translator; Jesse, Anthony, and I would cook. Chris would help in the kitchen and document everything. We'd base this cookbook on the trip and everything we learned—except I didn't want to learn anything. The site of the pop-up was Chris's aunt's restaurant in Shenzhen.

Chris: Shenzhen's one of these places in China that has gone from a suburb to a massive industrial city in a mindbogglingly short amount of time. My aunt is wealthy and owns a stately banquet restaurant primarily so she can entertain guests. I'd never seen it before this trip; I found it to be way more lavish than the shopping mall where it's located. It's called Capistrano. There's a glassed-in wine room, two concierges, and numerous private dining rooms full of paintings and sculptures.

It was awesome; the main dining hall was enormous—a little ridiculous, really. The kitchen had a room dedicated to roasting ducks and chickens and pork, and another room with multiple aquarium systems—both decorative and functional. One part of the kitchen was just dim sum. There were dozens of cooks.

    At that point, I had never seen the inside of a real Chinese banquet kitchen; I had only ever been in our little takeout restaurant. I was blown away to find they had a hierarchy like the French brigade system. The main wok cook came in—this mean-looking dude—and took off his shoes and put on a pair of slippers, like Mr. Rogers. Then he turned around, unlocked a drawer, and

pulled out a paper toque. Only then was he ready to work. When he got an order, one of his assistants would gather all the *mise en place* and hand each ingredient to him as he called for it. The woks were set over a pit made of cinder blocks, with burners in the center that erupted flames like jet engines. There were no handles on the woks—the chef just grabbed the edge of the wok with a folded piece of thin cardboard. When he finished the dish, he'd turn around to find a serving plate already pulled out and set down for him.

All I wanted was to cling to the wall and stay out of the way. But where you might expect them to be territorial, the cooks and chefs were embarrassingly accommodating. I was humbled, scared, in over my head. I didn't know what I would cook. Any confidence I had in my "Chinese food" drained out of me in an instant. These guys were legit. They were grabbing hot woks with their bare hands, for Christ's sake! I was in Genoa again, thrust into a scenario where I'd be cooking other people's cuisine for them. Only this time I didn't have the luxury of just making what someone told me to make. In Italy, I'd been told to make pesto, so I made pesto. Here I was supposed to cook *my* Chinese food.

But I already knew what Chinese people would think of my food. I worked with Sue and Liang every day and I knew what they thought about the food. *It's too spicy, it's too fatty.* So I reverted to my old repertoire. I made a menu with duck three ways, razor clam sashimi, mangosteens in Sauternes—the French-Japanese food I felt safe cooking. It would be fancy, and not something they could compare anything to.

Anthony: This was a total surprise to the rest of us. The whole premise of our trip had been to do a Mission Chinese Food pop-up to see what people in China would think of Mission Chinese Food.

Chris: But after a week of arguing about where to eat and disagreeing about what was good, and tiptoeing around one another, we were all too scared to say anything. I was afraid that Danny would just scrap the whole thing if we pushed it.

At its high points, the pop-up menu was a greatest-hits compilation of solid dishes I'd learned before I found my own voice. At its low points, some beautiful shrimp died a very ugly death. I wanted to make a dish of live spot prawns tossed tableside in a wok full of hot salt until they were just cooked through, but the kitchen staff could only manage to secure coarse ice cream salt and not the fine salt that would form a less porous cooking environment around the shrimp. We wheeled the first batch of prawns out into the dining

room and dispatched them quickly. But as service continued and the salt had less time to heat up in the oven between rounds, cooking times lengthened. By the end of the night, the shrimp were just sort of languishing in warm salt, dying of boredom.

I think back and wish I'd come up with a menu beforehand. I wish I'd been brave enough to serve Mission Chinese Food— or at least finish the dinner with a mapo tofu course. But I was so insecure about what we were doing. I resented Chris and Anthony for making me do this dinner.

At night, we were staying at a dumpy sex motel. The rooms were entirely circular, the bed was a circle with curtains around it. There were emergency gas masks in the

bathroom, and the only other amenity was a disposable-underwear dispenser. The dismal living situation only added to the misery. The closest restaurant was a McDonald's in the same shopping mall as Chris's aunt's restaurant, so we ate there every day, two meals a day.* I spent 95 percent of our time in Shenzhen on the same two blocks. I'll boil it down to this: It was my first chance to see and taste China, and I fucked it up.

---

* When Youngmi and I got married in Korea, I was excited for my dad to get out of Oklahoma and see Asia. But his taste in food is pretty white bread. I had tricked him into eating beef tongue tacos once. He'd tasted them and said, "Wow, this is really good beef."

When I said, "It's beef tongue," he gave me this look full of disappointment and betrayal and said, "Danny, that's just one thing you don't do. You can't screw with people's food like that."

"Dude, you liked it until I said it was beef tongue."

"It's horrible."

After that incident, I didn't really push it. On our first night in Korea, we went to a restaurant for *samgyupsal* and I explained to my dad that it was pork belly. "It's like bacon, but not smoked."

"It doesn't taste like bacon."

The next night, my mother-in-law-to-be felt bad for my dad, so she showed him where the closest McDonald's was. Every morning, when I showed up to scoop him from the hotel, I'd spot a few poorly hidden McDonald's bags, and after we went out to eat, he'd sneak back to the hotel and eat more McDonald's.

I frowned on it then, but I guess I am my father's son after all.

The period after our trip to China in 2012 was the fastest, strangest half year of my life. Mission Chinese Food continued its impossible upward trajectory—people from every walk of life lined up to cram themselves into the restaurant every night. Hipsters shared tables with chefs, tourists, bloggers, Silicon Valley executives, and Ferran Adrià. Martha Stewart came in one night. The occasional strung-out heckler would barge in from off the street to yell at customers for gentrifying the Mission. Whatever we'd set off had an energy of its own now, like an out-of-control chemistry experiment.

And New York City started whispering its siren song in my ear.

I had mixed feelings about the prospect of bringing Mission Chinese Food to New York. New York is to chefs what Hollywood is to bright-eyed aspiring actors—we show up with all of our earthly possessions and dreams of making it on the world's biggest stage. Most of us flame out and crash quickly. Failed actors and chefs alike end up working in crappy restaurants. New York had already rejected me once, and the chefs who had pushed me out were still there.

But after almost eight years of avoiding the city, I made my first visit to New York with Youngmi. She booked us a hotel across the street from Xi'an Famous Foods in Chinatown, and we stood outside with the snow crunching under our feet, eating spicy lamb burgers and hand-pulled noodles.

When I had walked out of my apartment in New York as a young cook, I figured I'd be back soon. I was finally back, but as a much different person. I went to Rockefeller Center with my wife to see the Christmas tree. I ate a bagel at Russ & Daughters and pastrami at Katz's—things that had never been part of my daily routine. When I was a young cook in the city, I rarely went out, I never got to experience the city. Now I was hooked.

I started flying to New York as often as work allowed for events or just for fun (Jesse was growing into the day-to-day chef in San Francisco*), and every time I showed up, a chef or food writer would

---

* Jesse just left Mission Chinese Food last year. He's always been too good a cook not to have his own place, but he's also too good a soldier to strike out on his own. I pushed and pushed him for years to assert himself and make the food at Mission Chinese Food his own. Our biggest fights were over his refusal to change the menu I'd put in place. It sucked to see someone so close to you, with so much skill, allow himself to stagnate. He's finally gone now, and I'm really happy, not because I don't love Jesse, but because I want to see him thrive.

ask me when we were going to open a Mission Chinese in New York. I guess they realized what was happening before I did. Anthony, who has never shied away from a challenge, told me that if I wanted to open in New York, he had my back.

After our trip to China, I'd made peace with Yelp, or minimally at least—I decided to stop making myself miserable over it. I've never made claims to be cooking authentic Chinese food. I have no formal training in Chinese food, and I look at that as a strength. The chefs I've worked for in the past believed in learning and doing things in a certain order, but I feel that our cooking boils down to a lot of split-second decision making and being brave enough to try new things. It's not a style for everyone. I don't delude myself into thinking we're revolutionizing cooking or restaurants or even Chinese food, but I'm proud of our fearlessness.

Chris: That's a pretty major turnaround from whining about the food in China to feeling confident and happy with your style of cooking.

Like I said, it was the fastest six months of my life. That's what happens when you're a young chef today. The restaurant culture is now built around celebrities, so at the first sign that you've got something unique on your hands, people descend on you. If you're going to survive, you have to learn to adopt a very specific mix of humility and pride. You need to be open to learning, but also not let outside influences dilute your own voice. I've matured tremendously, very quickly since we started Mission Chinese Food. It shows in the food: My cooking is less showy now as I've learned to practice some restraint, holding back an ingredient when a dish doesn't need it, or balancing flavors rather than trying to overpower people. But I've also learned to approach life in general more maturely.

When word started getting around that we were planning on opening in New York, I began hearing from the big New York food magazines. Early in 2012, Andrew Knowlton from *Bon Appétit* called to offer to take me on my first trip to Sichuan Province for a sort of chef-finding-his-inspiration profile (with Chris tagging along as my "translator"—his Chinese is awful). Unlike my first trip, I no longer felt intimidated by China and was resolved not to cheat myself out of a good experience. Sichuan cooking was my first experience with regional Chinese cooking—prior to that, like many people, I'd viewed Chinese food as one cuisine. But the truth is, just as much as any other cuisine, if not more so, Chinese cooking is defined by regional variations. Our first menus were heavy with Sichuan peppercorns and chiles, and it's what made us famous, but I had never tasted the real thing. We had no agenda or absurd pop-up dinner to cook this time—my only assignment was to eat and explore, to take a breath and immerse myself in Chinese food before diving into the madness of opening a restaurant in Manhattan.

* * *

I wanted to try everything: mapo tofu, twice-cooked pork, fish-fragrant eggplant, hot pots, rabbit heads. Of course, Sichuan Province laughs in the face of anyone who thinks they can experience everything in one go. From the moment we landed, our noses and palates were overwhelmed. We went to Chongqing specifically to try *la zi ji* (chicken stir-fried in a mountain of chiles and peppercorns), and when we emerged from the train, what I had thought was fog turned out to be a thick blanket of smog that smothered the city. Climbing three flights of stairs to the restaurant left us winded and sweating. There was no relief in the food—a plate of *la zi ji* kicks you in the face with the scent of toasted chiles. It doesn't help that you have to hunch yourself over the plate, hunting through a sea of red for crunchy bits of chicken. The entire time I was in Sichuan, I danced a thin line between being sick and being elated.

The "fly restaurants"—divey mom-and-pop places that are swarmed with diners at lunch and dinner—are where the best eating in Sichuan happens. (They're similar to pop-up restaurants; their name emphasizes their fly-by-night nature.) But we ran into surprising and delicious dishes in a number of different places, from a theme-parkish town called Huanglongxi, where a stew of fish heads gave off an incredibly fresh perfume of green chiles even after a long, slow simmer, to roadside diners in the middle of the countryside. A friend schooled us in fresh tofu: We ground fresh soybeans with a stone mill and cooked them over a wood-burning fire that gave off a horrible black-smoke stench that, fortunately, didn't make it into the tofu. In Chengdu, at one of the fly restaurants, we ate mapo tofu with creamy pork brains, bacon steamed in lotus leaves, and one of my personal favorite dishes: a simple, restorative bowl of stewed turnips and beef in clear broth. Chris still bugs me to try and re-create a plate with hand-rolled pasta shaped like eels, served with eels and tons of white pepper.

At another restaurant, we had a Chinese version of haggis: a pork stomach stuffed with rice, peas, and chopped offal. Up until that point, I'd thought of Sichuan food as universally spicy, numbing, and intense, but nothing we ate was as hot as the Sichuan food at home. *Ma* (numbing) was in perfect balance with *la* (spicy), and almost everything had touches of salty, sweet, and sour. You could taste the sweetness of the chiles, not just the heat.

At one point, we linked up with a chef named Yu Bo and in thirty minutes of shopping at the market with him, I learned more about Chinese food than I'd ever known. Yu Bo is probably the best-known Sichuan chef in the world. He cooks in a modern style but draws on his region's history, not unlike guys like René Redzepi or Alex Atala.

Chris: The difference is that he's a lone wolf. He's not part of a community of chefs that gets together and shares ideas. There's no one within hundreds of miles who cooks like him.

I won't flatter myself by saying Yu Bo and I are similar, but I do recognize in him the qualities of a chef that I admire and strive for most. He's always searching, always curious. He's open-minded and generous.

He's got all these American cookbooks that he can't read but bought anyway, which is funny because I have all these Chinese books I can't read but couldn't help buying.

The only time I saw Yu Bo angry was at a culinary school where Knowlton signed us up for a crash course in Sichuan cooking. Yu Bo stood by while these well-meaning instructors showed us exactly how much MSG went into each serving of fish-fragrant eggplant, mapo tofu, and twice-cooked pork. Yu Bo serves modernist food, but his heart and his background are in classic Chinese cooking, and it was too much for him to see these shortcuts being taught to young cooks. I'm by no means an anti-MSG crusader, but I was impressed by how much it bothered him to see his native cuisine perverted. I asked him to show me the proper way of making the same dishes.

At one of the California-Italian restaurants where I worked in San Francisco, I learned how to make *ragù alla Bolognese*. It was a multistage recipe with a half dozen different spices. First you'd sear all the meat in batches, then take out the fat, deglaze the pan, and add mirepoix and tomato paste. You'd add a buttload of rosemary and thyme and a ton of black pepper, stew it with tomatoes, and serve it over fresh noodles. But when I went to work for Paolo at Farina, he made me *his* version of Bolognese—the best I've ever tasted. There was one carrot, a piece of celery, an onion, and a bay leaf. There were different times to add certain things, building flavor one layer at a time. After that, I decided I'd never go back to the old way. It was the same thing with Yu Bo. He unlocked things for me, showed me pathways and approaches that were new to me but instinctive to him.

When I came back from Sichuan, I immediately got to experimenting. I adjusted the way I used Sichuan peppercorns, not just deploying them for the novelty of their tingling sensation. I realized that great mapo tofu starts with great bean paste (*doubanjiang*) and good peppercorns. Sure, you can integrate techniques to make it unique and add depth of flavor, but there were a lot of extraneous ingredients in our recipe. I was still going to use good-quality pork and braise it instead of sautéing it, but now I had these fundamental flavor references to draw on.

Everything had changed.

Catfish à la Sichuan

SERVES 2 (OR 4 AS PART OF A LARGER MEAL)

This recipe derives from a classic Sichuan dish that not many American diners are familiar with, possibly because its name isn't exactly awe-inspiring: "water-cooked fish." But the name does not do justice to how intense and complex the finished product is. Our version stays pretty close to its forebear: Fish fillets are dusted in cornstarch, passed quickly through hot oil, and then simmered in a pickled stock.

The finest example of water-cooked fish I've ever had was in Sichuan Province, at the rural roadside eatery of Chef Yu Bo's longtime apprentice, who had set out on his own. It was unreal—spicy, sour, herbal, and nourishing. I was baffled by how he was able to achieve such an aromatic and flavorful soup. I struggled to re-create it at home. We tried making a big batch of potent stock, but the flavors mellowed and became muted after sitting around for any period of time. It has to be made to order.

After further testing, I landed on another key to the dish: fat. We infuse hot oil with Sichuan peppercorns, fennel, star anise, and cloves, then pour it over the soup. It sizzles and releases an intoxicating cloud, then pools to form an insulating layer that keeps the broth ridiculously hot.

The broth, by the way, is a heady elixir of beef stock with pickles and their juices. Not for the only time, I'll emphasize this: I love the concept of surf and turf. It's definitely not vegetarian-friendly, but it's often the ticket to savory, surprising food. For the pickles, Sichuan Pickled Vegetables (page 192), Pickled Mustard Greens (page 195), pickled onions, pickled fennel, or even kimchi would all work. A twist from the American South—boiled peanuts and Old Bay—rounds things out. (You'd be surprised how complementary Sichuan and Southern flavors are.) To make it a one-pot meal, add some noodles to the mix. And, again, this soup is best made to order; even so, you'll have dinner on the table in about half an hour.

1. Combine the beef stock, doubanjiang, and sugar in a large saucepan and bring to a simmer over medium heat, stirring to dissolve the sugar.

2. Add the pickled vegetables and their liquid and return to a simmer over high heat. Add the mushroom powder, ground Sichuan pepper, and Old Bay and season with salt. Add the fish to the soup, along with the peanuts and minced garlic. (You want the garlic to retain a little bit of its astringent spiciness when you serve the soup.) If you're in the mood for noodles, now's the time to add them. Let the soup return to a simmer.

3. Meanwhile, get a wok or saucepan very hot and toast the dried chiles until they've got a little color to them, about 2 minutes. Add the star anise, whole Sichuan peppercorns, fennel seeds, and clove, and stir and toast until fragrant, then add the chili oil and Sichuan peppercorn oil.

4. In the 30 seconds or so it takes for the oils to get smoking hot, ladle the soup into a large serving bowl. Stand back a bit and carefully but quickly pour the hot oil through a sieve over the soup. It will sputter and sizzle but subside quickly. Garnish with the cilantro and serve immediately.

Note: To make boiled peanuts, just simmer whole unshelled peanuts in chicken stock or water until soft, 2 to 3 hours, then drain and remove the shells.

2 cups beef stock

2 tablespoons doubanjiang (spicy bean paste)

1 tablespoon sugar

1 cup mixed spicy vegetable pickles (see headnote)

½ cup pickling liquid from your chosen pickles

1 teaspoon Mushroom Powder (page 299)

½ teaspoon ground Sichuan pepper

1 teaspoon Old Bay Seasoning

Kosher salt

1 pound catfish fillets (or any firm white fish of your choosing), cut into 1-inch pieces (a 2-pound whole fish, cut into chunks, works great too)

¼ cup boiled peanuts (see Note)

1 teaspoon minced garlic

½ (12-ounce) package Korean sweet potato starch noodles, soaked for a few minutes in hot water (optional)

4 dried Tianjin chiles or other medium-hot red chiles, like chiles Japones

1 star anise

1 teaspoon green or red Sichuan peppercorns

½ teaspoon fennel seeds

1 whole clove

3 tablespoons Chili Oil (page 290)

1 teaspoon Sichuan peppercorn oil

1 cup fresh cilantro leaves

Chongqing Chicken Wings

SERVES 4 AS PART OF A LARGER MEAL

It's well known that the sign of a great dish is its ability to silence a large group of noisy people, enraptured by what they're eating. All you hear is slurping and crunching, silverware against plates, chopsticks clicking. When the dish in question is *la zi ji,* the predominant sound is a soft rustling, like dry leaves skittering across a sidewalk. It is the noise made by diners sifting through a monstrous pile of chiles in search of golden brown bits of chicken hidden in the sea of red.

I've encountered versions of *la zi ji,* a dish most commonly traced to the Sichuan city of Chongqing, that are 95 percent chiles, 5 percent chicken. Some people balk at the idea of going to a restaurant and paying for a plate of food that is mostly inedible. To serve *la zi ji* at Mission Chinese, I needed to up the chicken-to-chile ratio.

Chicken wings to the rescue.

I've been pursuing the ideal chicken wing for most of my career. I've dabbled in all manner of elaborate wing practices. I've cured wings, confited them in chicken fat, smoked them, and sous-vided them. I've been close a few times, but I'd never really settled on a method until I spoke to a friend whose mom worked at the Anchor Bar in Buffalo. The Anchor Bar is the supposed home of the original Buffalo wing. I prodded my friend, trying to get her to ask her mom for their secrets. Eventually I pried out of them that the key to a perfect chicken wing is to treat it like a French fry: parcook it, freeze it, and fry it. The freezing causes the liquid in the skin to expand and burst the cell walls, resulting in perfectly thin, crisp skin without any breading. Once I learned this technique, I never looked back.

This is how a lot of things work at Mission Chinese. We talk to people with a history of doing things right, and we learn from them. Then we consider how we can add something to what they've taught us, improve on it, make it our own. In this case, the addition of fried tripe to a plate of chicken wings is giving your guests 110 percent. I like mixing proteins and layering similar textures. Here, on the same plate, you get the crackly skin of chicken wings, still juicy on the inside, as well as the crunchy chew of fried tripe. Plus the papery toughness of those chiles, which, I should mention, you don't eat. Please stop coming to the restaurant and eating the chiles.

Note: You need to parcook the wings a day ahead, so don't start this recipe on Sunday morning thinking you'll have wings in time for football.

1. Preheat the oven to 350°F.

2. In a large bowl, toss the wings with the salt and ½ cup oil. Spread the wings out on a wire rack set over a baking sheet. Bake the wings for 15 minutes, or just until the skin appears cooked but not browned. Let the parbaked wings cool to room temperature, then lay them in a single layer on a baking sheet and freeze, uncovered, overnight.

3. The next day, clean the tripe thoroughly under cold running water, scrubbing vigorously to remove any grit. Put in a pot, cover with cold salty water by 2 inches, and bring to a boil over high heat. Boil for 10 minutes, partially covered, then reduce the heat to a simmer and cook for 2 to 3 hours, until the tripe is very tender. Drain in a colander, rinse under cold water, and cool completely.

4. Meanwhile, retrieve the wings from the freezer and allow them to thaw at room temperature for 1 to 2 hours.

5. Slice the cooked tripe into strips about ½ inch wide and 2 inches long. Set aside.

6. In a deep pot or a wok (or use a deep-fryer), heat about 4 inches of oil to 350°F. Meanwhile, pat the tripe strips dry with paper towels, then dredge them in the cornstarch, shaking off any excess. Working in batches, if necessary, deep-fry the wings and tripe for 4 to 6 minutes, or until golden and crispy. They should cook in about the same amount of time.

3 pounds chicken wings (either mid-joints or whole wings)

¼ cup kosher salt, plus more as needed

½ cup vegetable or peanut oil, plus 8 to 10 cups for deep-frying

½ pound honeycomb tripe

½ cup cornstarch, for dredging

4 cups dried Tianjin chiles or other medium-hot red chiles, like chiles Japones

About ¾ cup Chongqing Wing Spice Mix (recipe follows)

7. Meanwhile, toast the Tianjin chiles in a hot, dry wok or skillet for about a minute over high heat, stirring continuously so the chiles cook evenly. Transfer to a plate.

8. Drain the fried wings and tripe, shaking off as much oil as you can (or let them briefly drain on paper towels). Then transfer to a large bowl and dust them generously with the spice mix, tossing to coat. Add the toasted chiles and toss well. The chiles will perfume the dish, but they aren't meant to be eaten.

9. To serve, transfer everything—aromatic chiles and all—to a serving platter and present to your awestruck and possibly terrified guests.

Chongqing Wing Spice Mix

MAKES ABOUT 1 CUP

2 tablespoons whole Sichuan peppercorns
2 tablespoons cumin seeds
2 teaspoons fennel seeds
2 star anise
2 black cardamom pods
1½ teaspoons whole cloves
2 tablespoons plus 2 teaspoons sugar
1 tablespoon kosher salt
2 tablespoons plus 2 teaspoons Mushroom Powder (page 299)
2 tablespoons cayenne pepper

1. Toast the Sichuan peppercorns, cumin seeds, fennel seeds, star anise, cardamom, and cloves in a dry skillet over medium heat, stirring continuously until fragrant. In a small bowl, combine the toasted spices with the sugar, salt, mushroom powder, and cayenne.

2. In a spice or coffee grinder, grind the spice mix to a powder, working in batches if necessary. The spice mix will keep in an airtight container for about a week before losing much of its potency.

Hot-and-Sour Rib Tips

SERVES 4

During my second trip to China, our guide, Lillian, took us to an acquaintance's home in Chengdu for dinner. The woman's daughter worked halfway across the country in Beijing, and you could tell she missed her—she seemed happy to have people in the house to cook for. She showed us around her home kitchen and stuffed us with food as though we were her kids.

This is the dish that sticks with me from that dinner. It's so simple and homey—from start to finish, she had it on the table in about twenty minutes. She caramelized sugar with some *doubanjiang* (spicy bean paste) in a pan of hot oil, then added Sichuan peppercorns, chiles, and pork ribs. A little water and vinegar, a lid, and a little while later, out came the ribs, glazed, sticky, spicy, and sour. Spooned over a bowl of steamed rice, they were immensely satisfying.

This recipe is pretty true to the original (with the notable exception of the *shio koji* marinade), down to the cut of meat we use. "Now just what are rib tips?" you may ask. They're the lower section of the sparerib, usually trimmed away by the butcher when he or she is preparing nice squared-off St. Louis–style ribs. You can usually find them dirt cheap at an Asian market. Other butchers may have them hidden away in the walk-in if you inquire about them. Otherwise, just ask your butcher to split a rack of baby back ribs or spareribs into two pieces for you. A quick zip through his or her bandsaw will give you the next best thing.

Note: This recipe requires an overnight marinade.

1. In a large container or bowl, combine the rib tips with the shio koji and one of the beers. (If you need to cut the ribs into smaller portions to fit in one layer, go for it.) Cover with a lid or plastic wrap and refrigerate overnight.

2. The next day, drain the rib tips and pat dry. Slice the ribs into 1-bone chunks.

Special equipment: Pressure cooker

1½ pounds rib tips (see headnote), or baby back ribs or spareribs cut into 2-inch pieces

1 cup prepared shio koji (see page 303)

2 (12-ounce) cans cheap beer (such as Bud Light), or as needed

½ cup peanut or vegetable oil

¼ cup Chili Crisp (page 290)

1 cup palm sugar (chopped, if you bought it as a puck) or brown sugar

2 tablespoons doubanjiang (spicy bean paste)

⅔ cup Chinese black vinegar

1 tablespoon tomato paste

1 tablespoon fish sauce

2 bay leaves

2 star anise

1 black cardamom pod, crushed

1 teaspoon fennel seeds

1 teaspoon cumin seeds

1 teaspoon ground Sichuan pepper

Steamed rice, for serving

3. Set a wok or skillet over high heat and let it sit for about 3 minutes, until it's very hot. Coat the wok with about 2 tablespoons of the oil and add the rib tips. Allow them to sit for a minute to get a nice sear on them, then turn and repeat until they're seared on all sides. Once the meat is an attractive shade of brown, scoop the ribs out of the pan into a pressure cooker. (If you don't have a pressure cooker, you can cook the ribs in a saucepan with a lid. Simmer for 1 hour, or until the ribs are tender.)

4. Add the rest of the oil to the pan, along with the chili crisp, and cook for just a moment, then add the sugar, doubanjiang, and ¼ cup water and stir to dissolve the sugar. Add the vinegar, tomato paste, fish sauce, and all the remaining spices and bring to a simmer.

5. Transfer everything to the pressure cooker and top off with the remaining beer. The meat should be at least halfway covered with liquid—if not, add more beer or water. Lock on the lid of the pressure cooker and cook at full pressure for 25 minutes, then allow it to depressurize naturally.

6. Strain the liquid into a wok or pan (reserving the meat, of course), bring to a boil over medium-high heat, and cook until the sauce has reduced to a glaze, about 8 minutes.

7. Add the ribs to the sauce and stir to coat. Serve with rice.

New York,
Part II

Nothing had changed.

It's funny how perception can outpace reality. People around the country knew who I was and what Mission Chinese Food was, but they'd never tasted our food. I went on TV and made hand-pulled noodles with Martha Stewart. I had been to China twice in a year. Food writers were asking me for advice on cooking Chinese food.

But the reality was, I'd only been cooking Chinese food for a year, and we were still one small restaurant, in the same broken-down space, on the same shady block in San Francisco. I felt antsy, afraid of being a one-hit wonder. I wanted to test myself in New York again. Anthony knew this, and during one of my trips to the city, he told me to meet up with his friend Dennis. "I've known him for a long time. He's looking for a space for you."

Anthony explained that Dennis worked in finance and loved food and had his ear to the ground. I set up a meeting with him in Chinatown at East Corner Wonton, my favorite little now defunct noodle-soup shop. Soon this thirty-something Asian guy in a blue hoodie walked in. It was a Saturday morning and he had "late night" written all over him. But as hungover as he was, he was very excited to be up and meeting with me. We started walking toward the Lower East Side. Every now and then Dennis would press his face up to a window and say something like, "This place doesn't look like it's doing very well; we should talk to them." It was a trip. This couldn't really be how you opened a restaurant in New York, right?

Eventually he walked me over to a Thai restaurant on Orchard Street. My idea at that point was just to open a low-key takeout restaurant, something simple with minimal overhead, near a bar that could entertain our customers while they waited for food. This place looked perfect—a small counter in front, with a pass into the kitchen—and it was on a busy street full of bars. Tucked in the back, down a narrow corridor, was a small dining room in a covered patio. I would've been fine not having a dining room at all. But it was there, so we rolled with it.

Dennis set up a meeting with the owner. The whole thing was pretty sketchy and hard to follow. The gist of it was that we were speaking to a guy with a failing restaurant who was more than happy to offload the lease onto someone else. But it was cheap, and it was available. It felt right to me, so I called Anthony and he told me to go for it. He figured if I liked the space, it would be fine.

Anthony came out for a visit later, but we were already well into negotiations with the landlord by then. There were a number of shadowy side deals to be made, because the previous lessee had silent investors who had to be paid off. We really got shafted, to be honest. But we figured if we just did whatever it took to take over the lease, we'd be able to open the restaurant and everything would work out. We knew nothing. In San Francisco, we showed up at Lung Shan and cooked. I think back, and I'm terrified by how wet behind the ears we were. In my head, I was already arranging tables, designing the kitchen, imagining where customers would stand, thinking about the menu—I had no idea about building permits or codes, health inspections, fire inspections, community boards.

If we were smart, we would have had a contractor do a walk through of the space before signing the lease, and we would have checked the Building Department's website to see what outstanding violations were attached to the building. We should have done a lot of things, but we didn't. Dennis and Anthony and I walked through the building with our lawyer and she said, "You realize you're taking the building *as is*, right? Anything you discover later, you'll have to fix yourselves." And we said, yeah, sure, cool. The previous owner must have been licking his chops when he saw us walk in the door. The building wasn't up to code, and it was obvious just looking and listening to us—a wide-eyed chef from San Francisco and an investment banker—that we were clueless.

They had never pulled permits for any of the construction they had done in the building. The dining room had been constructed illegally, entirely out of plywood. The bathroom vented into the kitchen. The main exhaust tube from the kitchen was stapled rather than welded together, a fact that the fire inspector brought to our attention a week before we planned to open. Meanwhile, one of the restaurant's previous owners, who was a trained architect acquainted with all the building's problems, began texting and emailing to blackmail us for hush money. "I know that back structure is illegal—I built it. Unless you give me $5,000 by Monday, I'm going to report you." We passed his texts on to our lawyer and went about trying to open. We started paying the rent in January, thinking we'd open within a month or two. Idiots.

I had finally acquired enough money to pay off my student loan, and I'd promised my wife that I'd open a bank account for the first time in ten years and get my credit back in line when we moved to New York. Instead, I put all the money into fixing the restaurant and sold off some of my ownership shares to fund the rest. We were bleeding cash. There was no room for failure now—for the first time since we started Mission Chinese Food, we had something to lose.

* * *

In San Francisco, Sue and Liang took care of everything related to the business of running the restaurant. They have a remarkable and uniquely Chinese approach to doing so. Everything is solvable, everything can be done yourself. In New York, we tried to mimic the Chineseness of San Francisco. We didn't hire an accounting company until well after we'd opened. We had no HR department or business people—it was just me winging it.

It was so easy in San Francisco, why couldn't we do it again in New York? *We'll buy a restaurant that's not working, we'll move in, reshuffle a few things, and then we'll open. I'll hire Chinese wok cooks who don't have a lot of experience, and I'll teach them our way to cook.*

Everything backfired. The three Chinese cooks we hired didn't work out. The oldest, Peter, lost it and quit, probably because he was being picked on by the two smaller, quieter Chinese guys, Jin and Chin. There was something exceptional about our working relationship with Sue and Liang in San Francisco. We had started from a very innocent place, and they made it possible for us to grow. Liang would bug us occasionally about buying the restaurant outright and taking over, but at the end of the day, he knew we were all in it together. I think that those cooks in New York knew who we were, that we had a big profile. They looked us up, and they used the fact that we were going to be busy and that we needed them for leverage.

I thought about Sue and Liang and the San Francisco team often. I was fortunate to have another shot at New York. But if we made fools of ourselves here, it would affect the way people viewed our restaurant in San Francisco. It could affect the way people would view San Francisco as a whole. The truth is that New York is the big time. Since leaving San Francisco, I've caught a lot of flack about abandoning the Bay Area. I know it seems that way, but I hope that San Franciscans can see our little restaurant succeeding in New York and be proud.

Chris: I can't help but be reminded of a certain young kid, hoping to catch Emeril at Universal Studios. I asked the San Francisco crew separately about this, but tell me: You're in New York most of the time now; is San Francisco really as good as it was when you were there?

Meanwhile with Jesse and Greg

Chris: How do you two feel Mission Chinese San Francisco changed when Danny left to open New York?

Jesse Koide, head chef of Mission Chinese San Francisco: Danny is such a presence. When he left for New York, the restaurant lost that. People kept talking about how they missed the way he'd come out into the dining room. It's not in my nature to be so personable. I had to force myself to do it.

C: What changed about your job?

J: It took me a while to realize that I was actually running the place, and that I should be thinking about putting stuff on the menu. A younger chef would have jumped on that and maybe used it as their time to shine. Danny and Anthony would tell me all the time that I should feel free to change the menu. But to be

honest, Chinese food isn't what I think about when I'm trying to be creative. Eventually, I started adding things that I know how to do, which was also different from stuff that Danny would do intuitively. I would order different types of really nice fish and try to make crudos with Chinese and Japanese ingredients. We started ordering whole boxes of fish from Tsukiji market and doing sashimi specials. Stuff like that kept me more interested and occupied and happy than stressing out about trying to make a new noodle dish. Every time I did come up with something it just felt so contrived, like I was trying so hard to make it seem like Danny's food or to make it seem like it was cohesive with the rest of the menu.

Greg Wong, general manager of Mission Chinese San Francisco: I think the food quality stayed the same after Danny left. The biggest thing

that I missed was something so small. Every morning, Anthony, Danny, Grandma, and I would peel eggs in the dining room. Jesse would come out and everyone would sit around and talk. We had this little familial round table. That was a really nice time every morning. We talked about food, we talked about stupid stuff.

C: About six months after Danny left, the *San Francisco Chronicle* revisited Mission Chinese and questioned whether the restaurant was as good without Danny there. Did you feel like that was a fair question? That the restaurant was not as strong?

G: No, I would say that foodwise it's just as strong. The front of house was too relaxed. And after that point I tried to step it up. One thing I always tried to do when Danny was out here was listen really intently to how he would describe dishes. Part of his charm was that every time he came up with a new dish he was super stoked about it and he would talk about it to every single customer. He'd go up to every table. It's different not coming from him.

J: In my mind, the review didn't really complain about the food as much as the service. And maybe that was Michael Bauer's way of saying that things are different without Danny there.

C: Would you say the transition was difficult for you personally?

J: In the beginning, I was a little butt hurt about Danny moving to New York. He would say things like, "Well, the way we do it out there is better, so just do it that way." I would be like, "Well, you and I developed this way here, and it was awesome six months ago, and now all of a sudden it's worthless." But that kind of wore off. I realized he had wrapped his mind around a bigger picture. I started to realize he actually wants to be a restaurateur. And because of his personality, he'll become a great one. He doesn't like to spend ten hours on the line. Sadly, I do, but I also want to learn how to operate and run a restaurant. I'm not that great at it, but I know I can be good at it.

G: I always saw Danny as a kid with ADD. I was told when I started that he might leave at any time. I was originally a cook, and Anthony said, "Make sure you're writing things down, because if Danny leaves, we need this information." Danny's got this great sense of creativity, but sometimes with creativity you need outlets for it. That outlet ended up being Mission Chinese Food, but I don't think that was the plan. I was excited for him to go to New York, because I assumed he was going to do something new.

C: Did you feel any bitterness?

J: I never really felt bitter or neglected, even though it would be easy to feel that way, and we would joke about it. I tried to put myself in his perspective. If I was to go open another place, I'd have to walk away from the first place and make the second as good or better, then go back and check in and hope that number one was still good. You can't be in two places at once. I tried to put my feelings aside, because, sure, I'm in charge of San Francisco, but it's not about me.

G: The only thing I'd be bitter about is that he's hard to get in contact with. Sometimes I just want to be like, "Hey, jerk, respond to my questions. I know New York is keeping you super busy and it's important and it's good for all of us, but this is still your little original shop."

C: In a lot of ways Mission Chinese Food was still growing into a restaurant when Danny left, so you guys have had to grow with it. Do you feel like the experience of running Mission Chinese is instructive to you going forward, maybe opening your own place?

J: Sure. Almost every Murphy's-Law, worst-case scenario has happened since I've been here. Not very many restaurants do as much customer volume, whether it be delivery or eat-in. That kitchen is always putting out food.

C: Danny talks about how, after he left Farina, you guys didn't talk for almost two years. He said there was no falling out, it just kind of happened. How do you remember it?

J: We ran that place with Paolo, and then got to the point where we were both just doing the menu ourselves. There were days when I would come to work at twelve thirty, even though we didn't have to be there until one, but I could tell Danny had already been there for several hours. I'd go in the kitchen, and be like, "What's going on?" And he'd say, "Oh, nothing, I already made the menu and prepped everything." "What time did you get here?" "Oh, eight." I don't think he was even intentionally trying to prove that I wasn't needed; he was just really going for it.

And then he wore himself out and had issues with the owners, like everybody else did, and he ended up just walking out one day during lunch. So then I picked up, trying to do the same thing and prove to myself that I could run this huge place. I went through the same process: wore myself out, got into a fight with the owner, showed up the next day at noon, grabbed all my shit, and bounced. It was the only job I've ever walked out on, and from there I pretty much walked straight to Mission Burger, where Danny was, and said, "Hey, I just quit." I knew I didn't have to say anything more. Just showing up and saying hi to him was going to tell him enough.

C: Until Farina, you had always been a senior cook to Danny. Did it ever feel unnatural at Mission Chinese Food for Danny to be chef and for you to be his sous?

J: It was a little uncomfortable, because I felt like if we had stayed friends for that year and a half or so, I probably would've ended up being a bigger part of Mission Street Food. Mission Street Food was like a soul search for him and Anthony. And I was still at Farina, just chipping away.

I mean, when he really wants something to be a certain way because he really believes in it, that's when he can seem like a dick. But these things are easy to move on from. You just argue, and six hours later, you're having a beer together. Not a big deal.

C: That's interesting to me. If it were me, I'd say, "Screw you, long hair. I taught you everything you know."

J: It's not in me to remind people.

C: I would feel questionably happy for Danny if I had come up with him and then he was really successful. I feel like you guys are both purely happy for the success of the whole thing.

J and G: Yup.

I left San Francisco with someone running the kitchen who was more than capable as a chef: Jesse. By the time I headed for New York, he was already basically running the kitchen. Certainly you sacrifice some things when you go across the country to open a second restaurant. The energy in the room changes because I'm not there. But mostly the differences exist more in people's minds than in reality. You can't help people letting their feelings about the chef not being there affect their experience of the food. But when we went to New York, my San Francisco guys understood that this was something we should all be excited about. It's a new sibling in the family. They understood and they supported me, and I needed them.

Chris: Early on, you guys talked about keeping the New York restaurant as far beneath the radar as possible. You were almost not going to call it Mission Chinese Food at all. You even asked me if you could call it Ying Chinese Food.

We didn't want the expectations. We wanted people to find out about it gradually, but in New York City, before you get a liquor license, you need to go in front of the community board and explain why you deserve one. Food bloggers sit in on these meetings to get the scoop on the latest restaurant openings. So I figured if we had to let the cat out of the bag, it'd be best to have a proper newspaper announce it. I called the *Times* Dining Section to give them a heads-up, and that was it. People started showing up at the restaurant weeks before we were open.

Now, faced with an overly scrutinized, overhyped opening, I started freaking out. I didn't have Anthony nearby to share the weight. He was in San Francisco, where his wife was having a baby. I hired a scruffy go-getter named Allen Yuen to be general manager, and I lucked out in finding an unbelievably talented woman named Angela Dimayuga to be chef de cuisine. But I was Allen's boss, and he was looking to me for direction—so I did my best impression of someone who knows what he's doing. I yelled at contractors when they showed up late, haggled over equipment, hired cooks, and made design decisions off the top of my head. We painted the walls teal because someone had called me and asked what color I wanted the walls, and when I looked down, the first color I saw was teal.

How (Not) to Design a Restaurant

Make what you will of this advice. As described in the next couple of chapters, the original location of Mission Chinese Food New York is closed, largely because of our naïveté (and the willingness of others to take advantage of that). As it turned out, the restaurant wasn't built to stand up to the volume of business we did. We needed a restaurant specifically designed to meet our unique needs, in the way that everything on a submarine is made specifically for submarines. But for a while, it was the happiest place. It felt familiar to people. It had the feel of a clubhouse, or a bar your dad built for his buddies in the basement. It was honest, and even though it had its problems, I loved it.

Tiling:

We didn't have any money, so we couldn't do any major renovations or structural improvements. The aesthetic came to us on the fly. We had to fix the floor in the back, and the cheapest material available was black faux-marble tile. It looks sleek and fancy in a Miami coke-house sort of way, but it's slippery as hell when it's wet. A terrible choice, but it was cheap. If you ate at Mission Chinese, you knew to be careful when you were walking through the dining room.

Seating:

Two of our staff members, Aubrey and Arley, built the banquettes out of plywood and lit them with fluorescent pink lights. Dennis recruited his dad to do some carpentry too. When I walked in and saw his sixty-five-year-old father slumped over saying, "I'm so tired," I had to yell at Dennis about why he'd forced his old man to build our restaurant.

Accoutrements:

We hung up a Chinese dragon because we had one in San Francisco, and it was easier than figuring out something new.

The Bathrooms:

I really liked the bathrooms at Isa in Brooklyn, where everything

about the restaurant was serious, and then you'd go to the bathroom and walk into this trippy space. We were just going to copy them exactly, but one night, while watching *Twin Peaks* at home, it dawned on me that if we were going to make going to the bathroom a weird, otherworldly experience, we might as well go all out. You'd step from the busy, noisy restaurant into a small, dim stall and be immersed in the haunting refrain from the *Twin Peaks* theme song. There were wood-paneled walls and a few sprigs of pine. A photo of Laura Palmer. And just like with *Twin Peaks,* if you said you didn't like our bathrooms, it would be because you didn't understand them.

The Menu Board:

My reference for the menu board at Mission Chinese was the menu at Landmark Diner, right near my apartment, but it could just as easily have been any of tens of thousands of cheesy backlit menus around the country. My wife took the pictures. I told her to put them on blue backgrounds, style them ridiculously ("Think cheeseburger next to a rose"), and overexpose them. She did a great job.

First thing every morning, I threw up from stress. I was losing my mind. I was ready to go, but the restaurant wasn't. I'd show up at the site first thing in the morning and the contractors wouldn't be there. I was training my cooks in my apartment because we couldn't legally cook in the restaurant. None of this will be surprising to any other New York restaurateur, but I had no idea.

It all came to something of a head one night in Brooklyn. I went to a show my friend Peter Meehan was playing with his band. I was already a little drunk, and we made a beeline for the bar when we walked in the door. I ordered five shots of bourbon for myself, Youngmi, Angela, and two friends. Suddenly, Andrew Knowlton sidled up next to me. Since our China trip, I'd moved to New York and I'd called Andrew repeatedly, but couldn't get him to call me back.

The truth is, I didn't have a lot of friends in New York, not real ones, at least. Andrew and I had bonded during eight days in China together, on a trip that was pivotal for me. But now it seemed like we were just summer-camp friends. When we got back to New York, we didn't hang out. I understand that that's what it's like to be a busy adult living in New York, but at the time I was existentially alone and grasping for some sort of buoy.

"Dude, what the hell, man? You never answer the phone."

Not reading how drunk I was, or how paranoid, Andrew smiled, said, "What's up?" and hugged me.

"Don't hug me! I could be on the side of the road dead. If I call you two weeks in a row, do me a solid and text me back and say what's up."

I had almost unconsciously been drinking the shots in front of me. I started punching Andrew in the stomach, a little too aggressively, ranting about how he wasn't a real friend. Real friends answer the goddamn phone. I was getting in his face, saying that nobody gives a crap about him or *Bon Appétit*. I was being an asshole, trying to get him riled up, and the less he reacted, the angrier I grew.

Chris: Well, in his defense, he told me that the bar was so loud that the most embarrassing part for him was that he kept having to say, "I'm sorry, what did you say?" And you'd respond, "I said you were a piece of shit!" "Oh."

But I don't exactly understand why you were so upset that

this guy wasn't calling you back. You'd only known him for a short time, after all. Were you worried that people who were being friendly to you weren't really your friends?

Yes. At that point, I was drinking eight or nine Tsingtaos every night in the restaurant space—just pounding them, not enjoying them. I'd get drunk and hungry, go home, order a boatload of Chinese food, and tell my wife that it was for research and development. I'd pass out until it arrived, then wake up and eat. She'd go downstairs to the door and haul up an entire box of Chinese food with enough sets of chopsticks for five people. Youngmi was saying, "This has to end, Danny."

Chris: Real quick, what would you order?

At the time, I had an idea to improve on moo shu pork, so I was ordering moo shu every night. I would try to order somewhat responsibly—fish with green chili pepper or whatever—but when you're drunk, you get a little reckless. Plus, I knew from working in Chinese restaurants that ordering seafood gets dicey when it gets late. By eleven p.m., that calamari has been sitting in cornstarch for a long time, you know what I mean? So I stuck to the old standbys. Mongolian beef. For a while, I'd always order Singaporean rice noodles because they don't overcook and get gummy. But, truth be told, it's my least favorite noodle. I always got combination fried rice or fried rice with salted fish and diced chicken and Chinese sausage. The point is, I was not living well. I wanted to lose weight but in New York it was just too easy to eat. There are so many places to choose from, and everywhere is open late.

Chris: You didn't want to lose weight because you were showing up in more magazines? Or because Uniqlo wanted you to model their clothes?

No, I'm not that vain. The Asian people around me make sure of it. They like to tell you if you've gained weight. If I was looking chubby, Sue or Liang would say, "Oh, you got fat. That's good; that means you're making a lot of money." Or when I'd say hi to Amanda, who works at the supermarket down the street from Lung Shan, she would always say, "Hey, you got fat." Thanks.

This is the absolute truth: I did the Uniqlo campaign because it was good business. I'm not interested in seeing myself on the side of a bus. When I sit down with my phone or laptop, I Google "Mission Chinese Food" before I Google myself. Mission Chinese Food is the important thing, and I am not Mission Chinese Food.

Chris: But I think people see you dressed in bright clothes, or swim trunks, or in all white or all black, with your long bleached hair, and they assume you're trying to be fashionable or avant-garde.

Anthony: Danny's always had flair in terms of personal appearance. Actually, he used to dress crazier.

If anything, I've toned things down. I used to wear dress shoes and tank tops in the kitchen. I shared a ladybug sweater with my wife. The fact that people talk about my hair or my clothes now is ridiculous. I'm not trying to be Kanye West. I'm not wearing a ski mask with eyeholes cut out to work. I wear all white because it's hot in New York in the summer. I wear swim trunks because you get a lot of water splashed on you in a kitchen.

Chris: Anthony, clearly, Danny has achieved a level of fame that we weren't expecting. Do you feel like he's changed as a person?

Anthony: Not to me. The only change is that sometimes he forgets what he's told me. He talks to a lot of people.

I feel bad about that. Anthony will listen to me tell an entire story, and it will gradually dawn on me that maybe he's already heard it. I'll have been talking to him for thirty minutes, and then I ask, "Wait, did I already tell you this?" And he'll just say, "Yeah, you did."

* * *

I strive to be a humble person. When I was younger, I spent a lot of time and energy being negative, criticizing other restaurants. When I landed in New York, I was nervous as hell. People in San Francisco told me that New Yorkers hated San Francisco, that they'd resent the idea that Mission Chinese Food could show them anything new. I made a conscious decision to be quiet, to be nice. If you don't come into a new city with an agenda to take over or undermine your peers, you'll save yourself a lot of headaches.

And so, for every bit of negative energy that came my way—construction delays, extortion threats—I tried to put twice as much positivity back into the system. In the middle of construction and recipe testing, we'd take a few hours to deliver staff meal to our friends' restaurants: heaps of savory, fatty salt-cod fried rice; enormous bowls of mapo tofu; crisp pork jowls with crunchy winter radishes; steamed rice studded with fragrant barley; and sometimes

even my pesto. We figured we were cooking anyway, no harm in making a little extra to share. The amount of goodwill that came back to us was unreal. Paul Liebrandt came and made us staff meal at Mission Chinese, for crying out loud. Chefs are people pleasers, and they respect good hospitality more than anyone else.

David Chang happened to be around when I brought his team lunch at Momofuku Ssäm Bar. I'd met Dave a few times. I just wanted to duck in and out and get back to work, but when Dave saw that we'd brought food, he grabbed me and had his entire staff stop working. He stood in front of them and gave a speech about how not long ago restaurants in New York used to have one another's backs. There was a sense of community that he said I was bringing back, and while it might not occur to his staff, the fact that we were bringing them lunch meant that we had spent time thinking about them. "This is an act of generosity that you need to remember and be thankful for. This is a dying thing, and it shouldn't be. It's a part of good cooking."

The next time I saw Dave was the night before we opened. I worked up enough nerve to ask him for advice.

"Anything you want, just ask me," he said. "What do you want to know?"

"What do I do?"

"What do you mean?"

I cleared my throat. "Well, we open tomorrow. What am I supposed to do, man?"

At first, he responded with positive vibes. "You've got this, man; you're going to be fine." But then he got on a roll. "Don't undersell yourself. Don't invest everything in your people, because they will screw you over. You don't want to hear this now, and believe me I would never want to hear this either, but you can't put all your eggs in one basket. You've got to value yourself; you've got to make sure that you look out for yourself."

I think he sensed he was crushing my spirit. "Also, you have nothing to worry about." At this point, Youngmi wobbled drunkenly over to us. "You have a beautiful wife, you're happy. You're doing it right." I nodded. "I look back and can't say that I did everything right. Don't listen to me. You're on the right path."

I pushed his warnings to the back of my mind and focused on what he was saying at that moment. I was alive, I was married. Anything else would be a bonus.

All right, I could do this.

Pork Jowl and Radishes

SERVES 4 (OR 6 AS PART OF A LARGER MEAL)

We'd come to a point about six months in at Mission Chinese Food in San Francisco where everything on the menu was spicy. I didn't want to get a reputation as just another Sichuan restaurant that brutalized customers with heat. This recipe was my olive branch to people with more sensitive tongues and tummies: an earthy umami plate of pork with just-cooked radishes. The fresh shiso and mint brighten things up.

Raw or nearly raw vegetables and herbs aren't something you typically come across in Chinese cooking. The Chinese people I know don't like to eat undercooked vegetables. (Chris's mom says she was totally baffled when she first moved to the States from Taiwan and saw her schoolmates eating salad.) It's too bad. In Chinese cooking—and Western cooking, for that matter—root vegetables are often tragically overcooked, braised to mush. When done properly, though, they can be tender but still hold on to their crunchiness, and they are the perfect complement to rich meats—like, say, pork jowl.

Jowls are likewise underappreciated, and frequently misunderstood. They're very fatty, so one's instinct is to cook them low and slow until all that fat has melted away. But we don't shoot for fall-apart tenderness—in Chinese cooking, it's all about textural variety. In New York, where we have proper ovens, we roast the jowls until just tender. In San Francisco, we put the jowls in cold oil, then bring them up to 350°F, turn off the heat, and let them slowly cool. It's the wrongest of wrong ways to confit something, where the idea is to gently cook in warm oil, but it works for jowls.

Because I love you, I'm also including an alternative to jowls, which can sometimes be tricky to find. In fact, this just might even be a better option: Hong Kong–style crisp pork belly.

Note: If you're using jowls, they need to be seasoned and refrigerated overnight before cooking, and then chilled thoroughly before finishing the dish.

2 pounds pork jowls, or
 1½ pounds Hong Kong–Style
 Crisp Pork Belly (recipe follows)
About 2 tablespoons kosher salt
6 to 8 cups rendered pork fat or
 vegetable or peanut oil, plus a
 little more for stir-frying
1 pound small radishes with
 greens (or substitute small
 peeled turnips)
1 tablespoon minced garlic
1 tablespoon fermented black
 beans
1 tablespoon soy sauce
½ teaspoon Mushroom Powder
 (page 299)
1 teaspoon cornstarch slurry (see
 page 292)
Leaves from 1 sprig fresh mint,
 coarsely chopped
2 shiso leaves, coarsely chopped
1½ tablespoons Fried Garlic
 (page 294)
Steamed rice, for serving

1. If you're using Hong Kong–style pork belly, skip ahead to step 5. If you're using pork jowls, slice the jowls across the grain into 1-inch-wide strips. (Think very thick, short strips of bacon.) Season the strips liberally with salt, set them on a wire rack over a baking sheet, and refrigerate, uncovered, overnight.

2. In a deep pot, immerse the pork jowl strips in enough fat or oil to cover by about an inch, set the pot over high heat, and bring the fat to 350°F. The jowls will begin to brown as the oil comes to temperature. Once the oil hits 350°F, cook for 5 to 7 minutes more, or until the meat has browned and about half the fat has rendered from the meat.

3. Using tongs or a slotted spoon, transfer the pork to a baking dish or baking pan. Carefully ladle just enough of the hot fat over the pork to cover it. Lay a sheet of parchment paper on the surface of the fat, cover the dish tightly with aluminum foil, and allow the meat and fat to cool completely.

4. Remove the pork from the fat, wrap it tightly in plastic, and refrigerate it for at least a couple of hours or as long as overnight; it'll be much easier to slice once chilled. (You can reserve the fat for another confit. Strain out the solids and store it in the fridge for up to 2 months.)

5. Bring a large saucepan of very salty water to a boil. Meanwhile, slice the pork (jowls or belly) into rough ½-inch cubes. Set aside.

6. Wash the radishes, including the greens, by swishing them around in a bowl of cold water. Depending on the size and type of radishes you're using, halve or quarter them, doing the best you can to leave the greens attached. (With turnips, you may want to remove the greens and discard any tough stems, reserving the tender greens.) Blanch the radishes and greens in the salty water until they're slightly softened but still crunchy, about 30 seconds. Drain in a colander and run under cold water.

7. Get a wok or skillet very hot over high heat and coat with a thin film of pork fat or oil. When the fat's shimmering, add the pork and stir-fry to warm it through and get a little color, about 3 minutes. Transfer to a plate.

8. Add the garlic to the wok and stir-fry until softened and fragrant. Add the fermented black beans and give them a quick stir, then add the radishes and return the pork to the wok. Stir-fry the ingredients briskly, then add the soy sauce and mushroom powder and give everything another quick toss. Add ⅓ cup water, then add the slurry, stir, and allow the liquid to come to a simmer and thicken into a glaze—it will happen quickly. Toss to coat the ingredients, adjust the seasoning with salt, and then scoop everything onto a serving platter.

9. Rain down the chopped mint and shiso over everything. If you used pork belly, put the whole or crumbled pork crackling on top. Finish with a sprinkling of fried garlic. Serve with rice.

Hong Kong–Style Crisp Pork Belly

MAKES ABOUT 3 POUNDS (CAN BE SCALED UP)

This is a very straightforward recipe I adapted from Marco Pierre White, after watching his videos online. When you really nail the recipe, you get an awesome crunchy rind and perfectly cooked meat.

1 (4-pound) piece skin-on pork belly
3 tablespoons kosher salt, plus more as needed
1 tablespoon sugar
Olive oil

1. Rub the fleshy side of the pork belly with the salt and sugar. Lay it skin side up on a wire rack set over a baking sheet and refrigerate, uncovered, overnight.

2. The next day, remove the belly from the fridge and let it rest at room temperature for 1 hour before cooking. Meanwhile, preheat the oven to 360°F.

3. Rub the skin side of the belly lightly with olive oil and salt it lightly. Pour about ½ cup water into a roasting pan and set a

rack in the pan—if the water touches the rack, pour off enough so that there is about ¼ inch of space between the water and the rack. Set the belly skin side up on the rack and slide the pan into the oven. Roast the belly for 1½ to 2 hours, peeking as little as possible, until the skin has bubbled and puffed and turned a glorious golden brown. If at any point the water evaporates, replenish it. (Alternatively, you can undercook the pork belly to medium doneness, about 1 hour, and then deep-fry the whole thing. The skin will only be about one third of the way to crisp and bubbling when it comes out of the oven, but will finish in the oil. This is how we do it at the restaurant, but it's probably too much extra work for home cooking.)

4.   Pull the belly out of the oven and allow it to rest for at least 20 minutes before slicing. Seeing as how the skin should have gone crunchy and the flesh beneath it should be tender—like, say, a loaf of bread—a bread knife works well for portioning. If you're planning to use the belly in the stir-fry with radishes (page 160), remove the skin in one piece before slicing the meat, then break up the crisp skin over the meat and vegetables, or just place the whole damn thing on top. If you're not serving the pork until the next day, you'll have to bust out the deep fryer. A 5-minute turn in 350°F oil will restore the texture of the crackling. It will feel slightly soft straight out of the oil, but not to worry—it will crisp up as it cools.

* * *

The first or second day after we opened, Jin and Chin, the Chinese cooks, sent their cousin in to talk to me. He told me that they no longer wanted to do prep work. They were tired, and they were here to cook, not slice vegetables. They wanted everything prepped and handed to them. They'd dump it into a wok, push it around, and then dump it out onto a plate. I was paying them well—nearly as much as Angela pulled in as the chef—but they thought they had me over a barrel. They kept saying, "This is your business. We don't want to leave, but if we have to work so hard, we will. This is your business. This is your business." We were wildly busy from day one, fighting just to keep pace. Still, I'd be damned if I was going to be held hostage. They'd already driven out our other Chinese cook. I told them if they didn't want to pull their weight, and if their families really didn't need their income, they could walk. And they did.

We were a few hours away from dinner service. I looked at my remaining three cooks and said, "Tonight, you're going to have to work the woks." They'd worked at places like Daniel and Blue Hill, and none of them had ever touched a wok. They looked at me with big doe eyes. I looked back at them and said, "I'll show you. I'll be with you, but you're going to have to learn fast." All night we alternated back and forth. I would cook, they would watch. I'd move to the other station and watch one of them, while showing the other something else. And in this way, we got through one service, and then the next. And then we were off to the races.

The *New York Times* gave us a glowing, impressionistic review that compared us to Led Zeppelin, and in their year-end roundup they named us the restaurant of the year. The James Beard Foundation nominated me as the best chef under thirty—the Rising Star Chef of the Year—and then again the next year. The second time, I won the award. Anthony and I flew to Copenhagen to present the Mission Chinese story at René Redzepi's MAD Symposium. And the restaurant kept getting busier. Every night we thought we'd fed as many people as we possibly could, and then the next day it seemed as if we fed a hundred more.

Articles about us cropped up everywhere, almost always with cultural references to the sixties and seventies. People saw us as beatniks, blues rockers. They talked about eating at the restaurant as a hallucinatory experience, about how we were taking hold of an ancient cuisine and redefining it. They talked about the heat and the numbing, and about feeling breathless but helpless to stop themselves

from eating more. I guess there *was* something profane and free-loving about what we were doing, but if I had to describe our restaurant, I would say that we were just flying by the seat of our pants.

With a kitchen we'd designed ourselves, and without the physical and cultural limitations of the Lung Shan space, the food got better—better than in San Francisco, better than I could have hoped. I could cook freely and improve dishes where we'd taken shortcuts before. We added little squares of crispy tripe to the Chongqing-style chicken wings. We replaced the braised beef cheek in our broccoli beef with smoked brisket. I was as happy with the mapo tofu as I'd been that first night at Mission Street Food, so we decided to put it on the menu twice: once by itself, and once mixed with thick bone marrow broth in the meatiest, spiciest bowl of ramen you've ever had.

Angela and I developed an ideal working relationship. From day one, she got it. She thrived in our narrow New York City kitchen, which, with the flames of three woks firing at once, was like working inside a furnace. I'd taken her to San Francisco to show her what that restaurant was about—a cramped, run-down place held together by sheer force of will and a shared sense of purpose—and she brought the same energy to New York. I didn't have to worry about leaving her to run the restaurant when I went back to check on San Francisco.

It was the best I've ever felt. I'd come back to New York, where I'd fallen on my face at the beginning of my career, and succeeded. I came intent on learning from mistakes—not just my mistakes, but those of other chefs. I wanted to examine how they'd failed me, how I'd failed them, and build something new. I treated my staff like friends, paid everyone well, hung out with them after work. I emphasized camaraderie above everything—I didn't want a divide between the front and back of the house, or between the staff and me. We had nightly reports on sales, what had gone right and wrong, what VIPs had come in. In the kitchen, everything was about efficiency and consistency. We portioned out our *mise en place* ahead of time, used an intercom system so our expediter could be heard over the roar of the woks and the music, turned every available space into storage, did anything to keep up with the demands of the dining room. I would take the ideas we developed in New York and return to San Francisco to share them. And in the middle of it all, Youngmi got pregnant with our son, Mino.

Chris: A year or so in, the restaurants were bustling—probably still getting busier—and it didn't seem like you were faltering at all. The

Internet was buzzing about you opening in Brooklyn, Oklahoma City, Paris. And in private, you were definitely beating the drum for opening more places.

We desperately needed a commissary—somewhere we could do our prep work and stage our delivery orders. There just wasn't the space to make more food in the restaurant. Same in San Francisco—the place runs off one oven with a broken temperature regulator. I had begun daydreaming about multiple production hubs, improving the existing restaurants, adding new ones, trying out new concepts. I did a pop-up restaurant in Oklahoma. I flew to Paris to scout locations.

Friends and other chefs would ask how I expected to open in another country when I already had two restaurants separated by the width of a continent. They warned me that I needed to shore things up at home before looking abroad—the volume and pace we were working at were increasingly untenable. But that's what I was trying to address. I figured more restaurants meant less pressure on the existing locations, and more money to work with. There are plenty of restaurateurs with restaurants in multiple countries; they don't have to be in one place all the time. If you install capable people in your restaurants, you can trust them to run things when you're gone. Paris was a ways out, but I definitely had my sights set on big things.

Chris: Nothing ever seems that far off with Mission Chinese.

Mapo Ramen

SERVES 4

Since our mapo tofu recipe is easily made in large batches, here's another way to use it. Combined with thick, gelatinous, super-fatty bone marrow broth, it makes for a bonkers bowl of ramen: ideal for a cold night, but total suicide in the summer. I wouldn't exactly recommend making this recipe from scratch—it requires a fridge well stocked with various homemade condiments from the rest of this book. But if you've got it, flaunt it.

1. Bring a pot of water to a boil. Meanwhile, heat a wok or large saucepan over high heat. Add the oil, ginger-scallion sauce, garlic confit, and miso and cook for about a minute, stirring continuously with a wok ladle or spatula and smashing the garlic against the sides of the pan. Add the broth to the wok along with 6 cups water and bring to a simmer. Season to taste with salt.

2. Drop the ramen noodles into the boiling water and cook for about a minute, until just tender. Drain the noodles thoroughly and divide them among four large bowls.

3. Pour the hot broth over the noodles. Top each bowl with about a cup of mapo tofu. Nest a soft-cooked egg into each bowl. Garnish with the chili oil, Sichuan peppercorn oil, fried garlic, and toasted nori. Serve piping hot.

1 tablespoon oil from Smoked Garlic Confit (page 305), or substitute vegetable or peanut oil
¼ cup Ginger-Scallion Sauce (page 295)
10 to 12 Smoked Garlic Confit cloves (page 305)
¼ cup shiro (white) miso
6 cups Bone Marrow Broth (recipe follows)
Kosher salt
1 pound fresh ramen noodles
About 4 cups Mapo Tofu (page 62), warmed
4 Soft-Cooked Eggs (page 306)
Chili Oil (page 290), for drizzling
Sichuan peppercorn oil, for drizzling
¼ cup Fried Garlic (page 294)
1 sheet nori, quartered and toasted (see page 299)

Bone Marrow Broth

MAKES ABOUT 8 CUPS

This isn't like other stocks where you want to simmer everything gently. Boiling is necessary to emulsify the fat into the broth.

3 or 4 (3-inch-long) marrow bones (about 2 pounds)
1 (4-inch) square dashi kombu, wiped with a damp cloth
A 3-inch piece daikon, peeled

1. In a large stockpot, combine all of the ingredients with 1 gallon of water and bring them to a boil over high heat. Skim any gray scum that rises to the surface in the first few minutes, then reduce the heat to medium-high and keep the stock at a boil (or at least a strong simmer) for 3 hours. Don't let the liquid reduce by more than half—if it gets lower than that, add a little fresh water.

2. After 3 hours, remove the pot from the heat and allow the broth to cool to room temperature. Strain through a fine-mesh strainer, discarding the daikon and kombu and reserving the bones and loose marrow. Using a butter knife, scrape any marrow that hasn't already fallen out of the bones and combine it with the marrow you strained from the broth in a blender.

3. Blend the marrow with a ladle of stock into a very fine puree, then pour it back into the broth. Strain the broth once more through a fine-mesh strainer, cover, and store in the refrigerator for up to a week.

MISSION CHINESE FOOD

龍

山

小

館

Closed

They closed us down.

The health inspector came into Mission Chinese New York one night when I was in San Francisco working an event and said he had found mouse droppings in our basement garbage area. The agency shut us down that night. Put a yellow notice in the window and told us we couldn't serve food to people.

Allen called me from New York to tell me. I don't know that I can convey the weight of the helplessness and utter humiliation I felt in that moment. It was like having your hands tied behind your back, closing your eyes, and being knocked down and swallowed by a wave.

Short of poisoning and killing someone, there's nothing worse you can have happen at your restaurant. I was a failure. Before that night, when people criticized my appearance, or questioned our accolades, I could point to the restaurant as evidence of my worth. If I ran into an old chef who made me feel small, I could walk back to Mission Chinese and be rejuvenated. I feared all that was gone. I looked at myself in the mirror. My hair went down to the middle of my back and I wore whatever I wanted to wear in the kitchen. I let everybody do whatever they wanted, and I was three thousand miles away from New York when this happened. I didn't look like a chef, and I certainly wasn't acting like one.

I went downstairs to the event space where I was scheduled to cook, did my job, came back upstairs, and locked myself in my hotel room. The next morning, René called me.

Meanwhile with René Redzepi

What follows is a conversation we had with René Redzepi at the third edition of his MAD Symposium in Copenhagen. It was an absurdly beautiful day on the island of Bornholm, and the symposium speakers were cooking lunch together. Our talk came on the heels of two major developments for his restaurant Noma: (1) for the first time in four years, it was not the highest-ranked restaurant on the World's 50 Best Restaurants List; (2) about sixty cases of Norovirus—a fairly common stomach illness—were traced back to the restaurant and a staff member who had not taken proper precautions to prevent the spread of his own case of the illness.

Danny: My wife and I are having a baby.

René Redzepi: Whoa!

Danny: I don't know if you remember or not, but we were outside of that wonton noodle place in New York, and you said to me, "Chef, have a kid. Don't wait for things to get slower for you; it's only going to get more busy."

René: Of course. You think that you're busy now? You'll never have more time than now.

Danny: Is it better? Things get better, right?

René: Of course. It changes, though.

Danny: To me, all the things that I thought were important before—as far as events and travel—are less important. I have to slow down.

René: Well, it depends on how you want to do it, Chef. The way I've noticed my friends, there are two types

of parents, roughly speaking. There is the type of parents who fall in love with their kids and fall out of love with each other, and their whole life gets changed. And then there is the type of parents who have kids and they fall in love with the family and the family just does everything together.

Danny: That's how I feel I am going to be.

René: And if you do that, it's the most wonderful thing to see your little child run around your restaurant, picking up the flowers, "Can I take these home with me?" And then, of course, the conversations that you have change. I used to have conversations with David Chang, before kids, and we would say—and this is honest to God the truth—"You know what? If I die in the process of making this restaurant, I'm fine. We are just going to go crazy. It's just going to be crazy, crazy madness."

I remember as a child I read this book by a guy called Willard Motley. It was called *Knock on Any Door,* and there was this line like "Live fast, die young, and have a good-looking corpse." When I was starting to become a cook, I thought, *Wow, that's the idea.* And then, the kids arrived. I don't feel I've slowed down in the way that I want to explore my profession and what I do—

Danny: But it's grounded you more, having a child?

René: You work for other things, other reasons.

Chris: Did having kids change your goals professionally? Does it make making money more pressing?

René: Yes, it does. I try hard to find a balance between the fun of work and the ways through your restaurant, through your profession, through your dedication, to make a healthy living where you provide a sound future for your family. But I'm lucky. My father was a dishwasher. My mother was a cleaning lady. She still is. I am already doing much better.

Chris: It does feel as though ever since Noma lost the number one ranking, you've become determined to get it back. Everybody who's eaten at the restaurant this year has

been saying it's nuts how good it is right now—how much better it is than last year. It's like losing the top spot was a threat to your livelihood.

Rene: To me, it's not the 50 Best that did it. Not at all.

Chris: What was it?

René: I'm not going to lie—if they tell me I won 50 Best again, I'll be happy. [Editor's note: He did, and he was.] Why I became angry and really hungry again is because I don't want us, with the quality of guys working right now, to be known as the team that brought the Norovirus into our restaurant. No way, man. I don't want us to be remembered for that.

Chris: So that cut deep.

René: You cannot imagine. In some ways it doesn't matter— the restaurant is still full every night. And it sounds childish, even selfish. Other people might say, "Who the fuck are you? We have eight guests on a Tuesday. You have nine thousand people on the wait list." But it just did something to us. The thing is that there have been two huge news items that ever came out of Noma. The first was when we won number one. And the second was equally big: Norovirus. There is no way we're going to have that be the last word about us. There's no fucking way.

I told the team that this year we work a little more. We're a little more angry. A little more clear. A little more clever. A little more everything.

Danny: It's a reinvention.

René: And that can only happen if everybody feels the same way. What it did to us, we became closer.

Danny: Seeing the kitchen work last night was magical. It was amazing.

Chris: Danny's opening a Mexican restaurant in New York now, and he knows he can't capture lightning in a bottle over and over again. But you think that adversity is important to success.

René: Of course. In a sense, having the Norovirus was amazing for us. Just falling to number two in the rankings would never have done what the Norovirus did to us. Never. People were crying. So did I. We couldn't have this on us. I just couldn't have that we were the team that did this to Noma.

Chris: You're a well-grounded guy, and you put in a lot of work, but there was a bit of a rocket ship aspect to what happened to you when Noma became number one. And on a smaller level, Danny's career trajectory has been—

René: More.

Danny: What are you talking about?

René: Come on! Come on!

Danny: We had one good year.

René: It's a product of the time. Now you can achieve what you have in a year. Five years ago, maybe it was possible, but a little slower. Ten years ago, much slower. Before Twitter, Facebook, bloggers . . .

Chris: Or before there were guys like you who paved the way first.

René: The only thing is: Do not fall in love—do not become emotionally attached—to success. Do not let it become like your second child. It will ruin you. It will eat you up the moment that it moves on.

The best chef in the world had heard from Copenhagen that we were shut down. He was well positioned to console me, having been through a similar situation himself, and I couldn't help but be flattered that he was calling, but I needed to get back to New York as soon as possible.

When I landed, I called a few friends for advice, and they all told me we needed to reopen immediately to demonstrate that whatever problems we had were solvable within twenty-four hours. We scrubbed and cleaned the restaurant. We cemented over any openings we found in the walls.

Chris: Was it the staff's fault? Wasn't it their responsibility to keep the place clean in the first place? Or was it your fault for letting things slide. My perception at the time was that you let them off easy.

You can't blame them—it was my fault. They weren't neglecting anything I'd told them to pay attention to, or doing anything against my wishes. We'd passed multiple health inspections in the past. There was nothing ever wrong with the food—they were on top of that. There were no problems in the kitchen. The violations occurred down in the basement area. One of the main sources of the problem was a locked unfinished boiler room that we had no access to. Only after we were closed did we get the landlord to open it up and show us what a disaster it was inside.

My staff was responsible for the restaurant, but we were running the restaurant so hard we were burning it out. I wanted to be successful, I wanted to be busy. We were overworking the building. A year of being open seven days a week, doing four hundred covers a day, in a thousand square feet, closing for only four hours a day, it was too much.

These are not excuses. These are the circumstances and warning signs I should have heeded: Right behind our property, construction crews had demolished a building to make way for a high-rise condo. When you start digging a hole in the Lower East Side, you're unleashing a wave of displaced rodents on the surrounding area. Our restaurant wasn't sealed properly. The dining room was basically a shack built on a patio elevated over a dirt plot. The previous building owner who had tried to blackmail us was now reporting us to the health and building departments.

Chris: So you knew what was coming and what had to be done. Why didn't you do it?

We knew what had to be done, but we couldn't afford it. We couldn't afford to close the restaurant, or to pay $300,000 to rebuild the dining room. And, more than that, we didn't want to. We should have closed and rebuilt, but we didn't. We cleaned and patched, and I met with a Department of Health expediter for advice on how to reopen as quickly as possible. We had the inspectors back out, and they gave us their approval.

I was confident, and we reopened less than two days after the DOH closed us. There was a fair amount of backlash. Reading the comments online wasn't awesome. Some people took a racist view of it: We were a Chinese restaurant, no wonder we were filthy. I hated the idea that we were a dirty restaurant, but there was no reason to argue. We'd been closed down by the health department. I kept a low profile. I didn't go to restaurants, I didn't drink. Business slowed down for a while. We took the opportunity to launch citywide delivery. Things picked up again. In fact, they got downright crazy again. We had some of our busiest days after our closure.

And those few weeks after being shut down ended up being a happy time, actually—we'd made it over a huge hurdle.

* * *

But the health department came through again a month later, between lunch and dinner. The inspector walked downstairs with a flashlight and got on his hands and knees and crept around for hours, searching for mouse droppings. He came back and told us he'd found 122 droppings, and he was closing us again. I told him there was no way—I'd been down there and seen nothing. I was in disbelief. I showed him our clean exterminator report. He looked at me and said, "I'm sorry, you should have stayed here overnight with the exterminators and made sure that they were doing their job." And he was right.

I called the same friends I'd called before. They told me to hide the notice, to make up some reason we were closed. "They'll fine you a couple grand, but you gotta hide it." I told them, no, we were going to face facts. We could keep up this cycle of closing and cleaning and reopening. But nothing short of rebuilding the restaurant was going to solve it.

Anthony: The restaurant was like this old, beat-up hoopty that we'd driven cross country. It had somehow managed to get us from point A to point B—and even to point C, really—but when we arrived at our destination, the transmission fell out and the engine caught fire.

**When Mission Chinese New York closed the second time, we were
two weeks away from opening another restaurant down the street,
Mission Cantina—a Mexican place I'd been dreaming of since
landing in New York.** I can't say that Mission Chinese Food being
shut down helped Mission Cantina. The food wasn't as good as it could
have been if I'd given it my full attention. There were no four-hour waits
outside, like there had been at MCF.

When we closed, I tried to transfer as much staff as I could over
to the new restaurant. But I had to let some of them go. Others didn't
want to stay. When Mission Cantina got a lukewarm review, more of
them left. It's hard to focus on crafting recipes when you spend all
day in meetings with lawyers and realtors and business people.

I scoured New York for a new location for Mission Chinese Food
for the better part of a year. We had multiple deals and leases fall
through at the eleventh hour. I was gun-shy in the kitchen, questioned
myself. The food at Mission Cantina is just now finally getting to the
place I intended.

This was a low.

* * *

I'm really sorry.

I'm sorry that this happened. I'm sorry for my cooks, I'm sorry for
our customers.

My priorities weren't in line. I wasn't at the restaurant enough—I
traveled too much. Don't get me wrong, I was there every moment
I could be, but I wasn't where I needed to be. I was working the
dining room and working on the menu. I should have focused on
the less glamorous, more serious parts of the job, like watching our
exterminators or figuring out how to repair the space. We rushed
headfirst into a bad deal. We didn't take the time to close down and
rebuild when we should have, and we felt the consequences of that
shortsightedness.

But I don't feel sorry for myself, and I hope nobody feels sorry for
me either. Some people can work their entire careers and not achieve
half the success we have. I'm not bragging, I'm saying we've been
extraordinarily fortunate already.

I'm glad that things happened the way they did. I'm not glad we got
shut down, of course, but I'm grateful for the lesson. Amazing things were
happening to us at an unbelievable clip. I wasn't mature enough to handle

all of it—there's no way I could be. Things were going so well for us, and we were just doing whatever the hell we wanted. The entire ordeal had the effect of focusing me, teaching me humility and perspective. For months, I was face-to-face with the prospect of losing everything. Our ambitions for Mission Chinese Food were sky-high before we closed. But we weren't truly ready then.

* * *

On September 5, 2014, we signed a lease on a new space. I swear to you, things will be tighter. I'll hold people accountable: my staff, my contractors, myself. We won't rush. We'll be deliberate. We'll do things right.

Chris: But Mission Street Food, Mission Chinese Food—they exist because you guys never hesitated. Eating at Mission Chinese New York was incredible because of the chaotic energy in the room.

We were young, we didn't know what we were doing.

Chris: Don't you worry that you'll lose something without that wild energy?

Maybe we will lose something if we're less wild. Maybe people won't come back if we don't have that raw edge or that manic spirit. But now we have two strikes against us. We're not infallible. We need to take control. We need to be a better restaurant.

I know the new Mission Chinese Food will be great. I'm excited to put my head down and cook Chinese food again. Anytime a friend came into Cantina while Mission Chinese was closed, I'd throw together an order of fried rice or pork jowl for them—I couldn't help myself. I know you're afraid this experience broke me. I know you're worried I won't have the same courage or spark that I used to. Don't worry about me.

The experience forced mc to grow up. I look at this cookbook as a document of a specific time and set of experiences: the early years of Mission Chinese food, the end of my twenties, growing up as a chef. In the time since we started writing this book, we opened a restaurant in New York, closed it twice, and reopened in a new location. I worried at each of these junctures whether the book would still be relevant when it finally came out.

Chris: But in a lot of ways, the book is better for it. It's been there with us, written as all these ups and downs happened. The recipes at the restaurant are still evolving—the ones in the book are just the most recent ones—and the story is certainly incomplete.

I'm better for it too. I see now how I can actually realize the things I want to do. A year ago, I was nowhere near the chef or person I needed to be. I could say I wanted to open in Paris or Oklahoma or Afghanistan, but I wasn't ready. We're prepared to be a more sound restaurant now.

And at the heart of everything, it's what we want. It's like being a musician. You start out as a hungry band, rough around the edges. As you keep playing, you get more polished. Some people may resent it if you're cleaner or more sophisticated. But the bottom line is we have to do this. We can't be irresponsible. We can't be a young punk band forever.

Fried Hainan Chicken Rice

SERVES 4

Hainan chicken rice is the best way to eat chicken. There, I said it. If you aren't already acquainted with this magnificent invention, it is this: perfectly steamed chicken, shocked in ice water to create a thin layer of gelée between the skin and meat, and then sliced and served with aromatic rice flavored with chicken fat, along with sides of soy sauce, salted chiles, and ginger. It's straightforward, comforting, clean, and customizable to your taste.

It's also an extremely difficult dish to nail. The chicken should be just cooked through—you want to see a tiny bit of pink at the bone—and you need to shock it at the precise moment when the fat and juices are still trapped under the skin. It's a dish that can really suck, but if you find someone who's got it dialed in, someone who's made it thousands of times, it's life affirming.

I'd never been completely happy with any of my versions of the dish, because even if none of them were trying to be a proper Hainan chicken rice, they just weren't as good. Fast-forward to the weeks following the closing of Mission Chinese in New York. Frank Falcinelli and Frank Castronovo offered us a space in their restaurant in Brooklyn, Frankies Spuntino 457, to do a few pop-up dinners and keep ourselves busy. Even so, our chef, Angela Dimayuga, started going a bit stir-crazy. One day I brought her some *shio koji*—an intensely umami Japanese condiment made of rice, salt, and mold—and told her to mess around with it. Angela being Filipino, and Filipinos being great lovers of fried chicken, she marinated some chicken in the *koji*, fried it, and served it over rice, with fermented green chiles, preserved lemons, and salted cucumbers. It was the first version of chicken rice I've been truly proud to serve. It's also a testament to what you can come up with with too much time on your hands.

Speaking of time, if you plan to prepare your own *shio koji*, along with all the accompanying sauces for this dish, it will take you about three weeks. Consider that before planning a weeknight meal around it.

Note: This recipe calls for deboning the chicken. Take your time with this and don't freak out if you don't do a perfect job. If you get confused, feel free to refer to the many videos available online. Basically you're just trying to create two chicken halves with as few bones as possible. If you mess up and cut the bird into more than two pieces, it's no big deal.

1 (3- to 4-pound) chicken

2 scallions, trimmed

2 garlic cloves

1 (4-inch) piece fresh ginger, peeled and cut into ¼-inch-thick coins

Kosher salt

½ cup prepared shio koji (see page 303)

1 bay leaf

1 tablespoon whole black peppercorns

8 to 10 cups vegetable or peanut oil, for deep-frying

½ English cucumber, or 1 lemon cucumber, peeled and thinly sliced

3 cups steamed jasmine rice (about 1½ cups raw rice)

½ cup Fermented Green Chili–Lemon Kosho Condiment (recipe follows)

1. Debone the chicken: Starting with the breast side down, make a long incision along the entire spine of the bird. Next, working one side at a time, use a boning knife to carefully peel the flesh away from the rib cage, making small incisions as close to the bone as you can. Slice through the cartilage that connects the thigh to the body, and proceed all the way to the top of the breast bone. Slice through the skin to separate half of the chicken—one breast, leg, thigh, and wing—from the carcass. Debone the thigh. Finally, slice off any big pockets of fat you find and reserve them with the bones.

2. Thinly slice the scallions. In a mortar and pestle or a food processor, grind or process the scallions with the garlic, half the ginger, and a healthy pinch of salt until you have a bright green paste. Combine the paste with the shio koji in a small bowl and mix well.

3. Season the chicken with salt, then pour the scallion paste over the chicken and use your hands to rub it thoroughly into the meat—really get it in there. Put the chicken on a wire rack set over a baking sheet and refrigerate, uncovered, for 3 days.

4. Meanwhile, combine the reserved chicken bones, including the carcass, the remaining ginger, the bay leaf, and peppercorns in a large stockpot and add water to cover by 2 inches. Bring to a simmer over medium-high heat, skimming off any gray scum that rises to the top early in the simmer, then allow it to gently bubble over low heat for 5 hours.

5. Strain the stock and discard the solids. Transfer the stock to a medium saucepan, bring to a boil over high heat, and let it bubble away until it has reduced down to about a cup of ultra-flavorful concentrated stock. Let cool to room temperature and then refrigerate until ready to serve.

6. The day you're cooking the chicken, place the cucumber in a bowl and sprinkle generously with salt. Set aside for 30 minutes.

7. At long last, you're ready to fry some chicken: Retrieve the chicken from the fridge and allow it to rest at room temperature. Meanwhile, heat 4 inches of oil to 325°F in a deep pot or a wok, or use a deep fryer. Fry the chicken in batches until crispy, brown, and just cooked through, about 8 minutes. Pull the chicken from the hot oil and let it rest on a rack set over a baking sheet for a few minutes.

8. While the chicken rests, reheat about ¼ cup of the concentrated chicken stock.

9. To serve, slice the chicken into about 8 pieces, combine the warmed stock and the rice in a large bowl and mix well, then scoop the rice onto a serving platter and top it with the fried chicken. Serve with the salted cucumbers and chili-lemon condiment on the side.

Fermented Green Chili-Lemon Kosho Condiment

MAKES ABOUT 1 CUP

This is a combination of two condiments—salted chiles and lemon kosho. Either is a good sauce for poultry or pork, but for the Fried Hainan Chicken Rice, we blend them together. Pour the condiment into a small container with a tight-fitting lid and top off with a layer of olive oil to prevent air contact, and it'll keep for up to 2 months. Use as you would any delightfully bright hot sauce.

Note: This sauce takes 3 weeks to 1 month if you preserve your own lemons. It only takes 1 week if you buy preserved lemons rather than making them.

2 store-bought preserved lemons (or 2 lemons, plus the juice of 2 lemons,
  and ¼ cup kosher salt)
Kosher salt
3 or 4 Anaheim chiles
1 to 2 tablespoons ume vinegar
About 2 tablespoons extra-virgin olive oil

1. If you have a month to spare to preserve your own lemons, stand each whole lemon on end and bisect it down the center, leaving it attached at the bottom. Turn the lemon 90 degrees and repeat, creating an almost-quartered lemon. Spread the lemons open and salt generously, using about 1 tablespoon salt per lemon.

2. Pack the lemons tightly into a clean jar and cover with the fresh lemon juice. Seal tightly and leave the jar in a cool place to ferment for 3 to 4 weeks, giving it a good shake every day.

3. Meanwhile, stem the chiles and halve them lengthwise. Salt very generously, using about 2 tablespoons salt. Pack the chiles into a jar or container with a tight-fitting lid—a glass pint jar works perfectly—and set in a cool place. Let the chiles ferment for 4 or 5 days, giving the container a good shake once a day. You want the chiles to break down a bit and just begin to go limp, but you don't want them to develop any mold—the salt should help prevent this. Once they've gone a bit flaccid, pulse them in a food processor into a puree, transfer them to another container, and store them in the refrigerator.

4. When the lemons have softened considerably and the skins have become slightly translucent, pull them out and finish quartering them. Use a knife or spoon to separate the flesh from the rind and transfer the flesh to a food processor. Lay each piece of lemon rind flat against a cutting board and use a knife to fillet off as much of the white pith as you can from the zest; discard the pith. Add the zest to the lemon flesh and pulse to a puree. Voilà, lemon kosho.

5. Put all the chiles and half the lemon kosho in a bowl and mix well. Adjust to taste, adding as much of the remaining lemon kosho as you desire. Season with the ume vinegar, then finish with a good glug of extra-virgin olive oil and stir well.

Appetizers

Pickles

Pickles probably aren't the first things that come to mind when you think of Chinese food. But pickles—lacto-fermented salt pickles as well as vinegar-brined pickles—are plenty common in Chinese cooking, particularly in Sichuan cuisine. They might not show up in the five or six Sichuan dishes that most Americans know, but you'd be surprised how often you encounter pickles in Sichuan Province.

Walking through the touristy streets of Huanglongxi there, I wandered into numerous shops that were filled wall to wall with barrels of pickles—young ginger, bamboo, chiles, crosnes (a kind of little tuber also known as "Chinese artichokes"). And for each vegetable, there were two or three pickle variations. Fermentation yields so many different flavor profiles—think about the many vastly different styles of wine, cheese, and beer there are. Pickling, as it turns out, is one of the most rewarding parts of learning to cook Chinese food.

Some of the pickles that follow are meant to be eaten on their own as snacks, others are components of or garnishes for other dishes. From time to time, pickling liquid serves as the acidic element in our stews or braises. In general, we don't use as much sugar in our pickles as you might find in Japanese, Korean, or American pickles. Ours veer more toward savory and sour.

When we started out, none of us knew squat about pickling, but we did a little research and went after it full steam. I encourage you to do the same, and to mess with these recipes as much as you please.

Sichuan Pickled Vegetables, Two Ways

Sichuan pickles are the first thing I want customers to eat when they sit down at Mission Chinese. They're crunchy and refreshing, and they cleanse your palate, but they also have a sour-and-salty kick that whets your appetite for what's ahead.

Giardiniera-Style Sichuan Pickles

MAKES 5½ CUPS; SERVES 8 TO 10

1. Combine the onions, carrot, cauliflower, cabbage, and jalapeños in a container just large enough to hold everything with about 2 inches of headspace. Add enough cold water to cover the vegetables by 1 inch. Stir in the salt—this will both season the vegetables and keep them crunchy. Cover with plastic wrap or a tight-fitting lid and refrigerate overnight.

2. The next day, drain the brine from the vegetables and replace with enough rice vinegar to cover. Stir in the garlic, peppercorns, chili crisp, and chili oil. Cover and refrigerate to pickle for an additional day.

3. Serve the pickles in a bowl with a few spoonfuls of the brine. Sprinkle with the Sichuan pepper and chopped cilantro and finish with a drizzle of chili oil. The pickles will keep as long as you still find them appetizing—at least 2 weeks and they'll keep getting more pickled.

½ red onion, diced (about ⅔ cup)

½ white onion, diced (about ⅔ cup)

1 carrot, diced (about ½ cup)

½ head cauliflower, cored and cut into small florets (about 1½ cups)

½ head green or purple cabbage, cut into 1-inch squares (about 2 cups)

3 red jalapeños, thinly sliced

½ cup kosher salt

About 5 cups rice vinegar

6 garlic cloves, sliced

1 tablespoon whole Sichuan peppercorns

1 tablespoon Chili Crisp (page 290)

½ cup Chili Oil (page 290), plus more for garnish

Ground Sichuan pepper

Chopped fresh cilantro

½ head napa cabbage, cut crosswise into 1-inch-wide ribbons (about 2½ cups)

1 white onion, diced (about 1⅓ cups)

1 red onion, diced (about 1⅓ cups)

1 carrot, diced (about ½ cup)

3 serrano peppers, cut into thin rounds

1 large bunch red radishes (about 13), cut into thin rounds

3 tablespoons kosher salt

2 (12-ounce) cans Budweiser or other light and delicious beer

1 tablespoon fish sauce (optional)

Sichuan peppercorn oil

Chopped fresh chives

Toasted fennel seeds

Beer-Brined Sichuan Pickles

MAKES 6 CUPS; SERVES 8 TO 10

1. Put the cabbage, onions, carrot, serranos, and radishes in a bowl and massage with the salt. Add the beer and fish sauce, if using, and give everything a stir.

2. Pack everything into a large container with a tight-fitting lid. Lay a piece of plastic wrap directly on the surface of the vegetables. Seal with the lid, place in a warm spot—above your fridge, for example—and allow to ferment for 2 to 3 days.

3. Remove the plastic wrap. The pickles are now ready to go but can be refrigerated for up to a few weeks. To serve, put the pickles in a bowl and top with a trickle of Sichuan peppercorn oil and a scattering of chives and toasted fennel seeds.

Chili-Pickled Long Beans

**MAKES ABOUT 2 CUPS;
SERVES 6 TO 8 AS A SNACK**

You can cut these crunchy, spicy pickles into whatever size fits your needs. Left as ½-inch pieces, they can be topped with chili oil, sugar, and salted chili condiment for a mouth-puckering snack. Chopped into ¼-inch nubs, they make a sharp topping for rice or garnish for Sizzling Cumin Lamb (page 224) or Steamed Fish Cheeks (page 230).

1. In a wide-mouthed jar or other container with a tight-fitting lid, combine the beans, serrano, habanero, shrimp, if using, fennel, cumin, kombu, and ginger. Add enough soy sauce to completely cover the beans. Lay a piece of plastic wrap directly on the surface of the liquid, then seal the container. Place the pickles in a warm place for 3 to 5 days, depending on the temperature (3 days at about 80°F and 5 days at about 70°F).

2. The pickles are ready when the beans have fermented somewhat and developed a bit of a funky flavor. There may be a small amount of white mold on top of the soy sauce. Relax—it's perfectly normal and, in fact, a good sign. Just skim off the mold and proceed. If you like funkier pickles, allow them to continue fermenting. Otherwise, store the pickles in the fridge. They'll last indefinitely in the soy sauce or for up to a week if drained. You can reuse the soy sauce for further pickling projects or to cook with, but beware: It will have taken on a good amount of spice from the chiles.

3. To serve, put the pickled beans in a bowl and top with plenty of chili oil, sugar, and salted chili condiment.

½ pound long beans, cut into ½-inch pieces

1 serrano pepper, cut into ⅛-inch-thick rounds

½ habanero pepper

1½ teaspoons dried shrimp, soaked in hot water for 15 minutes, drained, and finely chopped (optional)

1½ teaspoons fennel seeds

½ teaspoon cumin seeds

1 (4-inch) square dashi kombu, wiped with a damp cloth

1 (1-inch) piece fresh ginger, peeled and bruised with the side of a cleaver or heavy knife

About 1 cup soy sauce

Chili Oil (page 290)

Turbinado sugar

Salted Chili Condiment (page 302)

Pickled Mustard Greens

MAKES 3 CUPS

2 pounds mustard greens, washed, dried, and thick stems removed

2 garlic cloves, thinly sliced

About 2 tablespoons kosher salt

1 cup thinly shaved red radishes

1 tablespoon dried shrimp, soaked in hot water for 15 minutes, drained, and finely chopped (optional)

½ cup shiro shoyu

1 (4-inch) square dashi kombu, wiped with a damp cloth

Sliced thin, these pickles make excellent toppings for rice porridge or our Dan Dan Noodles (page 243).

1. Slice the mustard greens lengthwise in half and toss in a large bowl with the garlic and a generous sprinkling of salt. Massage the greens gently to wilt and bruise them slightly. Taste for seasoning—the raw greens should be as salty as you'd like the finished pickles to be (about as salty as a potato chip). Add the radishes, shrimp, if using, and shoyu to the greens and toss to mix.

2. Place the kombu in the bottom of a 9-inch square nonreactive baking dish, then add the salted mustard leaves in neat layers. Top with any liquid remaining in the bowl and place a piece of plastic wrap directly on the surface of the greens. Cover tightly in two layers of plastic wrap and leave at room temperature for 2 to 4 days, depending on the temperature (2 days at 80°F, 4 days at 70°F), giving the greens a toss once a day. The salt will draw water out of the mustard greens. Ideally, after the pickling period, the greens will be completely covered with kombu-infused juice.

3. Remove the pickled leaves and slice as you see fit, then refrigerate in the pickling brine in an airtight container for up to a month.

Dill Pickles

MAKES ABOUT 2 CUPS; SERVES 6

These sour pickles cut through the fat of Smoked Beef Brisket (page 36) or Fried Pigs' Tails (page 236).

1. Combine the cucumbers and onions in a medium bowl and salt them generously. They should be as salty as you want your final pickles—about as salty as a potato chip. Add the garlic, dill, and spices and toss to mix. Cover the bowl tightly with plastic wrap and refrigerate overnight.

2. The next day, drain off any liquid that has leached out of the onions and cucumbers. Douse the vegetables with the white vinegar and marinate, covered, for 3 to 4 hours in the fridge.

3. Drain off the vinegar and store the pickles, covered, in the fridge. They'll last for a week. Add more chopped dill before serving.

1 pound Persian or Kirby cucumbers, cut into ¼-inch-thick coins

½ white onion, sliced (about ⅔ cup)

About 1 tablespoon kosher salt

1 garlic clove, minced

2 sprigs fresh dill, leaves picked and chopped, plus additional for garnish

1½ teaspoons whole black peppercorns

1½ teaspoons fennel seeds

1 teaspoon red pepper flakes

1 cup distilled white vinegar

Pickled Red Onions

MAKES 2 CUPS

These accessorize our Stir-Fried Sweet Peas (page 256) and Sizzling Cumin Lamb (page 224).

2 cups red wine vinegar
½ cup sugar
1 garlic clove, thinly sliced
1 bay leaf
1 large red onion, cut into large dice

1. Combine everything but the red onion in a saucepan and bring to a simmer over medium heat, stirring to dissolve the sugar. Remove the saucepan from the heat, add the red onion, and allow the liquid to cool to room temperature.

2. Refrigerate the onions in their liquid in an airtight container. They will keep for at least a week.

Chili-Pickled Pineapple

MAKES ABOUT 4 CUPS

1 small pineapple

1 (4-inch) square dashi kombu, wiped with a damp cloth and cut into 5 or 6 pieces

1 serrano pepper, cut into ⅛-inch-thick coins

⅔ cup sugar

2 cups rice vinegar

3 chiles de árbol

This is the perfect accessory for the Tiki Pork Belly (page 218)—the heat and acid make a nice contrast to the sweetness of the soy caramel and the richness of the pork belly. You could also try the pickles as a pizza topping or as a rim garnish for a Mai Tai or an exotic Shirley Temple.

1. Trim and peel the pineapple. Halve it lengthwise and then halve it again into quarters. Remove the core, then cut the flesh into ½-inch-thick wedges. (You can slice the pineapple into smaller pieces once it's pickled.)

2. Place some of the pineapple wedges in the bottom of a heatproof container—a wide-mouthed 1-quart glass jar is ideal—and top with a piece of kombu and a few pieces of serrano pepper. Layer on more pineapple, kombu, and serrano, and repeat until you've filled the container; there should be very little room to spare.

3. Put the sugar, vinegar, and dried chiles in a saucepan and bring to a simmer over medium heat, stirring to dissolve the sugar. Pour the liquid over the pineapple, covering the fruit completely. Top with a piece of plastic wrap directly on the surface of the brine. Seal with an airtight lid or two layers of plastic wrap and leave at room temperature overnight.

4. Store the pickles in the fridge for up to 2 weeks—after that, they will probably be too sour. Fish pineapple chunks out of the brine as you need them and slice to your desired size. Once you've eaten the pineapple, the pickling liquid can be reused, but note that it will have developed a considerable kick.

Tiger Salad

SERVES 6 AS PART OF A LARGER MEAL

In the years between being chased out of New York as a young cook and my return, I tried to keep tabs on what was happening in the city food-wise. Around 2005, a restaurant called Xi'an Famous Foods started getting a lot of buzz for its northern Chinese cooking. I followed along online and admired what I read about it.

One of the menu items that caught my attention was something called Tiger Salad, described as a mix of raw herbs and vegetables—cilantro, chiles, celery, scallions, and bell peppers—with a sesame dressing. Sounded pretty refreshing to me. So, without ever having tasted the real deal, we started trying to make our own version in San Francisco.

What we landed on was a fresh rice noodle sheet wrapped around a variety of fresh herbs and lettuces that we dressed in a Japanese-style vinaigrette. At the sushi restaurants where I'd worked, we often acidulated grated daikon (*daikon oroshi*) with ponzu to create a dressing for grilled fish or tempura. And that's essentially our vinaigrette for the Tiger Salad. When we landed in New York, we added the liquor from steamed mussels to the dressing for a fancy touch.

I sometimes daydream about further updating this salad or replacing it with something new, but it's my wife's favorite dish. It will be on the menu forever.

Note: This recipe is delicious with or without mussels, and if you omit them, it's actually a vegan dish. Just skip steps 2 and 3.

1. Prepare the vinaigrette: Combine all the ingredients in a medium bowl with ½ cup water and whisk until blended. Cover with plastic wrap and refrigerate until ready to use.

2. In a large saucepan with a tight-fitting lid, heat the olive oil over high heat until it shimmers. Add the garlic and shallot and give them a stir. When they begin to sizzle and smell fragrant, add the mussels. Douse with the wine, cover the pan, and steam the mussels until they open, 2 to 3 minutes. Transfer the mussels, with their liquor, to a bowl and let cool slightly.

VINAIGRETTE

1 shallot, minced

1 (4-inch) piece daikon, grated on a Microplane

2 tablespoons grated peeled ginger

½ cup soy sauce

¼ cup rice wine vinegar

¼ teaspoon yuzu kosho (see page 309)

¾ teaspoon yuzu juice (or substitute a 50:50 mix of lemon and lime juice)

2 tablespoons extra-virgin olive oil

2 garlic cloves, sliced

1 shallot, sliced

1½ pounds mussels, scrubbed and debearded

½ cup white wine or chicken stock

2 cups mixed greens—your choice of mesclun, tatsoi, mizuna, chrysanthemum greens, shredded napa cabbage, and/or pea shoots

4 cups mixed fresh herb leaves, such as Thai basil, parsley, tarragon, dill, and cilantro

3 (8- to 10-inch) round sheets fresh rice noodles, homemade (recipe follows) or store-bought

½ English cucumber, peeled and shaved lengthwise into ribbons with a mandoline or vegetable peeler

3 shiso leaves

2 tablespoons Chili Oil (page 290)

1 lime, cut into wedges

1 sheet nori, toasted and crushed into flakes

3. Pluck the mussels out of their shells, discarding any that didn't open along with the empty shells. Let the mussels cool in their liquor until both reach room temperature. Then add the mussels and liquor to the vinaigrette, stir, and set aside.

4. Combine the greens and herbs in a large bowl and toss to mix.

5. Lay a rice noodle sheet on a cutting board or work surface and place a few slices of shaved cucumber in a row down the center. Follow with a large heap of lettuces and herbs and one third of the mussels. Dress liberally with vinaigrette, then gently but firmly roll the noodle sheet up into a cylinder about 2 inches in diameter. (If the noodle won't stay rolled, remove some filling.) Repeat with the remaining noodle sheets and filling ingredients.

6. To serve, cut each roll into two or three segments and arrange on a platter. Garnish with the shiso leaves, tearing them into pieces, the chili oil, lime, and toasted nori flakes.

Fresh Rice Noodles

MAKES 5 TO 7 SHEETS

1. Combine the rice flour and tapioca starch in a medium bowl. Slowly whisk in ¾ cup water, taking care to work out any small clumps that may form. Continue to add up to another ¾ cup water, until you have a batter with the consistency of heavy cream.

2. Ready the steamer. Using a paper towel, lubricate the inside of the pie pan with oil. Give the batter a stir, then pour enough of it into the pie pan to form a very thin layer—it should just coat the pan without any gaps. Set the pie pan in the steamer and steam for 1 to 2 minutes, until the noodle sheet has completely set. Allow the noodle sheet to cool in the pie pan just until you can handle it, then lightly rub the surface with oil. Use an offset spatula and your fingers to transfer the noodle to a sheet of parchment paper, oiled side down, then oil the other side of the noodle. Repeat the process, building a stack of rice noodles. Cover with a damp towel, and use within a couple of hours.

Special equipment: 8- or 9-inch pie pan and bamboo steamer or steamer pot with an insert large enough to hold the pie pan

1 cup rice flour
½ cup tapioca starch
About ½ cup vegetable oil

Beijing Vinegar Peanuts

SERVES 2

PICKLED FENNEL

1 small fennel bulb with fronds

½ cup Chinese black vinegar

¼ cup soy sauce

1 (1-inch) piece fresh ginger, peeled and finely julienned

2 chiles de árbol, toasted in a small dry skillet

1 teaspoon whole Sichuan peppercorns

1 cup Fried Peanuts (page 294)

8 Smoked Garlic Confit cloves (page 305)

1 tablespoon extra-virgin olive oil

Turbinado sugar

Fennel seeds

The peanuts in this recipe are sort-of pickles. They're served doused in Chinese black vinegar and play nicely with the spicy, sour fennel.

1. Remove the stalks and fronds from the fennel bulb. Reserve the fronds, covered with a damp paper towel, in the fridge. (You can toss the tough fennel stalks or save them for stock.) Use a mandoline to shave the bulb crosswise into thin slices. Be careful!

2. Combine the sliced fennel, vinegar, soy sauce, ginger, toasted chiles, and Sichuan peppercorns in a container with a tight-fitting lid and seal. Let everything mingle overnight in the fridge.

3. To serve, put the peanuts in a serving bowl and top with the smoked garlic cloves and some pickled fennel, then add enough of the pickling liquid to almost cover the peanuts.

4. Mince about 1 tablespoon of the reserved fennel fronds and combine with the olive oil. Spoon the mixture over the peanuts and finish with a sprinkling of turbinado sugar and fennel seeds.

Smashed Cucumbers with Sesame Paste and Salted Chili Condiment

SERVES 4

In 2012, René Redzepi invited Anthony and me to speak on the subject of appetite at the second MAD Symposium in Copenhagen—a two-day gathering of chefs, scientists, artists, farmers, and other food people I deeply admired. We were scared out of our minds to be in an enormous circus tent full of our heroes, ostensibly there to teach them something about food. So we kept it simple. Everyone in the audience received a little portion of this dish: cucumbers topped with sesame paste and our salted chili condiment. For the demonstration, we sprinkled on a little ground Sichuan pepper, to give a sense of the numbing sensation created by Sichuan peppercorns. Chris was onstage with us, preparing a few platters of Sizzling Cumin Lamb (page 224) that filled the tent with the scent of spices, rendered lamb fat, onions, and bay. The cucumbers were crunchy and fresh, and we served cheap Chinese beer as an accompaniment. We didn't serve the lamb. The idea was to stoke people's appetites—i.e., make them hungry.

It worked—they invited us back the next year to cook lunch for MAD3.

I love this dish for those sentimental reasons, and also because of how it takes a few ingredients and elevates them. The sesame paste is basically just tahini enhanced with *shiro shoyu*. Bruising the cucumbers helps them absorb more flavor. You tend to lose some of the sometimes-annoying seeds too. This is an excellent complement to a Sichuan meal, spicy and cooling at the same time.

Note: The cucumbers marinate overnight, so plan ahead. Use the extra sesame paste to make hummus.

2 English cucumbers, quartered

About 2 tablespoons plus 1
  teaspoon kosher salt

1 garlic clove, thinly sliced

1 teaspoon fish sauce (optional)

1½ cups sesame seeds

½ cup sesame oil

3 tablespoons shiro shoyu

Sugar, if needed

3 tablespoons Salted Chili
  Condiment (page 302)

1. Lay the pieces of cucumber flesh side down on a cutting board, working with one piece at a time. Place the side of a large knife on top and press down with your palm to crush the cuke. You're not looking to demolish it, just bruise it a little bit. The flesh will become juicier and slightly darker in color as the cell structure is compromised.

2. Cut the smashed cucumbers into batons about 2 inches long and ½ inch thick and transfer them to a bowl. Salt generously; you'll need just under 2 tablespoons salt. The cucumbers should be as salty as you'd like the final product—about as salty as a potato chip. Add the garlic and fish sauce, if using, to the cucumbers and give everything a toss. Cover the bowl with plastic wrap and refrigerate overnight.

3. Preheat the oven to 325°F.

4. Spread the sesame seeds on a rimmed baking sheet and toast in the oven for 8 to 10 minutes, stirring twice to prevent the seeds from burning. They should just begin to deepen in color and become aromatic.

5. Transfer the warm sesame seeds to a small food processor (or a mortar and pestle), add the remaining 1 teaspoon salt, and process or grind to a smooth paste. (Work in batches if you have a particularly small food processor, allowing time for the blade to cool down in between sessions; if the blade gets too hot, it can further cook the sesame seeds, causing them to turn bitter.) Processing the seeds should take about 3 minutes total, or longer if the blade of your food processor is dull. At first the seeds will just bump and grind against one another, but soon they will start to break down and release oil and pulp. Eventually the mixture will be a smooth, thick paste, like creamy peanut butter but thicker.

6. With the food processor running, drizzle in the sesame oil, then pulse until the paste is the consistency of pancake batter. Thin with water, if neccessary. Add the shiro shoyu, give it another pulse, and taste. If the paste is bitter, add a bit of sugar. (The sesame paste can be made ahead, covered, and refrigerated for a couple of weeks.)

7. To serve, drain the cucumbers and transfer them to a small plate or bowl. Smother with a generous spoonful of sesame paste and then the salted chili condiment.

Shaved Pork Belly with Ma La Vinaigrette

SERVES 4 AS PART OF A LARGER MEAL

This is one of my go-to dishes at Sichuan restaurants: thinly sliced cold pork belly drenched in a sweet vinaigrette made spicy with plenty of raw garlic. The pork belly is chewy and fatty, almost like thick noodles. But the truth is, what really makes this dish addictive, at restaurants, at least, is the MSG. If, like many people, you only know MSG by reputation and not by taste, MSG (monosodium glutamate) is savoriness distilled into sugarlike crystals. I have no qualms about MSG, except to say that using MSG usually means you're taking a shortcut that sacrifices the depth of flavor you get from building umami naturally. There are lots of tall tales about MSG and how it causes headaches and nausea (a phenomenon often referred to by the quasi-racist term "Chinese Food Syndrome"). I can always taste when something has MSG in it—it makes my mouth dry in the same way too much salt can—so I don't use it, although there's no scientific evidence for the idea that it can make you sick. But the point is, you can easily omit MSG from Chinese cooking—you just have to compensate by upping the umami level another way. For this dish, we make a vinaigrette that is more well rounded than the traditional version, with layers of spicy and numbing, sweet and sour, and savory flavors.

The other key to this recipe is shaving the pork belly thin. This task can be simplified tremendously with a deli slicer. When I started spending more time in Chinese restaurants, I noticed that a lot of them had deli slicers. Were they all serving shaved pork belly? No. They use them to trim thin slices off large blocks of frozen meat for stir-fries. My guess is you don't have a deli slicer at home. No problem. Just do your best with a really sharp knife—chilling or lightly freezing the belly first helps—or enlist your friendly meat counter.

Note: This recipe requires an overnight cure.

1 pound skin-on pork belly

1 tablespoon plus 1 teaspoon
kosher salt

2 teaspoons sugar

1 cup mung bean sprouts

½ English cucumber, shaved
lengthwise into thin slices with a
mandoline or vegetable peeler

1 teaspoon minced garlic

2 scallions, thinly sliced

About ½ cup Ma La Vinaigrette
(recipe follows)

1 tablespoon Sichuan peppercorn
oil

1 tablespoon turbinado sugar

1. Rub the fleshy side of the pork belly with the salt and sugar. Set it skin side up on a wire rack set over a baking sheet and refrigerate, uncovered, overnight.

2. Pull the belly out of the fridge and let it sit at room temperature for at least half an hour, still resting on the rack set over the pan. Meanwhile, preheat the oven to 350°F.

3. Slide the pork into the oven and roast for about 1 hour. You're looking for the belly to be just cooked through and still bouncy to the touch. The skin shouldn't crisp or bubble or brown much. Remove the belly from the oven, cover it loosely with foil, and let it cool to room temperature.

4. Once the belly is completely cooled, wrap it tightly in plastic wrap and pop it into the freezer.

5. After about an hour, the pork should be firm and nearly frozen. Retrieve it from the freezer. (Alternatively, you can leave the belly in the freezer overnight and thaw it out a bit when you're ready.) If you've got a deli slicer, that's crazy—but good on you. Shave the belly against the grain into ⅛-inch-thick slices. If you don't have a slicer, do your best with a sharp knife.

6. To serve, lay down a bed of the bean sprouts on a platter. Top them with a tangle of the pork belly and cucumber slices. Sprinkle on the minced garlic and scallions, then dress liberally with the vinaigrette. Drizzle with the Sichuan peppercorn oil and scatter the turbinado sugar over everything to finish.

Ma La Vinaigrette

MAKES ABOUT 2¼ CUPS

This recipe makes more than you need for the pork belly, but it's difficult to make in a smaller batch. Thankfully, it holds for a week in the fridge and is great on noodles, salad, or roasted meats.

⅓ cup sugar
3 tablespoons vegetable or peanut oil
½ cup Chinese black vinegar
¼ cup soy sauce
½ cup Chili Crisp (page 290)
2 tablespoons minced garlic
¼ cup Fried Garlic (page 294)
1½ teaspoons ground Sichuan pepper
1½ teaspoons Mushroom Powder (page 299)

1. Combine the sugar and oil in a small saucepan. Cook over medium heat, stirring occasionally, until the sugar has melted and turned amber. Immediately add the black vinegar, soy sauce, and ¼ cup water (this will stop the caramel from burning) and stir to dissolve any hardened bits of sugar, then remove from the heat.

2. Add the chili crisp, minced garlic, fried garlic, Sichuan pepper, and mushroom powder to the pan. Let the vinaigrette cool to room temperature, then refrigerate until ready to use.

Shaved Pork Belly and Octopus Terrine with Married-Couple's Vinaigrette

SERVES 6 AS PART OF A LARGER MEAL

6 (¼-inch-thick) slices Octopus Terrine (recipe follows)

½ English cucumber, shaved lengthwise into long thin slices with a mandoline or vegetable peeler

⅔ pound cold Shaved Pork Belly (page 206)

½ cup Married-Couple's Vinaigrette (page 299)

¼ cup fresh cilantro leaves

¼ cup chopped scallions

2 shiso leaves, chopped

The inspiration for our octopus terrine came from Paolo, the Genovese chef I worked with at Farina. He used to make a beautiful *mortadella di polpo* by tightly packing octopus tentacles and pistachios into a terrine mold and setting it with a gelée, then shaving the terrine into thin mosaics of cross-sectioned tentacles. We combine the terrine with our Shaved Pork Belly for a surf-and-turf appetizer.

The dressing for this protein bonanza comes from a traditional Sichuan dish called Married-Couple's Beef, named for a pair of 1930s Sichuan street vendors who made the most outstanding plate of spicy beef bits: lean meat, tripe, tongue, and lung, stewed, sliced thin, and served cold. My version—call it Korean Guy's Surf and Turf—has the same fatty, chewy textures but is made with octopus and pork belly.

Shingle the terrine slices on a platter, then top them with the intermingled cucumber and shaved pork belly. Dress liberally with the vinaigrette and shower with the cilantro, scallions, and shiso. Serve.

Octopus Terrine

MAKES ONE 8-BY-4-INCH TERRINE; SERVES 6 TO 8

Note: The terrine needs to set overnight in the fridge.

1. Combine your eight-armed sea beast(s) with the celery, onion, carrot, and bay leaf in a pressure cooker. Halve the tomato and squeeze its insides into the cooker, then toss it in. Add the stock, salt, and kombu and bring to a simmer over high heat. Cover with the lid, lock it, and cook at high pressure for 25 minutes. Allow the cooker to depressurize naturally. (If you don't have a pressure cooker, double the amount of stock and simmer the octopus, partially covered, for 1 to 2 hours, depending on whether you're cooking 1 large octopus or several small octopi. You could also supplement the stock with 1 teaspoon powdered gelatin bloomed in ¼ cup water.)

2. Remove the octopus from the pressure cooker. Strain the stock and discard the solids.

3. Line one terrine mold with two layers of plastic wrap, leaving a 4-inch overhang of plastic on each edge of the pan. While the octopus is still warm, cut off the legs and lay them lengthwise in the terrine mold (the heads can be sliced and snacked on, or used in a salad or pasta). Trim the legs as necessary to fit and alternate the fat ends and narrow ends so that the legs are packed snugly in the mold. The skin of the octopus will have cooked down into a slippery purple goo that wants to slide off the meat. Try to preserve as much of this as you can—the gelatin in the skin is what will hold the terrine together. Spoon in enough octopus stock to fill in any open spaces and cover the legs. Reserve the remaining stock (you'll use some in the Married-Couple's Vinaigrette).

4. Fold the plastic overhang over the octopus. Fit the second terrine mold on top of the octopus and weight it down with a couple of cans, a container of leftovers, whatever. Refrigerate overnight.

5. Carefully unmold the terrine by grabbing the plastic wrap and lifting it out of the pan. Thinly slice it as you would a loaf of bread.

Special equipment: Pressure cooker and two terrine molds or loaf pans (roughly 8 by 4 by 4 inches)

4½ pounds whole octopus (1 large or 2 or 3 small ones), beaks removed

1 celery stalk, coarsely chopped

1 large yellow onion, coarsely chopped

1 large carrot, coarsely chopped

1 bay leaf

1 large tomato

4 cups pork or chicken stock (8 cups if you don't have a pressure cooker)

2 teaspoons kosher salt

1 (4-inch) square dashi kombu, wiped with a damp cloth

1 teaspoon powdered gelatin (optional)

Pigs'-Ear Terrine with Sichuan Salsa Verde

SERVES 6 (WITH LEFTOVERS)

The first course at a Chinese banquet is more often than not a platter of cold appetizers called *leng pan:* **steamed chicken, slices of lean beef, pickled jellyfish, century eggs, pickles, that sort of thing.** It'll spin around on a lazy Susan, and people will pick off their favorite bits as it passes by. It's a surprising way to start a meal—refreshing and cool, but also chock-full of interesting textures and pungent flavors.

This terrine of braised pigs' ears suspended in gelatin is my homage to a *leng pan* platter. Pho spice bags—store-bought sachets filled with Vietnamese cinnamon, cloves, ginger, anise, and allspice—are a fantastic shortcut for imparting the ears with loads of flavor. The dressing is a cross between chimichurri and sauce gribiche—a classic French sauce with eggs, pickles, capers, and herbs—and it brings an herbal lift to the whole dish. Serve this alongside the Shaved Pork Belly (page 209) for the full effect of a Chinese cold platter. Trust me, your friends and family will be warmed up for anything if you start them off with a plate of cold ears and belly.

Alternatively, if cold pork isn't your cup of tea, you could deep-fry the ears after they've been braised. The same sauce works just as well as a dip for crunchy pig parts.

Note: The ears must be salted overnight and the terrine must then be refrigerated overnight before serving.

1. Use a razor or blowtorch to scrape or scorch the hair from the ears, then rinse them thoroughly under cold running water. Put the ears in a container with a lid, salt them generously, cover, and refrigerate overnight.

2. The next day, braise the ears: Preheat the oven to 350°F.

Special equipment: 2 terrine molds or loaf pans (roughly 8 by 4 by 4 inches)

8 pigs' ears
Kosher salt
10 cups beef stock
1 pho spice bag (available at Asian markets and online)
1 teaspoon dried orange peel
1 bay leaf
1 to 2 teaspoons rice wine vinegar
1½ teaspoons powdered gelatin
¼ cup finely chopped fresh chives
¼ cup finely chopped fresh tarragon
1 carrot, finely diced
2 celery stalks, finely diced
¾ cup cooked chickpeas (canned is fine)
3 Belgian endives, halved lengthwise
Sichuan Green Peppercorn Salsa Verde (recipe follows)

3. Meanwhile, bring a large pot of water to a boil. Rinse the pigs' ears again, then blanch them in the boiling water for 5 minutes. Drain and set aside.

4. Combine the beef stock, spice bag, orange peel, and bay leaf in a medium pot and bring to a simmer over high heat.

5. Spread the pigs' ears out in a Dutch oven or roasting pan. Cover with the pho-spiced broth, then lay a sheet of parchment paper on the surface of the liquid. Cover the pot with the lid or a double layer of foil. Pop the pan in the oven and braise for 3 to 4 hours, or until the pigs' ears are completely tender. If you pinch a thin part of an ear, your fingers should go all the way through it. Allow the ears to cool for 30 minutes in the hot broth.

6. Extract the ears from the braising liquid and set aside. Pour the braising liquid into a saucepan, bring to a boil over high heat, and cook until the liquid has reduced by about half, until you have approximately 4 cups of liquid. Remove from the heat and taste, adjusting the seasoning with salt and the acidity with the rice wine vinegar as necessary—keep in mind that the broth will taste milder when cold.

7. Sprinkle the gelatin over ¼ cup cold water and let bloom for 5 minutes, then add to the pho-spiced broth, stirring to dissolve the gelatin. Let the broth cool to room temperature.

8. Skim off any fat from the cooled broth, then add the chives, tarragon, carrot, celery, and chickpeas and give everything a stir.

9. Line one terrine mold or loaf pan with plastic wrap, leaving a 4-inch overhang on each edge. Arrange a layer of pigs' ears in the mold, then scatter some vegetables on top. Add another layer of ears and veg, and repeat until you've stacked all the pigs' ears and vegetables in the mold. Top with enough cooled broth to almost reach the top layer of ears. Fold the overhanging plastic over the terrine, top with the second terrine mold, and lightly weigh it down with a few cans. The weight should compress the ears enough to bring the liquid completely over the ears. Refrigerate overnight.

10. To serve, carefully extract the terrine from its mold, using the plastic wrap to lift it out, and unwrap it. Cut it into ½-inch-thick slices and arrange on plates. Cozy half an endive next to each slice, and top with the salsa verde.

Sichuan Green Peppercorn Salsa Verde

MAKES ABOUT 1½ CUPS

¼ cup capers, soaked in water for 1 hour to desalinate
1 lemon, or as needed
1 tablespoon Sichuan green peppercorns (available at some Asian markets and online; see page 303)
2 tablespoons minced shallots
½ cup fresh flat-leaf parsley leaves, finely chopped
½ bunch fresh chives, finely chopped
Leaves from ½ bunch fresh tarragon, finely chopped
1 anchovy fillet, minced
1 garlic clove, minced
¼ cup extra-virgin olive oil, or as needed
Kosher salt

1. Drain the capers, mince them, and scrape them into a small bowl.

2. Zest the lemon into the bowl. Juice the lemon and strain the lemon juice into the bowl.

3. Toast the green peppercorns in a small dry skillet until fragrant, then grind them in a spice or coffee grinder. Add the ground pepper to the bowl, along with all the remaining ingredients. Stir to combine, then taste for seasoning. Add more salt, more lemon juice, or more olive oil if needed. The salsa will keep for only about a day, covered, in the fridge.

Entrées

Braised Pork Belly

MAKES 2 TO 3 POUNDS (CAN BE SCALED UP)

Our pork belly recipe is Anthony's from the Mission Street Food days, when his signature dish was a flatbread sandwich stuffed with crisp pork belly, jicama, and cilantro aioli. The first time he made the dish, he started with a strong stock in which he braised the belly, further fortifying the stock with pork flavor. For each subsequent batch of pork belly, he reused the same braising liquid. This is a deeply Chinese practice, in which liquid can be recycled in perpetuity and becomes known as a master stock.

This recipe is a good launching point for your own master stock. Start with chicken stock, and eventually you'll end up with a rich, porky master stock. Just remember to bring the strained stock to a quick boil after each use and then cool it quickly in an ice bath. Freeze it between braises, and don't add any more soy sauce. The master stock will eventually become too salty to serve, but it's unlikely that it will become too salty for braising. If you feel like you've reached that point, you can always dilute it with some fresh stock.

1. Prepare the spice rub: Toast the pepper, fennel, coriander, and star anise in a dry skillet over medium heat until fragrant, about 2 minutes. Grind the toasted spices in a spice or coffee grinder, then combine them with the salt, sugar, and cayenne in a small bowl.

2. If necessary, cut the pork belly into smaller pieces that will fit in a Dutch oven or small roasting pan. Use a sharp knife to score the skin/fatty side of the belly in a diamond pattern, making the cuts about ⅛ inch deep and 1½ inches or so apart. (Scoring facilitates the fat rendering, but be careful not to slice into the meat itself.) Give the belly a vigorous rubdown with the spices. Wrap it in plastic and refrigerate it for at least 1 night, and preferably 2 nights.

3. When ready to cook the pork belly, preheat the oven to 325°F.

SPICE RUB
1 teaspoon whole black peppercorns
1 teaspoon fennel seeds
1 teaspoon coriander seeds
1 star anise
¼ cup kosher salt
¼ cup sugar
2 teaspoons cayenne pepper

1 (3- to 4-pound) pork belly (skin optional)
8 cups Rich Chicken Stock (page 301) or master stock (see headnote)
1 bay leaf
3 garlic cloves, smashed and peeled
½ cup dark soy sauce, plus more as needed
Kosher salt, if needed
About ¼ cup vegetable or peanut oil

4. Meanwhile, bring the stock to a simmer in a large saucepan. Add the bay leaf, garlic, and soy sauce—ideally, it will be as flavorful as a rich ramen broth. Adjust the seasoning with more soy sauce or salt. Keep warm.

5. Heat a large skillet over high heat and add the oil. (If your pan's too small to handle the belly, use the roasting or braising pan you intend to cook the belly in.) Beginning with the fat/skin side, sear the pork belly on both sides. The fat will render from the first side, helping to brown the pork; if more than ¼ inch of fat accumulates, drain some off and discard or reserve it for another use. When both sides of the belly have achieved an attractive bronze hue, transfer the belly to your braising vessel, fat side up.

6. Cover the pork belly with the warm stock. Place a sheet of parchment paper directly in contact with the surface of the braising liquid. Pork belly has a tendency to float, so the parchment will keep the surface from drying out. Cover the whole pan tightly with a lid or two pieces of foil.

7. Transfer the pork belly to the oven and braise for about 3½ hours. You're looking for the meat to shred apart easily but not to lose all its fat or dwindle too much in size. Keep in mind that the meat will continue to cook in the hot liquid after you remove it from the oven. Pork belly is extremely fatty and succulent, but it's absolutely possible to overcook it.

8. Unless you plan on serving the belly immediately, allow it to cool completely in the braising liquid, then refrigerate. (Braised pork belly will keep for at least a week if left undisturbed in the braising liquid, and it can also be frozen—remove it from the liquid and wrap it tightly in plastic wrap and aluminum foil.)

9. If you're planning to fry small pieces of belly for preparations like Tiki Pork Belly (page 218), remove it from the pan, squeegee off the gelatinized braising liquid, and then cut the meat while it is still cold. You can also reheat the belly—whole or portioned—in the cooking liquid.

Tiki Pork Belly

SERVES 4 AS PART OF A LARGER MEAL

Pork belly is the cut of the people. Ever since fine-dining restaurants rediscovered it in the mid-2000s, it's been unavoidable. Everybody loves pork belly. We're not above it—we ain't proud.

No question, a pork belly is a fine piece of meat—fatty and flavorful. But to make it properly takes time and attention: brine it, braise it, cool it, portion it, and crisp it. I don't believe in simply cooking pork belly into pudding-like softness and calling it a day.

Our first belly preparation was just big fat fried squares of pork with hoisin sauce and shaved cucumbers. The dish has changed dozens of times since then, but pork belly is always on the menu in San Francisco. This is our most playful edition. It's a nod to the old-school pink-tablecloth Chinese restaurants where the food often got conflated with Polynesian food. Lots of pineapple and maraschino cherries and kitsch. It's sweet and salty and sour and a little bit funny.

Note: If you'd rather not bust out a fryer, or are low on vegetable or peanut oil, you can panfry the pork instead—in which case you should cut the belly into ¾-inch-thick slabs rather than 2-inch cubes.

SOY CARAMEL

About 1 tablespoon vegetable or peanut oil

¾ cup sugar

1 cinnamon stick

2 star anise

1 teaspoon fennel seeds

⅓ cup soy sauce

2 tablespoons fish sauce

8 to 10 cups vegetable or peanut oil, for deep-frying

1 pound Braised Pork Belly (page 216), chilled and cut into 2-inch cubes

1 cup Chili-Pickled Pineapple (page 199), cut into 1-inch pieces

10 canned mandarin orange segments

¼ cup unsweetened coconut flakes, toasted

¼ cup macadamia nuts, coarsely chopped

4 maraschino cherries

4 cocktail umbrellas (optional)

1. Prepare the soy caramel: Heat a small nonstick saucepan over medium-high heat and coat it with a thin film, about 1 tablespoon, of oil. Pour the sugar into the pan and cook, stirring occasionally, until it has melted and caramelized into a light amber color, about 5 minutes. Add the dry spices and toast in the caramel for a few seconds, then add the soy sauce, fish sauce, and 2 tablespoons water. The liquid will hiss and bubble and the caramel may solidify. Stir continuously until any hardened caramel has dissolved into the liquid.

2. Strain the hot caramel through a heatproof fine-mesh strainer into a heatproof bowl (or just pluck out the large spices) and reserve in a very warm place (like a hot water bath) until ready

to use, or rewarm when ready to use. It will thicken slightly as it cools.

3.   In a deep pot or wok, heat 3 to 4 inches of oil to 350°F, or use a deep fryer. Working in batches, if necessary, add the pork belly to the hot oil and fry until crisp and brown on all sides, about 5 minutes, then drain on paper towels.

4.   To serve, spoon a little pool of soy caramel onto a serving platter. Place the crispy pork belly pieces on top of the caramel and coat with more caramel. Artfully intermingle the pickled pineapple and mandarin orange segments in between and around the pieces of belly. Sprinkle the coconut flakes and macadamia nuts on top of everything, then finish with the maraschino cherries and cocktail umbrellas, if using them.

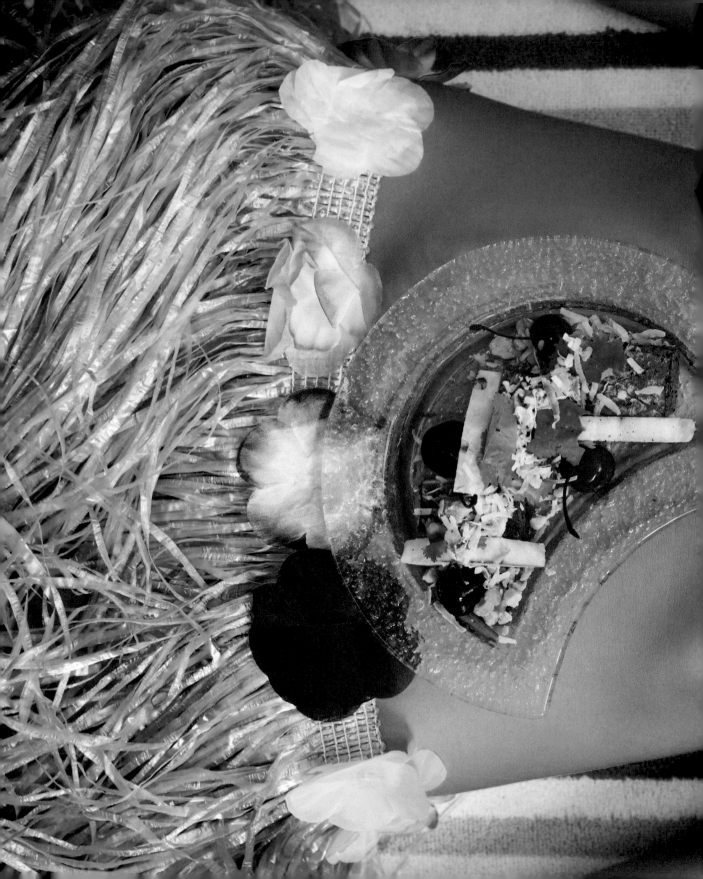

Pastrami

MAKES 2 TO 3 POUNDS (CAN BE SCALED UP)

Pastrami is a labor-intensive endeavor. Our method is a three-day process, and it doesn't even involve corning (salt-curing) the beef ourselves. At the restaurant, we use corned whole briskets to yield a variety of fatty and lean bites. Assuming you don't want to smoke an entire ten- to twelve-pound brisket, try to get a piece that is cut from the fattier end, commonly known as the "point."

From time to time, we'll serve a whole pastrami as an eye-popping—and sometimes soul-crushing—surprise to our friends at the end of a meal. But most often, we use this for our Kung Pao Pastrami (page 92). Leftover pastrami is great with eggs and hash browns, stuffed into *pupusas*, or, obviously, made into sandwiches.

Note: If you don't own a smoker, this shortcut will do the trick: Soak, rub, and cure the corned beef as directed in steps 1 and 2. Heat an outdoor charcoal grill until you can only stand to hold your hand 2 inches away from the grill grate for 2 seconds, and sear/blacken the corned beef on both sides. This will take a bit of time and careful management, as there's a difference between blackened and burned to a crisp. It's all right to flip repeatedly. Once it's blackened, remove the beef from the grill and allow it to cool to a temperature you can handle, then wrap the whole thing very tightly first in plastic wrap, and then in aluminum foil. Place the wrapped meat in a casserole dish and cook in a very low oven (200°F) for 5 to 7 hours, or until the meat is tender and the fat is melty.

Special equipment: Smoker rig of your choice and ¼ pound cherry, or applwood chunks, chips, or pellets

1 (3- to 4-pound) corned beef brisket from the point end
¼ cup kosher salt
¼ cup sugar
2 tablespoons freshly ground black pepper
1 tablespoon ground Sichuan pepper
1 cup yellow mustard

1. Put the corned beef in a large pot, add at least 1 gallon cold water, and soak overnight in the fridge to desalinate it.

2. The next day, combine the salt, sugar, and peppers in a bowl and mix well to make a rub. Drain the meat and pat it dry. Rub it all over with the mustard and then coat it with the rub. Lay the meat on a rack set atop a baking sheet and refrigerate, uncovered, overnight. The mustard and rub will dry out a bit, which will create a desirable "bark" when smoked.

3. The following day, smoke the brisket at 215°F for 8 to 10 hours, until the meat is jiggly and soft—it should fall apart under

moderate pressure. Start checking after 8 hours, but don't disturb it before then. Pull the pastrami from the smoker, wrap it tightly in aluminum foil, and let rest for at least an hour. Or, if you're not planning to serve it immediately, or want to portion it for Kung Pao Pastrami, allow the meat to cool thoroughly in the foil, then refrigerate before slicing.

Sizzling Cumin Lamb

SERVES 4

Some people swear they hate lamb. Others are okay with it, and a minority of people really love it, but lamb is rarely anyone's first-choice meat. The truth is, I don't think we eat enough lamb in this country to know whether or not we really like it. Most people have only ever had lamb chops or overcooked leg of lamb, scented with rosemary and garlic. My own experience with lamb was pretty limited until I discovered the glory that is cumin lamb. I'd had roast lamb in fine-dining restaurants and rotisserie lamb in shawarmas and gyros, but I'd never had anything like cumin lamb: earthy and fragrant, chewy and a little bit gritty from the crust of spice.

Cumin lamb is a dish common to both Sichuan and Muslim Chinese restaurants. It usually takes the form of thin strips of lamb coated in ground cumin, skewered, and grilled. Think of cumin and lamb as two separate halves of a heart-shaped locket—alone they are just curious shapes, together they form a full heart.

I got so excited about the combination of cumin and lamb that the smell of cumin lamb became the signature fragrance of Mission Chinese—we made sure of it. Mission Chinese San Francisco isn't much to look at. We love it, but I liken it to a divey music venue. Without the lights, the sounds, the fog, and the people, it looks like a real crap hole. In order to mask its homeliness, we have to distract the eye. Our cumin lamb, delivered sizzling on a fajita platter, cloaked in a wreath of smoke and steam, is one of those distractions. When it passes through the dining room, heads turn.

I prefer to use lamb breast for this dish, because it has a nice mix of succulent meat and rich, silky fat. Lamb ribs are a good substitute, and in a pinch, you can use double-rib lamb chops. When chopping the lamb breasts, you'll have to be assertive to get through the chine bones and cartilage. Alternatively, since you'll probably have to order a lamb breast from the butcher anyway, just ask him or her to do this for you.

Note: This recipe requires an overnight cure.

1 bone-in lamb breast (about 2½ lbs), cut into 2-rib chunks (see headnote)

SPICE RUB

1 tablespoon Mushroom Powder (page 299)

2 tablespoons kosher salt

2 tablespoons sugar

1 tablespoon plus 1 teaspoon cumin seeds, ground in a spice or coffee grinder

1 tablespoon freshly ground black pepper

5 dates, pitted and halved

1 yellow onion, halved and cut crosswise into ¼-inch-thick slices

1 serrano pepper, cut into ¼-inch-thick rounds

¾ cup (2-inch) pieces watercress

¼ cup Pickled Red Onions (page 198)

½ cup Chili-Pickled Long Beans (page 194), cut into ¼-inch nubs

1 tablespoon Fried Garlic (page 294)

1. In a large bowl or zip-top plastic bag, combine the meat and the spice rub ingredients (reserve 1 teaspoon of the cumin for garnish), and toss or shake to coat the meat. Cover the bowl with plastic wrap or seal the bag and refrigerate overnight.

2. The next day, preheat the oven to 325°F.

3. Lay the lamb pieces on a wire rack set over a baking sheet and roast for about 2 hours, checking on them frequently toward the end. The meat should be tender enough to pull away from the bone but not falling off.

4. Remove the lamb from the oven, immediately wrap it in aluminum foil to keep it moist, and let it rest for 30 minutes.

5. While the lamb cools, pour off the fat and drippings from the baking sheet into a tall heatproof glass container. The drippings will settle to the bottom and the fat will eventually congeal (you can speed this up in the fridge)—reserve the fat.

6. Unwrap the lamb. Set a fajita platter or large cast-iron skillet over high heat until it is very hot. Add 2 tablespoons of the reserved lamb fat—it should begin to shimmer and possibly smoke. Add the lamb chunks and sear, being sure to leave the chunks undisturbed for at least 1 minute to achieve a nice crust on the first side. Turn the meat and get a good sear on the other side too. (At the restaurant, we deep-fry our lamb breasts to get them crusty and brown all over, so if that's an option available to you, go for it.)

7. Transfer the seared lamb to a large bowl. Let the pan get really hot again over high heat. Add the dates and quickly sear them on one side, then add them to the bowl. Heat the pan once more, then spread the onion and serrano slices in an even layer in the pan and leave them undisturbed for about 2 minutes, so that they get a good sear, then stir until they're slightly soft, another minute or two. Ideally, the onions will have a bit of spring left in them, but they shouldn't taste raw.

8. While the onions and peppers cook, sprinkle the reserved 1 teaspoon cumin over the lamb and dates and give everything a quick toss.

9. To serve, scatter the watercress over the bed of sizzling onions, then arrange the lamb chunks and dates on top. Top with the pickled red onions, pickled long beans, and fried garlic. Just before you take the pan off the heat, spoon or squirt a couple of tablespoons of water along the edges to create a cumin-scented steam bath that is both theatrical and part of the final cooking of the dish.

Taiwanese Eggplant and Clams

SERVES 4 (OR 6 AS PART OF A LARGER MEAL)

I have never been to Taiwan, but this recipe came about because all my friends were talking about how cool Taiwan is, and I really wanted to seem like I was in the know. When I visit Taiwan someday, I hope I can get something like this dish. It's pretty good.

I'm only half kidding. There is a vague Taiwanese basis for this recipe, a dish called Three-Cup Chicken that's revered there. Like pound cake, the recipe is in the name: One cup each of soy sauce, sesame oil, and Shaoxing wine are simmered and reduced to make the sauce. A cup of sesame oil seemed like a hell of a lot to me, so we steered the recipe more toward the sweet side and used sugar instead.

You could swap in mussels for clams, but the brininess and chew of fresh clams are the best match for eggplant. Honestly, you could do a version with no shellfish at all and you'd still be golden. The real prize in this recipe is the eggplant technique. Eggplant can be a tricky vegetable to cook as it tends to suck up liquid—especially oil—and then expel it once it's cooked. The method in this recipe—a saltwater brine followed by a flash fry—gets the trick done. The eggplant cooks properly without becoming overly greasy. That also means this recipe requires some multitasking. Think of it as an Italian dish, in which the eggplant is the pasta and the clams are the sauce—ideally, the two parts will be rounding the corner to being perfectly cooked at the same moment and then mingle together to finish. If you're skilled enough to cook the clams perfectly while not overcooking the eggplant, come to me for a job. If not, don't worry—you'll get better with practice.

1. Combine the salt with 6 cups water in a large saucepan and stir over medium-high heat until the salt has dissolved. Remove the pot from the heat, add 6 cups ice water, and stir. Let the brine cool to room temperature.

2. Immerse the eggplant batons in the cooled brine. Let soak for an hour at room temperature. (You may need to set a plate on top of the eggplant to keep it completely submerged.)

3. Bring a large pot of water to a boil; have a spider or other strainer nearby. Meanwhile, in a deep pot or a wok, heat about 4 inches of vegetable or peanut oil to 350°F, or use a deep fryer.

4. Once the water is boiling and the oil is hot, set a wok over high heat. Get the wok very hot and coat it with a thin film of oil. Add the garlic, peppercorns, and basil. Sweat the aromatics for a few seconds, then add the Shaoxing wine, stock, soy sauce, oyster sauce, sugar, and black beans. Bring to a boil and boil for 1 minute, then add the clams and stir to combine. Reduce the heat to medium, cover, and let everything simmer until the clams open, about 5 minutes.

5. Meanwhile, drain the eggplant and shake off as much water as you can, then add it to the hot oil and fry for 3 to 4 minutes, or until it has softened but still has structure. Work in batches, if necessary, to avoid lowering the oil temperature too dramatically. Be very careful here, as the eggplant will steam and splatter when it hits the oil. As precarious as the situation seems, it's a good thing—the water escaping from the eggplant will prevent the oil from penetrating it. Once the eggplant is cooked, scoop it out with the spider, drop it into the boiling water, and blanch for just a few seconds. The hot water finishes the cooking and washes off any excess oil.

6. Scoop out the eggplant with the spider, shake thoroughly to drain off as much water as possible, and add to the wok with the clams. If you've timed everything perfectly, the clams will just be fully opening. Kick the heat up to high and toss everything for a minute or so to coat the eggplant and clams in a thin glaze.

7. Turn everything out onto a platter and shower with the torn basil and fried garlic. Finish with a spoonful of chili oil and a sprinkle of the turbinado sugar. Serve with steamed rice.

¾ cup kosher salt

1½ pounds Japanese eggplant, sliced into about 1-inch-long and ½-inch-thick batons (think steak fries)

8 to 10 cups vegetable or peanut oil, for deep-frying and sautéing

2 tablespoons minced garlic

1 teaspoon whole Sichuan peppercorns

2 cups fresh Thai basil leaves, plus a handful, torn (in a pinch, substitute sweet basil or a mix of sweet basil and mint)

2 tablespoons Shaoxing wine

1 cup chicken stock, boiled to reduce to ½ cup

1 tablespoon soy sauce

1 tablespoon oyster sauce

2 teaspoons sugar

2 teaspoons fermented black beans

2 pounds littleneck clams, soaked in water for 30 minutes to purge their silt, rinsed, and scrubbed

2 tablespoons Fried Garlic (page 294)

Chili Oil (page 290), for drizzling

1 tablespoon turbinado sugar

Steamed rice, for serving

Steamed Fish Cheeks, Ground Pork, and Chili-Pickled Long Beans

SERVES 4

One of the foundational eating lessons imparted by Asian parents to their children—and from those children to their non-Asian friends—is this: The cheeks are the best part of the fish. Just as the French prize the chicken oyster—that tender nugget where the thigh meets the body—the Chinese treasure above all the tiny morsel of flesh that's nestled behind the gills.

Since fish have but two cheeks, though, only the quickest on the draw will get one if you're serving a small fish. Fortunately, the cheek is a more shareable size on larger fish. This recipe uses meaty hockey puck–size cheeks from halibut or cod, which you can order in advance from most fishmongers, but if finding them proves difficult, you might ask for fish collars (or "wings" as they're sometimes labeled in Asian markets) instead. The chili-pickled long beans add a spicy, salty, umami punch, but you can swap in any spicy pickles you've got on hand.

⅓ pound ground pork

1 teaspoon fish sauce

1½ teaspoons sugar

1 tablespoon Ginger-Scallion Sauce (page 295)

1 tablespoon reserved pickling liquid from Chile-Pickled Long Beans (page 194)

1 pound halibut or cod cheeks

1 tablespoon sake

¼ cup Rich Chicken Stock (page 301)

1 tablespoon shiro shoyu

Salt and freshly ground white pepper

1½ teaspoons fermented black beans

1 (2-inch) piece fresh ginger, peeled and cut into very thin julienne

1 dried lotus leaf (soaked in warm water for 30 minutes)

About 2 tablespoons vegetable or peanut oil

1 tablespoon ground Sichuan pepper

2 chiles de árbol

2 garlic cloves, smashed and peeled

1. In a large bowl, combine the ground pork, fish sauce, sugar, ginger-scallion sauce, and pickling liquid and use your hands or a spoon to get in there and really mix everything together. Let the meat mixture marinate while you steam the fish.

2. Set a large flat bamboo or metal steamer in a stockpot filled with 1 inch of water. (If you don't have a steamer, you can set an overturned heatproof bowl in the bottom of the pot and balance the plate of fish on top of the bowl.) Bring the water to

2 tablespoons Chili-Pickled Long
    Beans (page 194), cut into
    ¼-inch nubs
1 teaspoon fennel seeds,
    toasted
1 jalapeño, preferably red, thinly
    sliced and soaked in rice
    vinegar for an hour
¼ cup yellow or green Chinese
    chives (or scallions), thinly
    sliced

a simmer over medium heat. Meanwhile, place the fish cheeks in a single layer on a rimmed heatproof plate or pie tin that will fit inside the steamer. Mix the sake, 1 tablespoon of the stock, and the shiro shoyu together in a small bowl, then pour it over the fish. Season the cheeks lightly with salt and white pepper. Scatter the black beans and julienned ginger over the cheeks and cover with the lotus leaf. Trim the leaf with a pair of scissors to fit if it's too unwieldy. Wrap the whole plate tightly in plastic wrap.

3. Set the plate in the steamer, cover, and steam for about 10 minutes—the fish cheeks should be just beginning to go opaque and flaky—they'll continue to cook as they rest. Set aside, still wrapped.

4. Heat a wok over high heat, then coat with the oil and heat until it shimmers. Add the Sichuan pepper, chiles de árbol, and garlic and stir-fry until fragrant—about 1 minute. Be careful not to let the aromatics burn. Add the seasoned pork to the wok and stir-fry, using a ladle or wok spatula to break up the pork as it cooks. When the pork is just cooked through, hit it with the pickled long beans and the remaining 3 tablespoons stock, and cook, stirring continuously, until the liquid has almost completely evaporated, about 1 minute. Remove the wok from the heat.

5. Unwrap the fish cheeks and remove the lotus leaf. Transfer to a serving plate and top with the stir-fried pork. Garnish with the toasted fennel seeds, sliced jalapeño, and chives.

General Tso's Veal Rib

SERVES 8 TO 10

Early on, we had a standing rule at Mission Chinese that we couldn't add a new protein to the menu if it cost more than $5 per pound. Since we stick to all-natural or organic meats, this meant choosing off cuts that weren't in high demand. If suddenly something we liked—say, beef cheeks—spiked in popularity, we were back to the drawing board. One day I noticed that veal breast was relatively cheap, so we ordered one.

With our tiny oven in San Francisco already working overtime, we didn't have room to accommodate any hulking pieces of meat. Luckily we found a market down the street with a rotisserie that agreed to take it on for us. We'd cure the breast overnight ourselves, then bring it over for the owner to strap onto the spit for a low-and-slow roasting.

What we got back was a perfectly roasted, succulent piece of meat. It would have been a shame to mess with it much, so we decided right off the bat that we'd break down the breast and serve it as big, Brontosaurus-size chops. But we cycled through a number of bad ideas on how to gussy them up. The answer finally came like a slap on the forehead. We worked in a Chinese-American restaurant. Certainly the cooks knew how to make General Tso's sauce, right? Anthony asked the cooks if they could make a batch, and the next morning there was a five-gallon soy sauce bucket of ruby-red General Tso's sauce—a gastrique-like glaze made from vinegar, sugar, dried orange peel, food coloring, and cornstarch slurry—waiting for us. Bingo. We've since tweaked the recipe, but it stays true to the original spirit: essentially a spicy sweet-and-sour sauce.

The most difficult part of this recipe will be sourcing the veal rib. If you can find an especially accommodating butcher who has whole veal breasts, ask him or her to saw the entire breast in half crosswise—resulting in two large chunks each about the size of a whole pork loin—and sell you one. If the butcher doesn't want to sell half a breast, invite more friends over (like, all of them) and double the recipe.

½ veal breast (5 or 6 ribs; 7 to
9 pounds)
⅓ cup kosher salt
⅓ cup sugar
2 tablespoons freshly ground
black pepper

GENERAL TSO'S SAUCE
1 cup sugar
1 cup aka zu (Japanese red rice
vinegar; see page 300), or
substitute red wine vinegar
1 cup Chinese red rice vinegar
(see page 301)
1 heaping tablespoon dried
hibiscus flowers
1 tablespoon vegetable
or peanut oil
1 tablespoon minced garlic
1 tablespoon Salted Chili
Condiment (page 302)
1½ teaspoons ketchup

8 to 10 cups vegetable or peanut
oil, for deep-frying
About 1 cup cornstarch, for
dredging
1 yellow onion, sliced
1 leek (white and light green
parts), quartered lengthwise,
cut into 3-inch pieces, and
thoroughly washed
2 teaspoons cornstarch slurry
(see page 292)

1. Slice the veal breast into 3 large chunks, about 4 inches wide. Use a boning knife to trim any obvious, unwieldy fat pockets, but don't go too crazy with it—you can always trim off more once it's roasted. Season the veal with the salt, sugar, and pepper. Wrap the pieces tightly in plastic and refrigerate overnight.

2. The next day, unwrap the meat and lay the pieces on a rack set in a roasting pan. Allow the meat to rest at room temperature for at least an hour before cooking. Preheat the oven to 300°F.

3. Slide the pan into the oven and cook for 2 to 3 hours, until the meat has an internal temperature of 140°F. Pull the hot veal out of the oven, wrap each piece tightly first in plastic wrap and then in aluminum foil to prevent moisture loss, and allow them to cool to room temperature.

4. If you see a lot of unrendered fat, go ahead and trim some off, but again, don't cut it all off—part of the deliciousness of veal breast is the fat. If you're not planning on serving the dish imminently, rewrap the meat in plastic and refrigerate; it will hold for a couple of days in the fridge. (In fact, it's easier to trim fat once the meat has been refrigerated. Remove the veal from the refrigerator a couple hours before frying.)

5. Prepare the General Tso's sauce: In a medium saucepan, combine the sugar and vinegars and cook over medium heat, stirring to dissolve the sugar. Add the hibiscus flowers, remove the pan from the heat, and allow the mixture to cool to room temperature, then strain the liquid and set aside.

6. Reheat the saucepan over medium heat and coat with the 1 tablespoon of oil. Add the garlic and sweat until softened, about 1 minute. Add the salted chili condiment and ketchup and stir until the mixture bubbles and steams, then return the

sugar-vinegar mixture to the pan. Boil over medium-high heat, stirring frequently to prevent burning, until the mixture has reduced to a syrupy consistency. Remove from the heat.

7. In a deep pot or wok, heat 4 inches of vegetable oil to 350°F, or use a deep fryer. Working in batches, so as not to lower the heat of the oil too much, dredge the veal chunks lightly in cornstarch, shaking off any excess, add to the oil, and fry to a crisp, browned, jerky-like texture on the exterior, 5 to 7 minutes; the interior will still be succulent. Rest the pieces of fried breast on a rack set over a baking sheet as you go.

8. To serve, in a large skillet, heat the sauce to a simmer over medium heat. Add the onion and leek and cook until just tender, 2 to 3 minutes. Add the cornstarch slurry and bring to a simmer, stirring continuously. Add the veal ribs to the sauce and toss to coat.

9. Transfer everything to a large serving platter. Have a slicing or steak knife at hand for carving.

Fried Pigs' Tails with Smoked Cola BBQ Sauce

SERVES 4 (OR 6 AS PART OF A LARGER MEAL)

Every pig has a tail. But when was the last time you ate one? It's a woefully underappreciated piece of meat. It's also mercifully cheap. It's odd that more people haven't discovered pigs' tails—they're like fattier ribs. And when fried, they go great with barbecue sauce.

A Chinese red braise—named for its dark mahogany color—is a classic way of preparing long-cooked meats. The braising liquid is sweet and salty, warmly spiced, and beautifully fragrant. It's good on a primal level. You can use this same recipe for other braises like pork belly, beef tendon, duck, or chicken.

Note: The tails need two days of prep: an overnight cure before braising and then a night in the fridge before frying.

1. Trim the pigs' tails down to 2-inch pieces. Season generously with the salt and sugar. Cover and refrigerate overnight.

2. Preheat the oven to 325°F.

3. Combine all the red braise ingredients in a Dutch oven and bring to a simmer over high heat. Add the pigs' tails and lay a sheet of parchment paper on the surface of the liquid. (Pigs' tails have a tendency to float, so the parchment will help keep them submerged and prevent them from drying out.) Cover the pot with the lid or two layers of aluminum foil.

4. Pop the pot o' tails into the oven and braise for 2 to 3 hours, or until the cartilage is soft but the meat is not yet falling off the bone. (The pigs' tails will continue to cook in the warm broth off the heat.) Remove the tails from the oven, remove the lid or foil, and allow them to cool thoroughly.

2 pounds pigs' tails
2 tablespoons kosher salt, plus more as needed
2 tablespoons sugar

RED BRAISE
1 tablespoon ground Sichuan pepper
1 star anise
1 cinnamon stick
2 garlic cloves
1 bay leaf
1 black cardamom pod, smashed
1 (4-inch) square dashi kombu, wiped with a damp cloth
1 cup soy sauce
1 (1-inch) piece fresh ginger, unpeeled, cut into ¼-inch-thick coins
1 cup packed dark brown sugar
1 (12-ounce) bottle cola, preferably Coke
4 cups chicken stock

8 to 10 cups vegetable or peanut oil, for deep-frying
¾ cup cornstarch
Smoked Cola BBQ Sauce (page 304)
Dill Pickles (page 196)

5. Remove the tails from the braising liquid and lay them on a wire rack set over a baking sheet. Refrigerate the tails, uncovered, overnight. If you like, boil the braising liquid, then cool—ideally in an ice bath—and refrigerate or freeze for use in your next braise.

6. In a deep pot or a wok, heat 3 to 4 inches of oil to 350°F, or use a deep fryer. Meanwhile, pull the pigs' tails from the fridge and let them rest at room temperature.

7. When the oil is ready, dredge the tails in the cornstarch, shaking off any excess, and fry them until crispy and brown—about 5 minutes. Work in batches, if necessary, to avoid lowering the oil temperature too dramatically. Transfer the tails to a paper-towel-lined baking sheet and immediately season with salt.

8. Serve the tails with the BBQ sauce and dill pickles.

Noodles

Hand-Pulled Noodles

SERVES 4

The first time my wife, Youngmi, and I traveled to New York City together, she booked us a hotel in Chinatown, across the street from one of the Xi'an Famous Foods locations. In the eight years I'd been away from New York, I'd entered into an online love affair with Xi'an Famous Foods, scrolling obsessively through their photos and menus, creating my own recipes based on nothing more than the names and descriptions of dishes they served.

The entire week we were in New York, it snowed, hailed, or rained. We ended up holing up in our hotel room, ducking out only for quick food runs. We must've eaten at Xi'an Famous Foods five times. Everything was great, but I fell especially hard for their hand-pulled noodles. Part of the charm of hand-pulled noodles is that they go against everything other noodles try to achieve. Italian pasta, Chinese soup noodles, Japanese ramen, soba, and udon—they're all intended to have uniform thicknesses and shapes that cook evenly. Hand-pulled noodles, on the other hand, are irregular, long and ragged, slippery, chewy and tender at the same time. The dough has to be extremely ductile (i.e., stretchable), allowing the cook to pull and tear it into noodles, while at the same time retaining plenty of bite.

I flew back to San Francisco determined to decode the secret to perfect hand-pulled noodles. I spoke to Chad Robertson, the dough whisperer from Tartine Bakery, and to Josh Skenes from Saison, who, in addition to being a Michelin three-star chef, is also fluent in Mandarin and travels frequently to China. I came away from our conversations thinking that the trick to the dough is either that it's overworked or it's super relaxed (likely aided by chemical dough conditioners). After two months of trial and error, I decided the real secret was this: Let it rest. Multiple rests loosen up the dough to a point where it can be stretched without ripping. As far as the pulling technique goes, I learned by watching others, both online and in person. (And, in a surreal turn of events, a quick Internet search will lead you to a video of me pulling noodles with Martha Stewart.) It's not terribly difficult—just go for it and don't be timid.

NOODLES

4 cups "00" pasta flour, plus more
   for dusting
½ cup grated Pecorino Romano
   (use a Microplane to grate it)
½ teaspoon kosher salt
3 tablespoons Chili Oil (page 290)
   or vegetable or peanut oil

SPICE MIX

1 teaspoon whole Sichuan
   peppercorns
½ teaspoon fennel seeds
½ teaspoon cumin seeds
½ teaspoon aniseeds
1½ teaspoons cayenne pepper
3 garlic cloves, minced
2 scallions, minced
About 2 tablespoons vegetable or
   peanut oil

DRESSING

⅔ cup Tiger Salad vinaigrette
   (page 200)
2 teaspoons cumin seeds, ground
   in a spice or coffee grinder
1 tablespoon Sichuan peppercorn
   oil
1 tablespoon Chili Crisp (page 290)
2 teaspoons sugar
1 tablespoon Chili Vinegar
   (page 291) or hot sauce

½ cup fresh cilantro leaves
½ cup minced scallions (white and
   light green parts)
About 2 tablespoons Chinese
   black vinegar

You can serve hand-pulled noodles in myriad ways—simply dressed with XO sauce, floating in broth, with rich braises, etc. But it was at a restaurant in New York called Henan Taste (now Spicy Village) that I discovered my favorite way of eating hand-pulled noodles: a dish called "big-tray chicken" (*da pan ji*), a platter of spicy, tingly, slightly sweet chicken bits and potatoes braised in beer and set atop a tangle of hand-pulled noodles. You can find a recipe for a fish version of big-tray chicken on page 272. I include a simpler dressing for the noodles with this basic recipe.

1. Prepare the noodles: Combine the flour and cheese in a little mound on a clean work surface.

2. Dissolve the salt in 1 cup cold water. Carve a little well into the center of your flour-cheese pile, fill it with the water, and stir with a fork or chopsticks, slowly bringing flour from the walls of the well into the water until the dough comes together enough for you to mix it by hand. Knead the dough just until it forms a loose ball, 3 to 4 minutes. Cover with a damp towel and let rest for 5 minutes.

3. Uncover the dough and knead it for 5 to 7 minutes more. My preferred method for kneading noodle dough is to repeatedly roll the dough out into a shoulder-width rope, fold it in half, and then roll it back out to a shoulder-width rope. The dough should become firm and relatively smooth and spring back when pressed gently with a finger. Roll the dough into a ball, cover again with a damp towel, and let rest at room temperature for 1 hour.

4. Cut the dough ball into 8 equal pieces. With the pieces cut side up, flatten each one into a ¼-inch-thick rectangle, roughly the length and width of a hot dog bun. Brush each piece with the chili oil—this will aid you in stretching the dough. Cover the pieces loosely with a towel and allow to rest for 1 hour more.

5. Meanwhile, prepare the spice mix: Toast the peppercorns, fennel, cumin, and aniseeds in a small dry skillet, then grind in a spice or coffee grinder. Combine the ground spices with the cayenne, garlic, and scallions in a small bowl. Add just enough vegatable oil to the bowl to make a paste, stirring well. Set aside.

6. Prepare the dressing: Combine all the ingredients in a small bowl and whisk together. Set aside.

7. Bring a large pot of salted water to a boil, then pull the noodles: Working with one piece at a time, grab both ends of a dough rectangle and pull, stretching it to shoulder width. Moving both arms in sync, flap the stretched dough up and down to generate a bouncing motion and slap the dough against the work surface. Repeat until the dough has stretched to about 3½ feet—five or six times ought to do it. Slapping the dough should create a seam down the center of the noodle. Use this seam to guide you as you tear the noodle lengthwise in half, stopping about an inch short of one end, so you have one very long noodle, about 1 inch wide and ⅛ inch thick. Dust with flour and set aside.

8. Drop the noodles into the pot of boiling water, give them a quick stir, and cook for just over 1 minute, until al dente. Drain well, then transfer to a bowl and dress with the spice paste and dressing to taste. Toss to combine, garnish with the cilantro, scallions, and black vinegar, and serve immediately.

Dan Dan Noodles, Three Ways

There are so many vastly different, totally likable versions of dan dan noodles—you can find them served cold or hot; sweet or spicy; topped with pork or vegetables; doused in peanut sauce, brothy, or dry. Between our two restaurants, we've served at least half a dozen versions ourselves. In the spirit of inclusion and variety, we're including three different recipes here.

"Real" dan dan noodles—named after the shoulder-mounted stick (*dan*) that street vendors use to carry their wares—are fresh noodles of spaghetti thickness, served hot and topped with pickled mustard greens and ground pork. They're sour with Chinese black vinegar and a little bit spicy with chili oil.

Our first version retains the mustard greens and black vinegar but is served cold, with fresh rice noodles, a sweet-and-salty sesame sauce, and poached shrimp. Version two is a meaty umami bomb—squid ink noodles topped with pork, Chinese sausage, squid, and peanut sauce spiced with yuzu kosho. The same peanut sauce accompanies fresh noodles (alkaline ramen or Chinese chow mein, your choice) in version three, which tangle in a bath of tingly lamb broth studded with tender pressure-cooked chunks of lamb.

Chilled Noodles with Sweet-and-Salty Sesame Sauce and Pickled Mustard Greens

SERVES 6

Note: If you don't want to make your own fresh rice noodles, you can substitute 1 pound of store-bought fresh rice noodles or 3 bundles of dried mung-bean vermicelli, cooked in boiling water just until al dente, about 1 minute, cooled in ice water, and drained.

SESAME SAUCE

½ cup tahini

½ cup unsalted roasted peanuts

½ cup Rich Chicken Stock (page 301)

2 tablespoons turbinado sugar

1 tablespoon Sichuan peppercorn oil

1 tablespoon light soy sauce

1 teaspoon fish sauce (optional)

1 tablespoon Ginger-Scallion Sauce (page 295)

Kosher salt

6 sheets Fresh Rice Noodles (page 202), cut into ¾-inch-wide ribbons

½ cup Chinese black vinegar

Chili Oil (page 290)

2 tablespoons minced garlic

1 cup Pickled Mustard Greens (page 195), thinly sliced

12 large shrimp, poached and peeled (optional)

½ cup store-bought fried shallots (page 295)

½ cup unsalted roasted peanuts, finely chopped

2 tablespoons flaxseeds, toasted

½ cup fresh mint leaves

½ cup fresh cilantro leaves

1. Prepare the sesame sauce: Combine all the ingredients except for the salt in a blender or food processor and pulse until everything comes together in a smooth sauce. Taste and adjust the seasoning with salt.

2. If you're using fresh rice noodles and they've gotten cold and hard, blanch them quickly in hot water. In a large bowl, toss the noodles with the vinegar, chili oil, and garlic, then divide among six plates. Divvy up the pickled mustard greens and the poached shrimp, if using, and drizzle any vinegar and oil left in the noodle bowl on top. Spoon a generous helping of the sesame sauce over each serving of noodles, then garnish with the fried shallots, peanuts, flaxseeds, and herbs.

Squid-Ink Noodles with Minced Pork and Peanut Sauce

SERVES 6

SPICY PEANUT SAUCE

⅓ cup peanut butter

⅓ cup tahini

½ teaspoon ground Sichuan pepper

1 (1-inch) square dashi kombu, ground to a powder in a
  spice grinder or blender

1 cup Rich Chicken Stock (page 301)

1½ teaspoons fish sauce

Juice of ½ lime

¾ teaspoon yuzu kosho or lemon kosho (see page 309)

KOSHER SALT

About 2 tablespoons lard or vegetable or peanut oil

½ pound cold Pork Jowl confit (see page 161), diced (about 1 cup), or
  ½ pound ground pork

¼ cup finely diced lap cheong (Chinese sausage)

¾ pound cleaned squid, tentacles removed and left whole,
  bodies cut into ¼-inch-wide rings

1 tablespoon fermented black beans

1 tablespoon plus 1 teaspoon light soy sauce

2 teaspoons sugar

1 cup (½-inch pieces) scallion greens

½ cup diced onion

1½ pounds fresh squid ink spaghetti or pappardelle
  (from an Italian grocer)

2 tablespoons Chili Oil (page 290)

2 tablespoons minced garlic

2 tablespoons Chinese black vinegar

½ cup fresh cilantro leaves

¼ English cucumber, peeled and sliced into matchsticks

2 teaspoons ground Sichuan pepper

2 teaspoons turbinado sugar

2 teaspoons toasted sesame seeds

6 (¼-inch-thick) slices oshinko or takuan (Japanese pickled radish;
  optional)

1. Prepare the peanut sauce: Combine all the ingredients in a blender or food processor and pulse until everything comes together in a smooth sauce.

2. Bring a pot of lightly salted water to a boil. Once it reaches a boil, get a wok very hot over high heat, then coat it with the lard. Add the pork and Chinese sausage and stir-fry until the meat is crisp and browned on the edges, about 2 minutes. Add the squid and black beans and stir-fry until the squid is just cooked, about 2 minutes. Season with the soy sauce and sugar, then add the scallions and onion. Give everything a good toss and remove the wok from the heat.

3. Drop the pasta into the boiling water and cook until the noodles are just al dente, about 2 minutes. Drain the noodles and toss them in a large bowl with the chili oil, garlic, and vinegar.

4. Divide the noodles among six bowls and top each bowl with a generous spoonful of the peanut sauce, followed by an equally generous scoop of the pork and squid. Garnish with the cilantro, cucumber, and sprinklings of the Sichuan pepper, sugar, and sesame seeds. Finally, if you managed to make it to the Japanese grocery store, nestle a little piece of pickled radish in each bowl.

Ramen Noodles with Pressure-Cooked Lamb in Numbing Broth

SERVES 6

Special equipment: Pressure cooker

2 pounds lamb cheeks (or boneless lamb shoulder), cut into 2-inch chunks
2 tablespoons kosher salt, plus more as needed
1½ teaspoons ground Sichuan pepper
1 teaspoon onion powder
1 teaspoon freshly ground black pepper
1 onion, unpeeled
1 (1-inch) piece fresh ginger, unpeeled
8 cups Rich Chicken Stock (page 301)
¼ cup vegetable or peanut oil or lard
1 carrot, coarsely chopped
1 celery stalk, coarsely chopped
2 star anise
1 cinnamon stick
2 tablespoons whole Sichuan peppercorns
1 bay leaf
Light soy sauce
Fish sauce
1½ pounds fresh noodles (your choice of alkaline ramen or Chinese chow mein egg noodles)
Spicy Peanut Sauce (page 245)
Chili Crisp (page 290)
Chopped fresh cilantro

Note: This recipe requires an overnight cure.

1. Sprinkle the lamb chunks with the salt, ground Sichuan pepper, onion powder, and black pepper, then spread them out on a rack set over a baking sheet and refrigerate overnight, uncovered.

2. The next day, take the lamb out and let it sit at room temperature for about an hour. Meanwhile, trim any dangling roots from the onion, halve it crosswise, and peel off the outer layer of skin from each half. Set both halves skin side

down directly over a gas burner and turn the heat to high. Let the flames lick and singe and blacken the skin, then scrape it off. If your onion has numerous layers of skin, repeat until you've reached onion flesh, then use tongs to turn the onions over and get some good char on the flesh side. Treat the ginger in the same way—burn the skin, wipe it off, and get some char on the flesh. (If you don't have a gas burner, use your oven's broiler.) Set the charred veggies aside.

3. Pour the chicken stock into a pressure cooker and bring to a simmer over medium-high heat.

4. Meanwhile, in a large skillet, heat the vegetable oil over very high heat until it's almost smoking. Working in batches—don't crowd the pan—sear the lamb. Be sure not to move the meat at first; let it get a beautiful golden brown on one side before turning the pieces, and only turn the heat down if the oil begins to smoke or the meat looks like it'll burn.

5. Add the browned lamb to the simmering chicken stock, then add the charred onion and ginger, carrot, celery, star anise, cinnamon, whole Sichuan peppercorns, and bay leaf. Cover the pressure cooker with its lid, lock it on, and cook at full pressure for 35 minutes. Allow to depressurize naturally. (If you don't have a pressure cooker, you can braise the lamb in a covered Dutch oven or roasting pan in a 325°F oven for about 2 hours, or until tender.)

6. While the pressure cooker depressurizes, bring a large pot of salted water to a boil.

7. Remove the lid of the pressure cooker and use a slotted spoon to scoop the lamb pieces into a bowl. Strain the broth through a fine-mesh strainer into another bowl, discarding the aromatics, and season with light soy sauce and fish sauce.

8. Add the noodles to the boiling water and cook just until al dente; drain.

9. Divvy up the noodles among six bowls. Nestle a few pieces of tender lamb in each bowl, then ladle over plenty of hot broth. Top with the spicy peanut sauce and garnish each bowl with a scoop of chili crisp and a sprinkling of cilantro.

Matcha Noodles

SERVES 2

Angela Dimayuga is the executive chef at Mission Chinese Food New York. I'll let her tell you about these noodles.

Over the year or so that the New York restaurant was closed, I jotted down small fragments of ideas as they came to me. As we prepared to open the new Mission Chinese Food in New York, Danny and I sat down and sifted through everything and started conceptualizing new dishes.

At the first Mission Chinese New York, we changed the menu constantly, always on the fly. Danny had so many ideas. He's obviously super creative, but often he would just come up with things, put them on the menu, and then test them afterward. Sometimes when we tested the recipe, we'd end up hating it but we were stuck working around what the menu said. Now, three years later, we're at a point where we talk about a dish together first—what we want in it, what the idea is, what the dish will be called—and then we make it. Sometimes it'll only take an hour to nail it, but that hour is more than we ever spent before.

For this dish we wanted to riff on the classic ginger-scallion noodles that you can get at any Chinese dive in New York. We wanted it to be vegetarian and approachable, and we wanted to use green tea as a seasoning. Green tea has a lot of savory flavors that you might not think about when you drink it. Your brain automatically puts green tea (aka *matcha* when it's in powdered form) in the sweet category when it's used in food, maybe because of the pastel color, maybe because we're just used to eating green tea ice cream. But matcha is toasty and vegetal, with a subtle bitterness.

The noodles we serve at the restaurant are custom-made for us by Sun Noodle in New York. We just told them we wanted a ramen noodle made with matcha and they worked with us to develop the recipe based on how we wanted to serve the noodles. They added a little spinach to it to give it a more vibrant green color, and we're really happy with the results. You can use whatever kind of fresh noodles you can get your hands on—this dish is totally fine with egg noodles or thick Chinese wonton noodles. The only way you can mess up this dish is if your water isn't at a hard boil. It has to be super hot so the noodles cook quickly and don't get gummy.

1. Bring a pot of water to a boil, and salt it well.

2. In a medium bowl, combine the ginger scallion sauce and mushroom powder with ½ teaspoon salt and ⅔ cup of the boiling water. Stir to combine.

3. Drop the noodles into the pot of boiling water, stir, and cook until just al dente—2 minutes, tops. Drain the noodles well and dump them into the bowl with the seasonings. Stir to combine, then transfer to a serving bowl, along with the flavorful liquid at the bottom of the bowl.

4. Drizzle the noodles with hoisin, then top with slices of radish and cucumber. Finish with a good dusting of matcha and serve immediately. The noodles will begin to stick together as soon as they get cold.

Kosher salt
2 tablespoons Ginger-Scallion Sauce (page 295)
½ teaspoon Mushroom Powder (page 299)
10 to 12 ounces fresh noodles (preferably alkaline ramen noodles)

GARNISHES
2 teaspoons hoisin sauce
Thinly sliced radishes
Thinly sliced cucumber
1½ teaspoons matcha (green tea powder)

Stir-Fried Chicken Parts

SERVES 4

If you're flipping through the book looking for things to ease you into wok usage, start with this one. This is a weeknight dinner-type dish designed to get you accustomed to using a wok. Also, to get you to cook with chicken tenders. Americans love chicken tenders, but nobody thinks to do anything with them except bread and deep-fry them. Chicken tenders are delicious. So are chicken hearts. By the way, there are chicken hearts in this dish. And chicken livers. Wait, don't freak out—you were enjoying them! Let's all eat more chicken hearts and livers too.

1. Soak the chicken hearts and livers in the milk for 30 minutes, then drain and season generously with salt and Sichuan pepper. Season the chicken tenders too.

2. While the chicken is soaking, prepare the vinaigrette: Combine all the ingredients except the salt in a blender or food processor and pulse until everything comes together into a smooth, loose dressing. Taste and adjust the seasoning with salt. Set aside.

3. Bring a pot of salted water to a boil. Add the vermicelli noodles and blanch for 30 seconds, or just until al dente, then scoop them out with a spider or other strainer, drain, and transfer to a serving platter.

4. Working in batches, blanch the chicken hearts, livers, and tenders for a few seconds—just long enough to cook the outside while leaving the insides rare—scooping them out with the spider and into a waiting bowl as you go.

5. Set a wok or large skillet over high heat and heat until it's very hot, about 2 minutes. Coat the wok with the vegetable oil, then immediately add the onions, chiles, and garlic, stirring vigorously for about 15 seconds, just until fragrant. Add the

¼ pound chicken hearts, halved
¼ pound chicken livers, cut into
  1-inch pieces
2 cups milk
Kosher salt
Ground Sichuan pepper
½ pound chicken tenders, cut into
  1-inch pieces

SESAME VINAIGRETTE
2 tablespoons tahini
¼ cup Rich Chicken Stock (page
  301) or regular chicken stock
1 tablespoon Fried Peanuts (page
  294) or roasted peanuts
1½ teaspoons sherry vinegar
½ teaspoon fish sauce
Kosher salt

2 bundles rice vermicelli
  (4 ounces), soaked in cold water
  for 30 minutes and drained
About 2 tablespoons vegetable or
  peanut oil
½ onion, cut into large dice
2 Thai bird's-eye chiles or
  1 serrano pepper, minced
5 garlic cloves, smashed and
  peeled
Pinch of sugar
1 teaspoon sesame oil
1 (1-inch) piece fresh ginger,
  peeled and sliced into thin coins
1 tablespoon Chili Oil (page 290)
½ English cucumber, thinly sliced

chicken parts, season with the sugar and sesame oil, and cook, stirring occasionally, until the edges of the chicken are burnished golden brown and the meat is cooked through, 3 to 4 minutes. Add the ginger, toss once, and remove from the heat.

6. To serve, offload the stir-fried chicken on top of the blanched noodles. Spoon the sesame vinaigrette over the chicken and finish with a drizzle of chili oil and the crunchy sliced cucumber.

Stir-Fried Sweet Peas

SERVES 4 AS PART OF A LARGER MEAL

You make your order at a Chinese restaurant. The waiter scribbles in his notepad, expressionless. You worry maybe you're ordering the wrong things or not enough food, so you ask, "Is that good? Should I get anything else?"

"Maybe some vegetables."

At this point, my go-to order is always sautéed pea shoots in garlic sauce. And without fail, I get my bill and I'm shocked to see that at $13, they're the most expensive part of the dinner. They're labor intensive. A cook has to sit in the back picking tough stems out of a huge bag of pea tendrils, which will cook down to a fraction of the original volume.

I wanted to use the same flavors in a dish that was more affordable. The idea would be to use pea shoots but add some textural variation and fill out the plate a bit. The solution is obvious: peas. Peas are a nice creamy counterpoint to the shoots. (Even when peas are in season, frozen petite peas can actually be better than larger, starchier fresh peas. Cheaper too.) It's a surprisingly rich dish. Good olive oil heated in a wok is almost buttery. The garlic is savory. For a plate made up almost completely of vegetables, this is remarkably hearty.

Note: Young pea stems are actually succulent and delicious, so don't discard them unless they seem tough. If they're young and tender throughout, just chop them down into 1½-inch lengths. If the pea leaves are more mature, the stems and stringy parts can be undesirable.

2 tablespoons extra-virgin olive oil, plus more for drizzling

1 cup fresh pea shoots, cleaned and stemmed (see Note)

2 tablespoons Green Chili Condiment (recipe follows)

2 cups small fresh peas or frozen petite peas

2 cups snap peas, sliced thin on a bias

1 tablespoon oyster sauce

¾ cup chicken stock

1 teaspoon kosher salt

1 teaspoon sugar

2 to 3 tablespoons Pickled Red Onions (page 198)

1 teaspoon ground Sichuan pepper

1. Set a wok over medium-high heat and coat it with the olive oil. When the oil begins to shimmer, add the pea shoots, immediately followed by the green chili condiment, and stir for a few seconds. Add the peas, snap peas, oyster sauce, and chicken stock, season with the salt and sugar, and stir-fry until

the peas are cooked but still al dente and the liquid has been absorbed and reduced to almost nothing.

2. Transfer to a serving platter and drizzle with extra-virgin olive oil. Garnish with the pickled onions and Sichuan pepper.

Green Chili Condiment
MAKES ABOUT 1 CUP

½ cup coarsely chopped jalapeño peppers
½ cup coarsely chopped serrano peppers
1 teaspoon salt
1 cup peanut or vegetable oil, plus more as needed
2 tablespoons chopped scallion whites
1 teaspoon minced peeled ginger
1 teaspoon sugar
1 teaspoon ground Sichuan pepper
1 teaspoon oyster sauce
1 teaspoon fish sauce

1. Pulse the jalapeño and serrano peppers and the salt in a food processor until the peppers are mostly broken down but still fairly chunky. Transfer to a heatproof bowl.

2. In a wok or heavy-bottomed saucepan, heat the oil to 350°F. Carefully pour the hot oil over the peppers while gently stirring them. Watch out—they will bubble and steam. Allow the peppers to cool completely.

3. Add the remaining ingredients to the bowl and stir. Transfer the condiment to a jar or a container with a lid and top off with just enough oil to cover. The condiment will keep for at least a week in the refrigerator, but let it come to room temperature before using.

Mongolian Long Beans

SERVES 4 AS A SIDE DISH

I'm not exactly sure why we call these Mongolian long beans— our recipes have a tendency to get away from their original idea. But because Chinese cuisine is so complex and, aside from the occasional nitpicker, nobody knows anything about it anyway, we don't get any complaints. At the end of the day, this is a really, really simple sauté, with multiple layers of spice from the chili crisp, dried chiles, and fresh horseradish. The beans are blanched and then stir-fried quickly so they retain their crunch.

1. Bring a pot of salted water to a boil. Blanch the long beans for 60 to 90 seconds—they should still be crunchy. Drain.

2. Gather all your ingredients and have them near at hand. Set a wok over high heat and get it good and hot. Pour the oil into the hot wok and swirl to coat. Add the garlic and sweat it for a couple of seconds, then add the chili crisp, chiles, and fermented black beans and stir-fry for 10 seconds. Add the blanched beans and onion, toss, and stir-fry for about 30 seconds to cook some of the rawness out of the onion. Add the mushroom powder, cumin, sugar, and soy sauce, toss a few more times, and scoop onto a plate.

3. Garnish the beans with the fried garlic and grated horseradish.

Kosher salt

2 cups (2-inch) pieces Chinese long beans (or substitute green beans)

2 tablespoons vegetable or peanut oil

1 tablespoon minced garlic

1 tablespoon Chili Crisp (page 290)

3 Tianjin chiles or other medium-hot dried red chiles, like chiles Japones

1 tablespoon fermented black beans

¼ onion, sliced (about ⅔ cup)

1 teaspoon Mushroom Powder (page 299)

½ teaspoon ground cumin

½ teaspoon sugar

2 tablespoons soy sauce

2 tablespoons Fried Garlic (page 294)

1 tablespoon grated fresh horseradish

Fish-Fragrant Eggplant

SERVES 4

Like mapo tofu, this dish is another greatest hit of Sichuan cooking that's been done and redone in thousands of different restaurants in thousands of different ways. But for the most part, fish-fragrant eggplant preparations fall into two camps: the battered-and-fried camp and the simply fried camp.

At its best, fried battered eggplant steams itself inside its batter shell, yielding tender eggplant with a crunchy exterior. But when the cooking isn't perfectly timed, it can turn out like french fries that've been cooked too long. The insides are all but disintegrated and what's left is just fried dough (which has its merits, but isn't really my thing). In Sichuan Province, they usually forgo the batter, and so do I.

Frying eggplant is notoriously tricky because of the vegetable's tendency to act like an ultra-absorbent sponge. Dropped straight into a deep fryer, eggplant will soak up buckets of oil and then spit it back out into your final dish. To avoid this, I take my cue from my time in Italian kitchens, where we'd brine eggplant in heavily salted water before frying it. Soaking the eggplant waterlogs them. When they go into hot oil, the water rushes out from the eggplant as steam, preventing oil from entering. In a nice mixing of cultures, we cook the eggplant a second time, as we learned from Liang and the wok cooks at Lung Shan: After the initial quick fry, the eggplant goes into boiling water to rinse off and finish cooking, and then, finally, back into the wok. It's a technique we also employ with our Taiwanese Eggplant and Clams (page 227).

As for the name of this dish, many people are surprised to find that the recipe neither contains fish nor is fishy. It's garlicky, somewhat sweet, slightly sour, herbaceous, and a little spicy. The term *fish-fragrant* refers to the aromatics and seasonings, which are the same ones used in traditional Sichuan fish cookery. We take some license with those ingredients too, but we're not the first to do so.

Note: To slice the eggplant into large diamonds, employ the "roll-cut" technique: First, slice off the stem with a cut on a 45-degree angle. Roll the eggplant a quarter turn and cut a 2-inch piece on the same diagonal. Roll the eggplant another quarter turn and repeat. Admire your work. The roll cut is pretty and eats well too.

¾ cup kosher salt

6 cups ice water

1 pound Chinese eggplant (about 3), "diamond-sliced" (see Note)

6 to 8 cups vegetable or peanut oil, for deep-frying

1 tablespoon Chili Oil (page 290)

2 tablespoons sugar

1 tablespoon doubanjiang (spicy bean paste)

2 tablespoons minced garlic

1 teaspoon ground Sichuan pepper

½ cup mushroom stock, if you have it, or chicken stock

2 tablespoons Shaoxing wine

1 tablespoon soy sauce

2 teaspoons cornstarch slurry (see page 292)

2 celery stalks, sliced thin on a bias

¾ cup (2-inch) chrysanthemum leaf pieces

¼ cup small fresh dill fronds

¼ cup fresh parsley leaves

2 tablespoons sunflower seeds, toasted

1 tablespoon Chinese black rice vinegar

1. Combine the salt with 6 cups water in a large saucepan and stir over medium-high heat until the salt has dissolved. Remove the pot from the heat, add the ice water, stir, and let the brine cool to room temperature.

2. Immerse the eggplant in the cooled brine. Let the eggplant soak for at least an hour at room temperature. (You may need to set a plate on top of the eggplant to keep it completely submerged.)

3. Heat 3 to 4 inches of vegetable oil to 350°F in a deep pot or a wok or use a deep fryer. Meanwhile, bring a pot of water to a boil.

4. Drain the eggplant and shake off as much brine as you can. Working in batches, if necessary, add the eggplant to the hot oil and fry until it's softened but still has structure, 3 to 4 minutes. Be careful, as the waterlogged eggplant is liable to hiss and steam something mighty, at least at first.

5. Scoop the eggplant out of the oil using a spider or other strainer and drop it into the pot of boiling water. Let the eggplant simmer for 10 seconds, then drain and transfer to a bowl. Set aside.

6. Get a wok or large skillet smoking hot over medium-high heat, then coat it with the chili oil. Add the sugar to the oil and stir to dissolve, about 1 minute. Add the doubanjiang, garlic, and Sichuan pepper to the wok and stir until softened and aromatic. Add the stock, Shaoxing wine, and soy sauce, scraping the pan to release any browned bits. Stir in the cornstarch slurry and bring to a simmer.

7. Add the fried eggplant and give everything a quick toss. Add the celery and chrysanthemum leaves and toss a few more times, just enough to wilt the greens a touch.

8. To serve, scoop everything onto a large platter. Scatter the dill and parsley over the top, sprinkle with the sunflower seeds, and drizzle with the vinegar.

Stir-Fried Corn with Chiles and Smoked Bamboo

SERVES 4 AS PART OF A LARGER MEAL

This recipe is Chinese by way of Mexico, where I ate simple tacos of roasted chopped pasilla peppers that captured my imagination. I loved the interplay of the corn tortillas and chiles and the minimalist vegetarian cooking.

As you might expect, San Francisco has a sizable vegetarian/vegan contingent. I don't mind accommodating them—vegetables are delicious. The thing is, though, vegetarians go nuts for "meatiness." Japanese cured bamboo (*menma*), which is smoked over fruitwood, gives this dish a crunchy, toothy anchor that conjures up the flavor of barbecue. It's a fine example of how you can take a prepackaged commercial product and elevate it to something really special.

I want to say this recipe takes the same minimalist approach as those tacos in Mexico, and it's true that the heart of this dish is built around just three ingredients—corn, peppers, and bamboo—but it's more likely you'll be cursing me as you scour the pantry for bonito flakes and wheel the smoker out of storage. On the bright side, almost everything can be done ahead of time and stored in the fridge until you're ready to cook. (And, hey, it's an excuse to smoke brisket, page 36; oyster sauce, page 100; oil, page 306; garlic confit, page 305; and cola, page 304, all at the same time.) Once you've got your *mise en place,* this dish comes together quickly.

Special equipment: Smoker and fruitwood chips

½ cup packaged sliced menma (Japanese cured bamboo), drained
About ¼ cup vegetable or peanut oil
6 ears corn, husked
1 cup bonito flakes (optional)
2 poblano peppers, seeded and cut into ½-inch pieces, or 5 Padrón peppers
1 cup loosely packed fresh Thai basil leaves (in a pinch, substitute sweet basil or a mix of sweet basil and mint)
1 tablespoon minced garlic
1 Thai bird's-eye chile
1 teaspoon oyster sauce
½ teaspoon sansho pepper
Extra-virgin olive oil
1 nori sheet, toasted and torn into pieces

1. Rub the menma with vegetable oil, which will help draw in more smoke flavor. Set up a smoker: At the restaurant, we line a hotel pan with foil, scatter wood chips onto it, and set it over two burners until the wood begins to smolder. Then the bamboo sits above the chips on a wire rack and more foil keeps the smoke contained for the half an hour or so of smoking. If you're not afraid of burning wood inside your

home, go for it. Otherwise, smoke the bamboo in a pan in an outdoor grill or electric smoker for 2 hours at 200°F.

2. Use a sharp knife to slice the kernels from each corncob into a deep bowl, then follow with a butter knife to scrape the remaining corn and "milk" from the cobs into the same bowl—pull the knife up the cobs, toward you, for the best results. Set aside.

3. Use a cleaver or heavy knife to cut the corncobs into 2-inch segments. Put as many cob pieces as you can fit into a medium saucepan, leaving an inch of room at the top. Cover with water, set the pot over high heat, and bring to a boil. Reduce the heat to maintain a simmer and cook, uncovered, for 1 hour.

4. Strain the corn stock, discarding the solids, and return it to the pan. Raise the heat to high, bring the stock to a boil, and cook until it has reduced to about 2 cups, 5 to 10 minutes. Remove the stock from the heat, add the bonito flakes, if using, and let steep for 10 minutes, then strain the stock and set aside.

5. Heat a wok or large skillet over high heat and coat it with a thin layer of vegetable oil. When the oil is almost smoking, throw in the peppers and toss for a minute or so to blister and char them. Add the basil, garlic, and chile and give everything a few stirs. Add the corn and its milk and the smoked menma and let the ingredients sit undisturbed for a moment to impart the smoky char of hot steel. Then toss and repeat until most of the corn has been charred brown on at least one side.

6. Add 1 cup of the reserved corn stock and stir as the stock is reduced to almost nothing. (Reserve the extra stock for soups or to make this dish again—it'll keep for a couple of days in the fridge.) Add the oyster sauce, give one last stir, and transfer to a serving bowl.

7. Garnish with the sansho pepper, a glug of good olive oil, and the nori.

Sweet Potato Leaves with Kabocha Squash

SERVES 4

I'd never thought of cooking with sweet potato leaves until I had them in a dish at Isa in Brooklyn, back when Ignacio Mattos was the chef. The next time I saw Sue and Liang in San Francisco, I asked if they knew where to get them. Of course they did. This is the magic of Sue and Liang. Another chef recently told me he'd become so desperate to know where to source Asian vegetables that he'd camped out in front of a Chinese restaurant to see where their early morning deliveries came from. We're pretty lucky to have Sue and Liang.

The leaves arrived at the restaurant on the heels of a night of moderate to heavy drinking. I was feeling hungover and in need of something brothy and restorative. So I devised this dish. It's vegan, umami rich, earthy, and sustaining.

At the end of the day, the sweet potato leaves aren't essential, although they do have a pleasant silkiness to them. You can substitute whatever succulent, leafy greens you like: e.g., pea leaves, amaranth greens, watercress.

Finally, there's going to be more squash than you need for this dish, so come up with some other uses for it—dumplings, baby food, risotto, soup.

1. Preheat the oven to 350°F.

2. Rub the flesh of the squash with 1 tablespoon of the olive oil and season with a generous pinch of salt. Place the squash flesh side down on a baking sheet and roast until it's tender but still firm enough to hold its shape, about 1 hour. Let cool slightly.

3. Slice 10 thin half-moons from the squash, then run your knife around the edges of each half-moon to remove the skin.

½ small kabocha or red kuri squash (about 2 pounds), seeded

3 tablespoons olive oil

Kosher salt

1 teaspoon minced garlic

½ pound sweet potato leaves or other tender greens (see headnote), rinsed and dried

½ cup dried adzuki beans or raw peanuts, boiled in Dashi (page 293) or chicken stock for 1 to 2 hours, until soft

1 teaspoon Mushroom Powder (page 299)

3 tablespoons Salted Chili Condiment (page 302)

½ block pressed tofu, or ½ block firm tofu, pressed and shaved on a mandolin or thinly sliced with a knife (see page 300)

Fish sauce (optional)

1½ teaspoons pumpkin seed oil (available at health food stores)

2 tablespoons squash or pumpkin seeds, toasted and hulled

Scoop the flesh out of the rest of the squash and pulse in a blender or food processor with just enough water to create a smooth, loose puree.

4. In a wok or medium saucepan, heat the remaining 2 tablespoons olive oil over medium-high heat until it shimmers. Add the garlic and sweat it for a few seconds, then add the sweet potato leaves and adzuki beans. Toss until the greens are just wilted, about 1 minute. Season the leaves with a pinch of salt and the mushroom powder, then add 3 cups water, 2 tablespoons of the salted chili condiment, and 3 tablespoons of the squash puree, and bring to a simmer. Add the half-moons of squash and the pressed tofu and return to a simmer. Season with salt and fish sauce, if desired.

5. Ladle everything into a serving bowl and garnish with the pumpkin seed oil, squash seeds, and the remaining 1 tablespoon of salted chili condiment.

Surprises

As a young cook, I never made enough money to eat at the restaurants where I worked. It's just a fact of our industry. You don't get paid enough, and you're working while everyone else is playing. One of the driving principles behind Mission Chinese Food has always been to serve food that our friends can afford. Here's another fact of our industry: When those friends are cooks and chefs, we crush them with food.

Part of it is about showing off: *Hey, look at all the cool stuff we're doing.* But part of it is also about acknowledging that we've all been in the same boat. On the one night that other cooks go out to eat, it's only right that we show them a good time. Now, there's definitely a balance to be struck between treating your friends to a few extra appetizers and burying them under an avalanche of dishes. We used to be really cruel about it. When chefs came in, we'd go out of our way to be over the top: start with Chinese food, then unload a crab boil onto the table, and then, just when they thought it was over, out would come the trays of barbecue brisket. It was especially fun to see the faces of their civilian dining companions contort with shock and delight. But I learned my lesson when David Chang repaid the favor.

Andy Ricker—the maestro of Thai cuisine and chef of Pok Pok— and I stopped in for a drink at Chang's restaurant complex in Toronto. We told the bartender that we couldn't eat, we had a dinner later that night, and that we'd come back to eat another time. Three minutes later, plates of pork buns and rice cakes appeared in front of us. Fine, this was to be expected. Then out came another wave. Oysters. Scrambled eggs with truffle. Three bowls of ramen. Dishes started showing up from everywhere—each floor of the building houses a different Momofuku restaurant. There were only two of us. We were struggling to move, let alone keep up. The chef came out to apologize and showed us an e-mail from Chang: "Kill them—send everything. They do it to everybody else."

So, we've eased back on the murderous generosity. But when a big group of friends comes in, we still like to bring a surprise to the table. And from time to time, when we're feeling frisky, we'll drop a platter of salt-and-pepper crab on a random unsuspecting table of guests. It's a deeply Asian way to eat—the best way, really: more food than you can possibly consume, everybody grabbing across the table. It's how I ate with my friends—Asian and otherwise—growing up. It's joyful. It's about plenty, and surprise, and sending people home with leftovers. If you're going to invite people over for a meal, really have them over. Be generous, be ridiculous.

Salt-and-Pepper Crab with Mapo Tofu

SERVES 6

1 live Dungeness crab

About 1 tablespoon kosher salt

About 2 teaspoons freshly ground white pepper

½ cup all-purpose flour

½ cup cornstarch

6 to 8 cups vegetable or peanut oil, for deep-frying

½ onion, thinly sliced

1 jalapeño, cut into thin rounds

2 teaspoons sugar

1 large serving Mapo Tofu (page 62), warmed

1 tablespoon Chili Oil (page 290)

3 tablespoons fried shallots, homemade or store-bought (see page 295)

3 tablespoons Fried Garlic (page 294)

½ cup fresh cilantro leaves

2 teaspoons ground Sichuan pepper

If you want to impress a group of Chinese people, make them salt-and-pepper Dungeness crab. Any older diners will applaud and let out an ecstatic, "Wahhhh!" It's truly one of life's more satisfying sounds.

At Mission Chinese San Francisco, whenever I was feeling mischievous at the beginning of dinner service, I'd walk down the street to the Chinese seafood shop and pick up a crab. I'd break it down, fry it, and bring it out as the last course for a table of friends. It has to be a spur-of-the-moment act. For one thing, you don't want crabs to sit around for too long—once a crab dies, it degrades quickly. More to the point, it's all about being spontaneous.

After we'd pulled this stunt a few times, people started telling me a legend about a similar secret off-menu item one could get at Spices—one of our muse restaurants. If you asked for it, they'd fry you up a platter of crab and then *cover the whole thing with mapo tofu!* I never went to Spices to confirm this. I didn't want it to not be true. That's why I started doing it myself.

If there's anything better than the look of appreciation on the faces of your guests when you give them a whole crab, it's the complete shock they experience when you cover the whole thing in molten mapo.

1. Clean the crab—a task made more comfortable with rubber gloves, and best done quickly to spare the crab any misery. Separate the top shell either by taking hold of a set of legs and pulling up on one edge of the shell or by inserting a paring knife into the back of the shell and popping it open. Reserve the top shell and its attached guts, and turn your attention to the body. Bisect the crab from front to back with a cleaver and pull out the gills with your fingers. Cut each crab between the

legs into 3 or 4 smaller pieces. Use a cleaver or shears to clip off the pointed last joints of the smaller crab legs. (The crab will continue to move involuntarily even at this stage, but it's certainly dead.)

2.   Tap on each leg with the back of the cleaver to crack it for easier eating. Season all the pieces liberally with salt and white pepper.

3.   In a deep pot or a wok, heat about 3 inches of oil to 350°F, or use a deep fryer. Meanwhile, mix together the flour and cornstarch in a large shallow bowl. (For a more tempura-like experience, you can add a couple of cups of soda water at this point to make a batter, but I prefer just to use a dry dredge.) Run each piece of the crab, including the top shell and guts, through the dredge and tap off any excess.

4.   Working in batches, if necessary, add the crab to the hot oil (fry the top shell last). Use a ladle or long spoon to stir it around and to douse any exposed bits of crab with oil. If you can keep the oil temperature at a steady 350°F, it shouldn't take more than a minute or two to cook the pieces to golden brown and perfect doneness. Transfer the finished pieces to a rack set over a baking sheet. Make sure you rest the top shell right side up, so that oil doesn't pool in it as it sits.

5.   Set a wok or skillet over high heat and let it sit for a minute, until it gets very hot. Slick the pan with a couple tablespoons of the frying oil, then immediately add the onion. Give the pan a few shakes and let the onion get a nice sear, then add the jalapeño. Again, give the pan a few shakes to get a good sear on the pepper. Add the fried crab, season everything with more salt and white pepper and the sugar, and toss a couple more times.

6.   Transfer the crab to a platter and smother it in the mapo tofu. Garnish with a good drizzle of the chili oil, the fried shallots, fried garlic, and cilantro. Sprinkle on the Sichuan pepper and serve immediately.

Henan Big-Tray Fish

SERVES 4

Chances are you haven't heard of this dish or, for that matter, of Henan food. Until recently, I hadn't either. When we were opening Mission Chinese Food in New York, we'd spend long days building out the restaurant and long nights drinking away the stress. The only real benefit to this cycle was our discovery of a place called Henan Taste, where we'd go to nurse our hangovers (it's now called Spicy Village).

Over the course of a few weeks, we ordered everything on the menu. The pinnacle was called Big-Tray Chicken: an enormous metal platter heavy with succulent chicken and potatoes braised in beer and warm spices. You had the option of adding hand-pulled noodles, which we always did. The chicken had been cleaved haphazardly into rough bits, with the occasional sharp bone protruding. The potatoes thickened the braising liquid into something between a soup and a glaze, and it was speckled with whole spices that we'd happily crunch on. Beer added a slight bitterness to the braise, a flavor we became completely obsessed with. It's why we started adding beer to our mapo tofu. And it's why we started making this dish ourselves.

I love watching customers dig into a whole fish. Their eyes light up when the plate arrives, and then they proceed to hunt for the very last morsel of meat, sucking sauce and cartilage off the fins and bones. You can make this recipe with chicken or pork shoulder, but fish is what I like best. Ours is a bit sweeter than the original—caramel is at the base of the sauce, and it complements the beer—and a little spicier and more numbing too.

This dish appears from time to time on the regular Mission Chinese menu, but it's here in the Surprises section because of a beautiful twist Angela once put on it. In a turn of sheer brilliance, she surprised us for staff meal by adding a batch of hot chicken wings to a platter of big-tray fish. The sauce coated the chicken like Chinese Buffalo wings, and Jesus wept. You don't have to add chicken wings, but I commend you if you do.

1 (1- to 2-pound) striped bass or other firm-fleshed fish, cleaned and scaled
Kosher salt

SAUCE SPICES

1 teaspoon cumin seeds
1 teaspoon fennel seeds
1 teaspoon whole Sichuan peppercorns
1 star anise
2 dried Tianjin chiles or other medium-hot red chiles, like chiles Japones
½ teaspoon whole black peppercorns
½ teaspoon whole white peppercorns

¼ cup sugar
¾ cup stout beer (like Samuel Smith Oatmeal Stout)
1 tablespoon sliced garlic
¼ cup doubanjiang (spicy bean paste)
2 tablespoons Shaoxing wine
4 cups fish or chicken stock (store-bought is fine)
2 teaspoons fish sauce
2 tablespoons soy sauce
1 teaspoon Mushroom Powder (page 299)
4 or 5 baby white turnips, peeled and cut into 2-inch chunks
1 purple sweet potato, peeled and cut into 2-inch chunks

4 to 6 cups vegetable or peanut oil, for deep-frying

Kosher salt

DREDGE

½ cup all-purpose flour

½ cup cornstarch

1 tablespoon cumin seeds, ground in a spice or coffee grinder

1 teaspoon ground Sichuan pepper

1 teaspoon kosher salt

Hand-Pulled Noodles (page 240), without spice mix or dressing

4 to 6 just-fried Chongqing Chicken Wings (page 135; optional)

1 tablespoon Chili Oil (page 290)

2 teaspoons Sichuan peppercorn oil

1 teaspoon ground Sichuan pepper

1 cup mixed fresh herbs, such as cilantro leaves, mint leaves, shiso leaves, fennel fronds, and/or dill

¼ cup sliced scallions

1 (1-inch) piece fresh ginger, peeled and julienned

1. Use scissors to snip off the dorsal and bottom fins from the fish, and score three deep diagonal slices into each side of the fish. Season the scores, body cavity, and head generously with salt. Refrigerate while you prep the sauce.

2. Toast all the sauce spices in a large saucepan over medium heat until fragrant, about a minute. Empty the spices into a small bowl and set aside.

3. Add the sugar and 2 teaspoons water to the saucepan and cook over medium heat, stirring occasionally, to melt and caramelize the sugar. When the caramel is amber, but definitely not burned, add the beer and stir to dissolve any hardened bits. Return the toasted spices to the pan, turn the heat up to high, and add the garlic, doubanjiang, Shaoxing wine, stock, fish sauce, soy sauce, and mushroom powder. Stir to combine and bring to a simmer, then reduce the heat to low. (If you like, you can make this sauce base a day or two ahead of time and refrigerate. Reheat before continuing.)

4. Add the turnips and sweet potato to the sauce, cover, and cook until the root vegetables are fork-tender but not falling apart, about 15 minutes. Remove from the heat and keep the pan somewhere warm while you fry the fish.

5. In a large saucepan or wok that will accommodate the whole fish, heat about 1 inch of vegetable oil over high heat until nearly smoking (375°F), or use a deep fryer. If you must, trim off the tail so the fish will fit in the pan. Meanwhile, bring a large pot of salted water to a boil for the noodles.

6. Mix together the dredge ingredients in a baking dish or on a large plate. Dredge the fish thoroughly, making sure to get the mixture inside its crevices, then shake off the excess as best you can. Grab the fish by the tail and lower the head into the oil on the side of the pan closest to you, then gently lay the rest of the fish in, away from you, to avoid splashing oil on yourself. Fry, turning once, until the coating is golden brown and the fish is just cooked through, about 4 minutes per side. Drain the fish on a paper-towel-lined platter or on a wire rack.

7. Drop the noodles into the boiling water and cook until they float, about a minute. Drain the noodles and add them to the pot of warm sauce. Toss and stir the noodles to coat.

8. Scoop the noodles, turnips, and sweet potatoes out of the sauce and onto a large platter, and top with the whole fish.

9. Return the sauce to the stovetop and cook over high heat until it has reduced by about a quarter. The starch from the turnips and sweet potato should help to thicken it. If you're the ambitious type and have the Chongqing chicken wings at the ready, toss them into the sauce and stir to coat.

10. If you're wingin' it, arrange the chicken wings around the fish. Spoon the sauce over everything, garnish with chili oil and Sichuan pepper, and cover with the herbs, scallions, and ginger. Serve immediately.

Beggar's Duck

SERVES 4 (OR 6 AS PART OF A LARGER MEAL)

Angela Dimayuga is the executive chef at Mission Chinese Food New York, where we serve this bad boy. She'll tell you about it.

Two or three weeks before we opened the second Mission Chinese Food New York, Danny and I watched a documentary about Cecilia Chiang called *Soul of a Banquet*. At that point, we were very close to having our menu locked down—everything except for the large-format section. There's a scene in the movie where they serve a beggar's chicken to this big table of excited guests. After the movie, Danny and I were gushing about how cool it was. I was kind of jealous.

So we tried it. We wrapped a chicken in lotus leaves, packed it in clay, sealed up the seams, and roasted it. It's a nerve-racking thing, not being able to touch the chicken or see it or measure the temperature. But when it works correctly, it's a really amazing way to cook—the ceramic shell locks in moisture and the meat comes out juicy and flavorful.

After a few successful attempts, we started tinkering. First, we swapped chicken out for duck, because duck is a little more luxurious and much fattier than chicken. To make sure that there's no way the duck was undercooked in the clay, we confited it first. To give it some color—usually beggar's chicken comes out a little pale—we glazed it with soy and sugar. And to give the dish a little more substance (and so that the duck doesn't just collapse into a sad heap), we stuffed it with sticky rice. We tried using other materials in place of the clay, but clay's the only thing that really works. Everything else gets soggy or cracks and looks ugly, and this dish is all about presentation.

We bring the duck out to the dining room on a silver tray, still in its clay shell, explain how we prepared the bird, and tell the story of beggar's duck. It's funny—the little spiel I give isn't something I've even looked into; it's just something we cobbled together from the Cecilia Chiang movie and conversations with people in the dining room. The story at this point goes like this: One day a beggar was gifted a chicken but had nowhere to cook it. He lived by a river, so he wrapped the chicken in a lotus leaf, then packed it in clay, and roasted it outdoors over coals. Thus, beggar's chicken.

Finally, we cover the duck with a napkin to prevent shards of clay from flying everywhere and let one lucky guest smash it open with a hammer.

Note: This recipe requires an overnight cure.

1. Remove the duck wings, and reserve for the duck sauce, along with the neck and any organs that the duck came with. Season the duck liberally inside and out with about ¼ cup salt, lay it on a wire rack set over a baking sheet, and refrigerate overnight.

2. Heat the oven to 275°F.

3. Place the duck in a Dutch oven and cover by about 1 inch with fat. Top with a piece of parchment paper, then cover tightly with a lid or foil. Carefully slide the pot into the oven and cook for 2 hours. Uncover the duck (leave the parchment), and let cool for about 30 minutes.

4. Meanwhile make the Duck Glaze: Add the sugar to a small saucepan over medium heat, and cook, stirring occasionally until the sugar is caramelized, about 6 minutes. Because the sugar is brown to begin with, it's hard to tell when it's caramelized and easy to burn! Use your nose more than your eyes. Once the sugar is melted, stir constantly until it just begins to smell like caramel. Add the Shaoxing wine immediately to stop the cooking.

5. Add the soy and dark soy sauces, and cook, stirring to dissolve any sugar that has solidified. Remove from the heat and allow to cool to room temperature.

6. Raise the oven temperature to 325°F.

7. Set a wire rack in a sheet pan. Insert a pair of tongs or a wooden spoon into the duck's cavity, and carefully lift it out of the oil. Drain as much oil as possible, and try your very best not to break the skin or spill oil all over yourself. Set the bird on the rack, and brush the skin with a couple layers of glaze, reserving 2 or 3 tablespoons. Slide back into the oven and bake for 15 minutes. Remove and allow to cool. This can all be done up to a day ahead. Store the duck in the refrigerator overnight and allow to sit at room temperature for at least 2 hours before proceeding.

Special equipment: 5 pounds moist high-fire clay (ideally purchased the same day you're going to use it); 1 full-size (16½-by-24½-inch) silicone baking mat; oil spray

1 whole duck, about 5 pounds
Salt
10 to 12 cups duck fat (or substitute lard or vegetable or peanut oil)

DUCK GLAZE
⅔ cup turbinado sugar
⅓ cup Shaoxing wine
⅓ cup soy sauce
1 tablespoon plus 1 teaspoon dark soy sauce

2 dry lotus leaves (page 299), soaked for 30 minutes in warm water

FILLING
1½ cups sticky rice (page 307), soaked in cold water for 4 hours
⅓ cup cooked chestnuts, rough chopped
⅓ cup pitted dates, cut into ¼-inch-thick coins

GARNISH
Rich Duck Sauce (recipe follows)

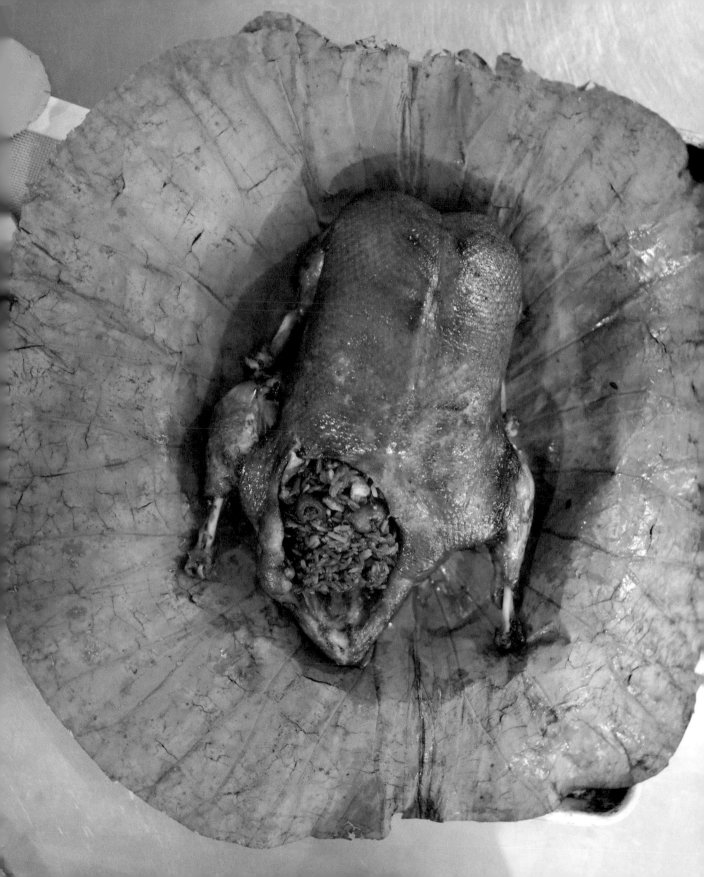

8.   Make the filling: Line a perforated pan or steamer with one of the lotus leaves. Drain the rice and spread it onto the leaf. Steam the rice in a large pot or rice cooker filled with 1 inch of water for 25 minutes.

9.   While the rice is still warm, mix in the cooked chestnuts, dates, and reserved duck glaze. Season to taste with more glaze. Use a spoon or your hands to pack the rice tightly into the cavity of the glazed duck. Set aside.

10.   Now comes the fun part. Set a silicone baking mat on your work surface and spray it with oil. Place the clay in the center of the mat. (Chances are you had to buy a big, 25-pound block of clay. No problem, just cut a slab with a butter knife.) Run a rolling pin under cold water, then use it to start pounding the clay flat. Roll the clay out into an unbroken piece of uniform thickness (about ¼ inch) that covers the entire surface of the mat. If you end up with a break in the clay, don't worry. Just use your fingers to press and seal it and keep rolling. Keeping the rolling pin wet will help prevent the clay from sticking.

11.   Lay a soaked lotus leaf in the center of the clay, and place the duck breast side up on the leaf, with the cavity nearest to you. Fold the left edge of the leaf over the duck, then the shorter ends (top and bottom), then finally the right edge. Pull the leaf taut and carefully flip the package over so that the folds are underneath the duck and the breast is now facing down.

12.   Now fold the left edge of the silicone mat over the lotus-wrapped duck, then gently peel the mat away from the clay. Repeat with the right side. Wet your fingers with water and rub the clay to seal any cracks or openings. Feel free to trim clay from the top and bottom edges to patch any openings. This is a pretty forgiving process— just make sure the package is completely sealed.

13.   Now carefully flip the whole package onto a parchment-paper-lined baking sheet. Allow the clay-wrapped duck to dry at room temperature for at least 1 hour. The clay should shrink a bit, turn lighter in color, and be dry to the touch before you roast it.

14.   Heat the oven to 375°F. Slide the duck in and roast for 1 hour. Don't open the door while the duck is roasting. Remove the duck from

the oven—the clay should be significantly lighter in color and hard to the touch. Bring it out to the table to wow your guests, cover with a napkin or towel, and tap with a mallet or hammer to break up the clay. Uncover, brush off the clay, and unwrap the lotus leaf to reveal your glorious duck. Spoon warm sauce over the top and serve.

Rich Duck Sauce

MAKES ¾ CUP

Wings, neck, and gizzards from 1 duck
1 (1-inch) piece ginger, peeled and thinly sliced
1 shallot, sliced
½ small carrot, sliced
1 clove garlic, sliced
1 bay leaf
1 teaspoon whole black peppercorns
2 juniper berries
1¼ teaspoons tomato paste
½ cup red wine
4 cups Rich Chicken Stock (page 301)
2 tablespoons butter

1.   Heat the oven to 425°F.

2.   Lay the duck parts out on a foil-lined baking sheet and roast until dark brown, turning once, about 12 to 15 minutes. Reserve.

3.   Heat a medium saucepan set over medium-high heat, then add the ginger, shallot, carrot, and spices to the pan and cook for 2 minutes. Move the ingredients with a spoon or spatula to create a little open space in the pan and add the tomato paste. Cook for 30 seconds, stirring constantly. Add the red wine and chicken stock, and use the spoon to scrape any bits from the bottom of the pan. Add the roasted duck parts and bring to a simmer, reduce the heat to low, and cook for 1½ hours.

4.   Strain and discard the solids, then return the broth to the pan. Cook over medium-high heat until the liquid has reduced to ¾ cup, about 15 minutes. Reserve until ready to use. To finish, bring the sauce to a boil, add the butter, and whisk to combine. Serve immediately.

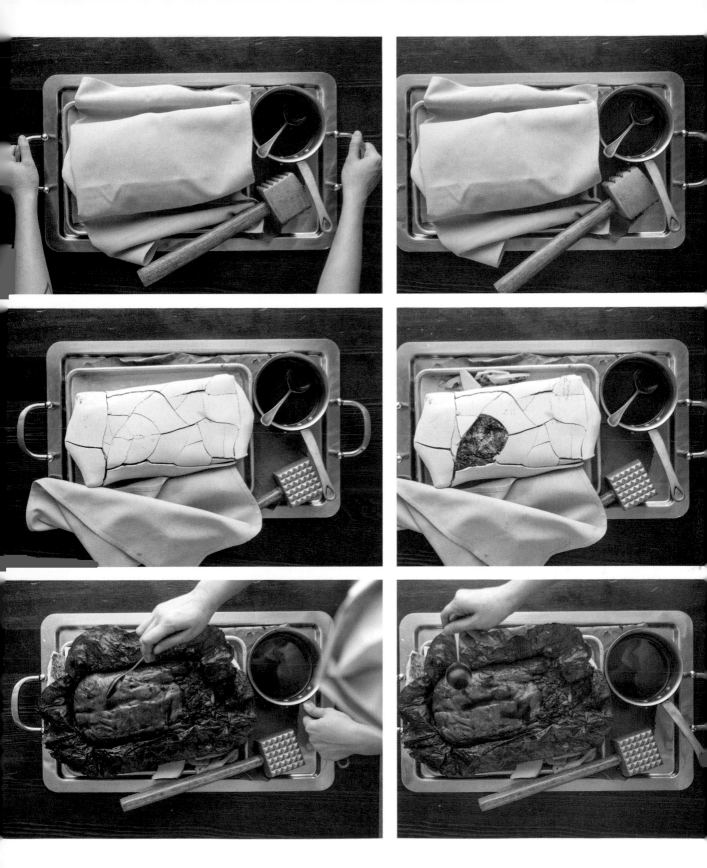

Sichuan Lobster Boil

SERVES A LARGE GROUP

When I was growing up in Oklahoma, my parents refused to eat seafood unless it was fried. As a concession to my more adventurous tastes, we'd sometimes have dinner at Joe's Crab Shack, where I could order a single-serving crab or lobster boil and my parents could get fried fish and french fries and hush puppies. Many chefs draw inspiration from memorable meals they had in their childhoods. Most of my childhood memories of special-occasion meals happen to revolve around chain restaurants. On the bright side, those restaurants taught me that a crab boil need not be restricted to the outdoors.

I love seafood boils—crab, crawfish, shrimp, lobster, whatever. It's such a communal, casual way to eat. You dump the cooked food onto the table, and you eat it. No utensils required. Maybe two people reach for the same piece of shrimp. No big deal. A seafood boil is the Western world's finest example of family-style dining. And Chinese food is all about family-style dining. Having a bucket of shellfish unloaded onto your table at a Chinese restaurant might seem to come a bit out of left field, but it doesn't feel that way to me.

One of my chef idols, Paul Liebrandt, was the first recipient of the crab boil treatment at Mission Chinese Food. We've busted it out quite a few times since then. At Chris's wedding, we brought great joy to a couple hundred guests, Asian and white alike, with a massive crawfish and shrimp boil.

The secret to a proper seafood boil is to cook the seafood just barely shy of done, then scoop it out and lock it in a cooler with gobs of butter and Old Bay. The crab and shrimp and lobster will finish steaming in their own juices rather than surrendering everything to the broth. That broth, by the way, is plenty delicious and should not be overlooked.

I'm not going to try and distill the art of the crab boil into exact steps, because part of the fun is winging it—pouring beers four at a time into a huge cauldron, kicking it up like Emeril with hot sauce, tossing sticks of butter into the cooler. It's fun and it's actually harder to mess up than you think.

You will, however, need some equipment:

- An enormous stockpot
- An ice chest big enough to hold all the seafood and vegetables
- A large spider or strainer
- A newspaper-lined landing place for all the food
- Crab crackers, bibs, Wet-Naps, and other picnic-y accessories

You can certainly pull off a crab boil inside, provided you have a commercial-strength gas stove that can heat a cauldron of bubbling seafood quickly and a way of keeping seafood juices from spilling all over your floor. If not, stick to the great outdoors. You can build a suitable fire pit out of nothing more than cinder blocks and a grate from a barbecue. Just build the fire in the middle of four cinder blocks, arrayed in a square or rectangle, balance the grate on the blocks, and set the stockpot on top of that.

As for what goes into the boil itself, well, that's up to you. Start with root vegetables and sausages as a base. Throw in some cheap seafood (shrimp and clams) to fill things out, and then add a luxury item (crab or lobster). Choose what to mix and match from the following:

- Corn
- Red potatoes
- Yukon Gold potatoes
- Yams
- Red and yellow onions
- Kielbasa
- Lamb merguez sausage
- Italian sausage
- Live crawfish
- Live clams
- Large head-on shrimp
- Live lobsters
- Live Dungeness crab
- Live blue crab

And, obviously, you'll need some starch to soak up the broth. Lots of crusty bread is an easy choice. Personally, I like to toss in Korean or Chinese rice cakes and make a soup once all the seafood is out of the boil. Speaking of the broth, here's the basic formula:

2 parts Rich Chicken Stock (page 301) or regular chicken or fish stock
2 parts water
1 part cheap beer (think Budweiser)

Season with your choice of:

• Old Bay Seasoning
• Scallion whites, smashed
• Garlic cloves
• Lemons, halved
• Bay leaves
• Black peppercorns
• Cinnamon
• Hot sauce (Tabasco, Crystal, etc.)
• Sichuan peppercorn oil
• Chili Crisp (page 290)
• Chongqing Wing Spice Mix (page 137)

Here's how this all goes down.

Start by cleaning and prepping all your ingredients. Scrub the lobsters and crab. Purge the clams in cold water. Husk the corn. Halve the potatoes. Peel and halve the onions. Et cetera. Get everything lined up so that all you are doing is throwing things into the pot, stirring, and then scooping them out. Once you get outside, you don't want too much work that you can't do with a beverage in your hand.

When you're all prepped, build a fire with a strong, steady flame and set the very large stockpot on the grate. Add stock, water, and beer and bring it to a boil. Season with your choice of the suggested seasonings—you want a very flavorful bath for the seafood to cook in, as salty and spicy as you'd want a soup to be.

Now you're ready to cook. The process is this:

1. Cook the different foods in individual batches to about 90 percent doneness.
2. Transfer to the cooler.
3. Season with Old Bay, hot sauce, and butter.
4. Let the food steam and rest in the cooler as you cook the other items.

You'll want to cook things in the greatest danger of overcooking last, meaning you'll start with the vegetables and sausages. Toss them into the boiling liquid and simmer until they're just about done, then transfer them to the cooler with the spider strainer. Throw a stick of butter in there with them, sprinkle on some Old Bay, squirt with hot sauce. Lock the cooler, give the whole thing a shake, and don't let anybody open it for a peek. Move on to the seafood. Assuming your fire is healthy and you bring the liquid back to a boil between each round:

- Shrimp will cook in 3 to 5 minutes.
- Crawfish in 4 to 6 minutes.
- Dungeness crab in 7 or 8 minutes.
- Clams and blue crab in 5 to 7 minutes.
- Lobsters (1½ pounders) in 8 to 10 minutes.

Proceed in roughly that order, adding each succeeding item to the cooler, along with another stick or two of butter, Old Bay, and hot sauce. Let everything ride out in the cooler for 5 or 10 minutes more while you bring the broth to one final boil. Add the rice cakes if you're using them. When you're ready, call your loved ones to the table and unleash the contents of the cooler onto a table. Be sure to have more hot sauce, Old Bay, wing spice, and plenty of lemon wedges on hand. Garnish with fried garlic and chopped cilantro. Dig in.

The Mission Chinese Pantry

Most of the recipes in this book are super easy, provided you have a well-stocked pantry full of Chinese spices and the various sauces and condiments we employ in the restaurant . . .

Most of the specialty ingredients called for in this book can be found at any good Asian market. You might not find all the Japanese ingredients at a Chinese market, or vice versa, and you might end up having to visit two stores to get everything you need. And if you don't have a brick-and-mortar Asian market nearby, your best resource is the Internet. Either way, a pantry filled with store-bought (and homemade) sauces, dried and fermented goods, and smoked things is vital to re-creating Mission Chinese Food dishes at home. Thankfully, most of these items will last for months in your pantry or fridge.

That said, I don't like the idea of you running out to buy a bottle of Sichuan peppercorn oil just to garnish one dish and then letting that bottle sit on your shelf for three years mocking you as you never use it again. Instead, start by taking a run through the book and formulate a menu or selection of dishes. Then commit to cooking Chinese food at least once a week for a month or two months, or whatever it takes to build up your pantry.

When it comes to shopping for jarred Chinese sauces, an Asian market can be a confusing wilderness. People tend to pick Chinese sauces at random, by price, or because of a vague hunch that they've had it before. But you would never go through the trouble of buying organic tomatoes and pasture-raised beef for an Italian pasta dish and then settle for Kraft Parmesan cheese, would you? With some of these products—*doubanjiang* (chili-bean paste) or fish sauce, for example—the flavor and quality can vary widely from brand to brand, even within the same price range. By all means, if you have preferences, stick to them, but if you want to use the same stuff we do, have a look at the photos accompanying the items in this section. Asian food labels can be maddeningly unclear, especially if you can't read the language—photographs really are the easiest reference for shopping. The labels are also how we often refer to things when we're talking to one another ("the sauce with the angry old lady on the jar").

Binchotan Charcoal: The finest Japanese charcoal, *binchotan,* is produced from oak charred at extremely high temperatures. It burns clean, with minimal smoke and fumes, and it's the charcoal traditionally used to cook *yakitori*; it can also be employed as a water purifier. It's pricey, hip, and sought after. We call for it only once in this book, for our *donburi* recipe (page 297), and it's perfectly reasonable to omit it. Just don't substitute other charcoal in its place.

Charred Chili Condiment: We use this condiment at Mission Chinese Food New York as a topping for canned anchovies that we serve with bread and butter. (Our favorite brand of anchovies, by the way, is Angostina Recca.) You can use this for anything to which you want to add heat and a little bit of funk. Consider it a fishier, more complex alternative to the Salted Chili Condiment (page 302).

MAKES ABOUT 1½ CUPS

1 pound fresh red Holland or Fresno chile peppers
1½ teaspoons fish sauce
1 teaspoon salt

1. Use your hands to pop the green tops off the peppers. (Slicing the tops off inevitably wastes too much perfectly good pepper flesh.) Place the peppers directly on a gas burner and char the outsides. You're not looking to fully blacken them as you would a red bell pepper. You only want to char 50 or 60 percent of the skin—there should still be some red.

2. Transfer the peppers to a food processor and pulse into ¼-inch pieces. Stir in the fish sauce and salt and scrape the peppers into a small nonreactive—plastic, porcelain, or glass—container. Place a piece of plastic wrap directly onto the chiles and press down lightly. Cover with a loose-fitting lid and leave at room temperature to ferment for 1 week. (If it's really warm, it might only take 4 days or so.) The peppers are ready when they've broken down a bit and look flaccid and limp, almost as though they've been cooked. You're not looking for them to smell super funky—they'll still smell and taste pretty fresh. If any white mold has formed, it's fine, just scrape it off. (Darker or other color molds are not okay.) Tighten the lid and store in the refrigerator until it no longer tastes good to you.

Chili Crisp and Chili Oil: For years, we referred to chili crisp affectionately as Old Lady Sauce, after the stern-faced auntie who graces the label of our favorite brand of the stuff, Lao Gan Ma. It's a hot-as-hell condiment, littered with crunchy dried spices and aromatics. You

should feel free to buy it from an Asian market, but by making it from scratch, you get two recipes for the price of one. Our house chili oil is a by-product of the chili crisp–making process. We use the condiment on all sorts of things: Dan Dan Noodles (page 243), Thrice-Cooked Bacon (page 96), and Hand-Pulled Noodles (page 240), to name a few.

MAKES ABOUT 2 CUPS CHILI CRISP
AND 3 CUPS CHILI OIL

4 cups dried chiles de árbol, stems removed

1 tablespoon whole Sichuan peppercorns

3 star anise

1 (3-inch) piece fresh ginger, peeled and thinly sliced

1 cinnamon stick (about 3 inches long)

1 black cardamom pod, smashed with the side of a cleaver or heavy knife

10 garlic cloves, coarsely chopped

½ cup Mushroom Powder (page 299)

3 tablespoons kosher salt

4 cups peanut or vegetable oil

½ cup sesame oil

½ teaspoon fish sauce

¼ cup Fried Garlic (page 294; optional)

½ cup store-bought fried shallots (optional)

1 tablespoon fermented black beans (optional)

1. Combine the chiles, peppercorns, star anise, ginger, cinnamon stick, cardamom, cloves, mushroom powder, and salt in a deep saucepan or heatproof bowl with at least 3 inches of room to spare.

2. In a separate pan, heat the oils to 375°F. Carefully but quickly pour the oil over the dry ingredients, using a heatproof whisk or wooden chopsticks to stir vigorously. The mixture will hiss and bubble and emit a fragrant cloud. Allow to cool completely.

3. Strain the oil through a fine-mesh sieve into a bowl, reserving everything. Pull out and discard the larger, woodier spices—i.e., the star anise and cinnamon—then use a mortar and pestle or food processor to crush and grind the remaining solid ingredients to the size of red pepper flakes. Season this mixture with the fish sauce, then reincorporate enough chili oil to form a thick, chunky salsa consistency. If you like, now is the time to add the fried garlic and the fried shallots. I like a little fermented black beans in my chili crisp too. The chili crisp and the remaining chili oil can be stored separately, covered and refrigerated, for months.

Chili Oil: See Chili Crisp and Chili Oil (page 290).

Chili Vinegar: This is our house hot sauce. You can squirt/spoon it onto noodles or greens, into barbecue sauce, or wherever you'd use a vinegary condiment like Tabasco or Frank's Red Hot.

MAKES ABOUT 3 CUPS

1 pound red Fresno chiles, thinly sliced
1 (2-inch) square dashi kombu, wiped with
  a damp towel
2 cups distilled white vinegar
1 tablespoon kosher salt

1. In a medium nonreactive
    saucepan, mix together the
    chopped chiles, kombu, vinegar,
    and salt. Cover, raise the heat
    to high, and bring the vinegar
    to a hard boil, then reduce
    the heat to maintain a simmer
    and cook until the chiles have
    become soft enough to break
    apart with a spoon pressed
    against the sides of the pan.
    Remove from the heat and let
    cool completely.

2. Strain the chiles, reserving the
    peppery vinegar and discarding
    the kombu. Transfer the chiles
    to a blender and add enough
    of the vinegar to cover. Spin
    on high power until the liquid
    and chiles have come together
    into a smooth sauce, about a
    minute. Too thick? Add more
    of the vinegar. This should
    resemble Tabasco, not Sriracha.
    Reserve the vinegar. The pectin
    in the chiles will cause the
    mixture to thicken a bit more
    once it cools; again, just add
    some vinegar to thin. Store in
    an airtight container in the fridge
    indefinitely.

Chinese Black Vinegar (Chiang Kiang Vinegar):
Black vinegar, made from glutinous (sticky) rice, has a musty grape taste and is sweeter than other rice vinegars. We generally use it as a finishing touch.

Chinese Chives (*Jiu Cai*):
These long, grasslike vegetables—known as *nira* in Japanese—have much more texture and flavor than regular chives. They're stinky in that good, cheesy/durian/fish sauce way, and have a strong leek-y, garlicky flavor. (They bear some resemblance to ramps but aren't quite as hard to come across.) There are both green and yellow (milder) varieties.

Chrysanthemum Greens:
Hollow-stemmed greens, also known as *tong ho* or crown daisies, these look a bit like carrot tops. They taste grassy and herbaceous and benefit from quick cooking that leaves them still crunchy, not wilted to mush.

Cornstarch Slurry:
Cornstarch slurry is the magic potion behind many Chinese restaurant sauces—everything from orange chicken glaze to broccoli beef gravy is made glossy and thick by the addition of a little cornstarch dissolved in water. We don't use as much of it at Mission Chinese Food as most Chinese restaurants do, but it still comes in

handy often. Just stir together equal parts cornstarch and water in a bowl. For 1 cup of sauce, 1 tablespoon of slurry will do. Be sure to give it one more stir right before adding it to the pan, and then let the sauce come to a boil before assessing the thickness and deciding whether or not to add more slurry.

Dashi: Dashi is as ubiquitous in Japanese cuisine as brown chicken stock is in French cooking. But rather than being extracted by long-simmering bones and vegetables, its flavor is coaxed out of smoked dried fish and kombu steeped in not-too-hot water. If you want a more intense, fusiony dashi, you can substitute chicken stock for the water. We've also included instructions for a "second-run dashi" that's made from the spent materials of the first dashi. It's much lighter, but it's a good cooking medium for long braises.

MAKES 8 CUPS

2 (4-inch) squares dashi kombu, wiped with a damp towel
3 cups tightly packed katsuobushi (see page 298)
Shiro shoyu

1. In a saucepan with a lid, combine the kombu with 8 cups water and bring to a very gentle simmer over medium-low heat, then remove from the heat—don't walk away and let the water boil. Cover and let steep for

10 minutes, then pluck out the kombu and reserve for the second dashi.

2. Add the katsuobushi to the saucepan, cover again, and allow to steep for 10 minutes more. Most of the katsuobushi should have sunk to the bottom.

3. Strain the dashi through a fine-mesh strainer or coffee filter. (If you're not going to make second-run dashi, you can slice the kombu for salads.) Season with shiro shoyu.

Second-Run Dashi

MAKES 8 CUPS

Spent dashi kombu and katsuobushi from above
Shiro shoyu

Combine the kombu, katsuobushi, and 8 cups water in a saucepan with a lid, bring to a gentle simmer over medium-low heat, and cook very gently for 10 minutes. Remove from the heat, cover, and allow to cool. Strain and season with shiro shoyu.

Doubanjiang: This spicy fermented bean paste is the cornerstone of mapo tofu. I think of it like chili miso. It's salty and has some heat to it, but it's not super hot. It's also not as funky

as other fermented bean pastes, and it brings a nice roundness of flavor to spicy dishes. There are non-Sichuan versions of *doubanjiang* that don't have chiles—to be precise, you're looking for *la* (spicy) *doubanjiang*. You can make your own—it's just chiles and fava beans fermented with salt—but I'd argue it's not worth the trouble. Having witnessed firsthand the careful dance of science and artistry that it takes to make this stuff, we opt to buy ours. We use a version imported by Union Foods. Lee Kum Kee does *not* make good *doubanjiang*.

Fish Sauce: Different versions of fish sauce can be found in countries from Scandinavia to southern Europe to Asia. Obviously, we stick to the Asian variety—made by letting anchovies ferment in salt until they've yielded a dark brown, stinky liquor. It's packed with umami and very salty. Squeamish eaters will hate the idea of it, but few can resist its call when it is tactfully deployed.

Fried Garlic: At the restaurants, fried garlic is a nutty, savory, crunchy-sticky garnish and an ingredient in some of our sauces. The garlic oil, a by-product of the frying process, is a nice pantry item to have on hand for sautéing or making vinaigrettes. Fried garlic that has become slightly stale can be "refreshed" in a 300°F oven for about 4 minutes.

MAKES ABOUT 1½ CUPS

2 cups garlic cloves
4 to 6 cups vegetable or peanut oil, for deep-frying

1. Pulse the garlic in a food processor, scraping down the sides of the bowl with a spatula between pulses, until uniformly minced.

2. In a deep saucepan or a wok, heat about 2 inches of oil to 300°F. Set a fine-mesh strainer above another saucepan. Add the garlic to the hot oil—it will cook very quickly, so be sure to get all of it into the oil at once—and stir continuously for about 1 minute. When it's barely golden—about the color of dried pasta—pour the hot oil and garlic into the strainer. Use a spoon to redistribute the garlic to promote drainage, then spread the garlic out on paper towels to absorb excess oil. The fried garlic will darken further as the heat carries over, and the finished product should be the golden brown color of a Nilla Wafer. Let the garlic drain and cool completely.

3. Once the garlic is cool, it can be stored for up to a week in an airtight container.

Fried Peanuts: Great as a garnish for salads, an ingredient in fried rice, or a topping for rice porridge—and the main ingredient in Beijing Vinegar Peanuts (page 203).

MAKES 1 CUP

4 to 6 cups vegetable or peanut oil, for deep-frying
1 cup raw peanuts (skins intact)
1 tablespoon kosher salt

1. In a deep saucepan or a wok, heat about 2 inches of oil to 325°F, or use a deep fryer.

2. Lower the peanuts into the hot oil and stir gently to promote even cooking. Once the nuts start to look chalky, they're almost ready. When the edges begin to brown, they're done. It should take around 90 seconds in all. Using a strainer or slotted spoon, remove the peanuts, draining them well, and transfer to a bowl.

3. Salt the peanuts while they're still piping hot, then transfer to a baking sheet lined with paper towels. Let the peanuts drain and cool completely. Once cool, they'll keep for up to 2 weeks in an airtight container.

Fried Shallots: You can fry shallots yourself: Just coat finely sliced shallots in Wondra flour, then deep- or shallow-fry in 325°F vegetable or peanut oil. But the store-bought stuff in a plastic container is

fine, especially if refreshed in a 325°F oven for 4 minutes.

Ginger-Scallion Sauce:
Ginger-scallion sauce is the cure for whatever ails your food. The ginger—a boatload of it in our version—brings herbaceous, quickly dissipating heat and the scallions add oniony brightness. It is a ridiculously versatile pantry item. Steamed chicken, roast duck, cold beef, fried noodles, soups, sauces—all stand to benefit from a spoonful of the sauce. I recommend having a jar in the fridge at all times.

MAKES 2 CUPS

¾ cup extra-virgin olive oil, plus more for storing
⅔ cup minced peeled ginger (about 5 ounces)
1 bunch scallions, thinly sliced
1 teaspoon kosher salt
1 teaspoon sugar
1 teaspoon fish sauce (optional)
1 teaspoon Mushroom Powder (page 299)

1. Heat a nonstick skillet over high heat for about 2 minutes, then add the oil and remove from the heat. Add the ginger, scallions, salt, and sugar and cook, stirring continuously, to wilt the scallions a bit and take the edge off the ginger. Allow the sauce to cool for a few minutes in the pan.

2. Season the sauce with the fish sauce, if using, and mushroom powder, then scoop it into

an airtight container (a wide-mouthed pint jar is ideal). The sauce is ready for immediate deployment on noodles, Hainan Chicken Rice (page 183), vegetables, tacos, etc. To store it, top it off with more olive oil to prevent oxidation and refrigerate, tightly sealed, for a week or even longer.

Hoisin Sauce: Although the Chinese name of this dark, gooey condiment translates as "fresh seafood sauce," it tastes nothing like seafood. It's sweet and warmly spiced, and you've likely had it with pho, Peking duck, Chinese barbecue, or mu shu pork.

Ikura **(Cured Salmon Roe):** Like most cooks, I reserve my deepest fan-boy respect for sushi chefs and the miracles they're able to achieve with minimal ingredients. This pantry item is a holdover from my days working at sushi bars, where the chefs taught me to end a sushi meal with uni (sea urchin) and *ikura nigiri*. If you can manage to score a skein of fresh salmon roe from a specialty fishmonger, try curing your own *ikura*. It's one of those things that seems impossibly tricky and better left to someone else—like carpeting your own house—but it's an impressive and rewarding skill to have. If you're unable to locate fresh salmon roe, you can soak store-bought salt-cured salmon roe procured from a specialty fishmonger in fresh water to desalinate it, then proceed with the curing process. We serve cured salmon roe as a topping for egg custards (pages 20 and 23) or VIP bowls of Westlake Rice Porridge (page 117).

1 skein (sac) salmon or trout roe
2 tablespoons shiro shoyu
2 tablespoons sake
1½ teaspoons mirin
1 teaspoon rice vinegar
Kosher salt, if needed

1. Soak the skein in a bowl of very hot tap water (120° to 130°F). The heat will break down the membranes, and some of the roe may turn a disheartening cloudy color—it looks like you've messed up, but you haven't. After 2 minutes, start agitating the roe with your fingertips or a pair of chopsticks. The skein will begin to break up, and the individual eggs will wriggle loose. The fresher the roe, the more easily this will happen. Strain the roe, transfer it to a large bowl, and submerge in plenty of cold water. Use your fingers to continue breaking up the eggs, removing and discarding the membrane. Little pieces of membrane will float to the surface, like peanut skins; discard these too. Pour off the water, replenish, and search for more membranes.

2. Once it's clean, drain the roe again and prepare your seasoning: Whisk together the

shoyu, sake, mirin, rice vinegar, and 2 tablespoons water; pour the mixture over the roe; and stir gently. The salt from the shoyu will restore the vibrant orange color to the eggs—rejoice. Cover and refrigerate for at least an hour. Taste and season with salt, if necessary. The cured roe will keep in the fridge for a couple of days.

Donburi

If you're taking the time to cure your own *ikura,* and you buy whole trays of uni, chances are you've got leftovers for *donburi*. And if you're the type of person who cures salmon roe and buys sea urchin, you're probably also the type who wants to poach your own monkfish liver. And I'm guessing you'd be interested in an overelaborate method of cooking sushi rice too. Cooking rice with kombu-wrapped *binchotan* charcoal gives the rice umami (from the seaweed), while the charcoal pulls impurities out of the water.

SERVES 4

2 cups sushi rice (preferably koshihikari)
1 (12-inch) sheet dashi kombu, soaked in water until soft
1 piece binchotan charcoal (see page 290)
¼ cup aka zu (Japanese red rice vinegar; see page 300)
1 tablespoon plus 1 teaspoon Dashi (page 293)

Poached Monkfish Liver (see page 298)
¾ cup ikura (cured salmon roe), homemade (see page 296) or store-bought
12 sea urchin tongues

1. Rinse the sushi rice in cold water, agitating the rice with your fingers, three times. Drain well.

2. Wrap the kombu around the piece of charcoal, then wrap in a piece of cheesecloth.

3. Put the rice in a medium pot or a rice cooker and set the wrapped charcoal on top of it. Cover with 2¾ cups cold water. Cook the rice as you normally would, simmering gently until the water is fully absorbed, about 15 minutes, if you're going the stovetop route. (If using a rice cooker, follow the manufacturer's instructions.)

4. Combine the vinegar and dashi in a small bowl. Drizzle the mixture over a rice paddle or a spatula onto the cooked rice, shaking the paddle to spread it over the rice. Cut the mixture into the rice, then use the paddle or spatula to flip the rice over, and cut again. Let the rice rest until no longer steaming hot.

5. Scoop the rice into four bowls and top with the monkfish liver, salmon roe, and uni. Luxuriate in its opulence.

Poached Monkfish Liver

SERVES 4

½ pound raw monkfish livers
About 1 cup kosher salt
About 1 cup rice vinegar
2 cups sake
1 cup mirin
1 cup shiro shoyu

1. Peel away any pieces of membrane hanging off the monkfish livers. Do the best you can to pluck out any obvious blood vessels too. Bury the livers in the salt for 15 minutes. Not to gross you out, but the salt may draw out some small worms—pick them out with a pair of tweezers and discard.

2. Rinse the livers in water, then dip them in the rice vinegar to rinse.

3. Combine the sake, mirin, and shiro shoyu in a small saucepan and bring to a simmer over medium heat, burning off some of the alcohol. Add any larger livers to the pan (reserve the smaller ones) and simmer for 3 minutes, or until they firm up slightly.

4. Transfer the poached livers to a heatproof container, along with any smaller livers, and cover them with the hot brine. Top with a piece of parchment paper and let cool to room temperature. Meanwhile, prepare an ice bath.

5. Pull off the parchment paper, nestle the container into the ice bath, and continue to cure for 1 hour.

6. Drain the livers. If any other membranes have loosened up, peel them off. Wrap the livers tightly in plastic wrap and refrigerate until ready to use, up to a couple of days.

Inari Age: These are thin slices of fried tofu used to make *inari,* the sweet, spongy pouches you see stuffed with rice at sushi restaurants. Cooked in sweetened dashi after being fried, they can be found sold as *inari age, ajitsuke inari age,* or seasoned fried bean curd.

Katsuobushi: Shaved flakes of dried, smoked bonito, primarily used to flavor dashi. There are a great many kinds and qualities of *katsuobushi,* but we have no real preference. Nothing we're cooking at Mission Chinese Food is delicate enough to necessitate a specific *katsuobushi.*

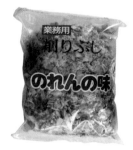

Lap Cheong: This term refers to a broad array of sausages. Chinese grocers may have several on offer—some made with beef, others with pork, and flecked with duck liver, glutinous rice, or blood. The one we use is the "standard" *lap cheong*: thin links of wrinkly, dried red pork sausage that are very sweet and a little smoky.

Lotus Leaves: These large (about 2-feet-wide) leaves come dried in packages of 10 or 15 from Asian grocery stores. Straight out of the package, they're pale brown and fragile and need to be soaked in warm or hot water to soften before being used to wrap rice or poultry. They impart a unique, vaguely medicinal, slightly floral perfume to whatever's inside.

Married-Couple's Vinaigrette: Married-Couple's Beef is a dish named after a fabled pair of Sichuan vendors who hawked a mighty fine plate of cold beef and offal. We use this spicy, tingly, sweet, savory dressing for our Shaved Pork Belly and Octopus Terrine, but it's terrific for salads or shredded chicken too. The recipe below uses a splash of octopus stock, which you'll have if you are making the octopus terrine, but if not, just substitute fish or chicken stock. The vinaigrette will keep in the fridge for a couple of days.

MAKES ABOUT ¾ CUP

½ cup octopus stock (from Octopus Terrine, page 209) or fish or chicken stock
¼ cup red pepper flakes
½ cup Chili Oil (page 290)
¼ cup minced garlic
2 tablespoons grated fresh horseradish
¼ cup sugar
1 teaspoon ground Sichuan pepper
2 tablespoons Sichuan pepper oil
2 tablespoons Mushroom Powder (see below)
2 tablespoons kosher salt
1 teaspoon Dijon mustard

1. In a small saucepan, bring the octopus stock to a boil over high heat and cook until it has reduced by half. Let cool to room temperature.

2. In a blender, combine the reduced stock with the remaining ingredients and ½ cup water and pulse until they are incorporated and the vinaigrette is emulsified. Store in the fridge, and give a healthy shake before using.

Menma: These fermented bamboo shoots are available presliced and packaged in Japanese markets. Although they're usually used as a topping for ramen, we smoke them and serve them with our stir-fried corn dish (page 262).

Mushroom Powder: This is the gentleman's MSG. It's umami incarnate, in powdered form. It makes dishes more savory, but since it's made primarily of powdered dried mushrooms, it lacks the stigma—unwarranted or not—of MSG. You can find mushroom powder at Asian markets or online, usually from Taiwanese producers. But a slightly less potent, and less mysterious, version is easily made at home. I wouldn't recommend making this in a large batch, as the flavor dissipates over time.

MAKES ABOUT ½ CUP

1 (1-inch) square dashi kombu
½ ounce stemmed, dried shiitake
  mushrooms

1. Use a pair of kitchen shears to snip the kombu into 4 or 5 smaller pieces, then grind it to a fine powder in a spice or coffee grinder or blender. Transfer to a bowl.

2. Grind the mushrooms to a powder and combine with the kombu. Store in an airtight container at room temperature. Like ground spices, this begins to lose its potency immediately.

Nori: These are the sheets of dried seaweed used to wrap sushi. They come in packages of anywhere from 10 to 100. We slice nori into squares or thin shreds to use as a garnish, but first it needs to be toasted. To toast nori, hold a sheet with your fingers or a pair of tongs and wave it quickly back and forth about 1 inch over a burner turned on medium heat for about 20 seconds. Rotate and repeat. Don't let the nori (or your hands) shrivel and burn. You just want the sheet to crisp ever so slightly and to get a little toasty.

Pressed Tofu: This is tofu that's been weighted down to squeeze out some of the water, resulting in a firmer product with more chew. You can find pressed tofu in most Chinese markets or prepare it yourself at home. To do so, line a baking sheet (or flat-bottomed colander) with three or four layers of paper towels or an absorbent kitchen towel. You can press a whole block of firm tofu, which will make it easier to slice thinner later, or for faster results, start by cutting the tofu into uniform slices about ¼ inch thick. Either way, put the tofu, whole or in a single layer, on the towel-lined pan and cover it with more paper towels or another kitchen towel. Weigh down the tofu with another pan or container and a couple of cans of soda/beer/soup (be careful not to add so much weight that you crush the tofu). Refrigerate overnight.

The next day, the tofu will have become firmer and chewier. If you pressed a whole block of tofu, slice it thin. (Note: If you're feeling lazy, freezing firm tofu and then thawing it out before slicing is a passable shortcut.)

Pumpkin Seed Oil: This oil, found in specialty groceries and health-food stores, tastes strongly of pumpkin seeds—a few drops'll do ya. It's potent.

Red Rice Vinegar:
Japanese red rice vinegar (*aka zu*) is made from sake lees and is not

to be confused with red plum (*ume*) vinegar (see page 307). This is the traditional seasoning for Edomae-style sushi (the first modern sushi). It's tart, of course, but also a little bit more fermented-tasting than other vinegars.

Chinese red vinegar is made from rice that's been inoculated with red mold, and has its own sharp, savory, slightly sweet flavor. You'll see it as a condiment for dumplings and soups at Chinese restaurants.

Rich Chicken Stock: Good chicken stock is as vital to Chinese cooking as it is to French. Rather than roasted bones and mirepoix, though, Chinese "superior broth" is flavored with chicken, Jinhua ham, dried scallops, scallions, and ginger. There are plenty of soups and noodle dishes in the Chinese canon that revolve entirely around this deeply flavorful, clean stock.

You can substitute regular chicken stock for most of the recipes in this book—I'm not going to judge you. But if you do make your own stock, you ought to give this one a try, as it's better suited to our recipes. It's a cross between classic "superior broth" and Fergus Henderson's "trotter gear"—a gelatin-rich chicken stock, fortified with pork feet.

MAKES ABOUT 6 QUARTS

1 (3- to 4-pound) chicken
1 pound chicken wings
1 pound raw ham hocks (or pork bones—ask your butcher to save some for you)
1 large leek, coarsely chopped and washed thoroughly
1 (4- to 5-inch) piece fresh ginger, peeled and cut into ¼-inch-thick coins
1 (4-inch) square dashi kombu, wiped with a damp cloth
½ cup dried scallops (optional—if you're feeling fancy)
5 ounces uncooked ham, such as prosciutto or country ham
2 to 3 tablespoons fish sauce

1. Pile the chicken (including the gizzards, neck, liver, and heart, if you have them), chicken wings, and ham hocks into a large heavy-bottomed stockpot and add cold water to cover. Bring to a boil over high heat, then remove from the heat and drain the chicken and bones with a colander. (I wouldn't bother with this step for a normal chicken stock, but this first boil is good for removing the impurities and funk that sometimes come with boiling pork hocks or bones.)

2. If you're using pork bones, give them a quick rinse and scrub under cold running water. Return everything to the stockpot and add the leek, ginger, kombu, scallops (if using), and ham. Cover with cold water by 1 inch and bring to a boil over high heat. Reduce the heat to a simmer and skim off any gray-white impurities that have risen to the surface. Partially cover the pot—resting the lid on a pair of disposable chopsticks balanced on either

edge of the pot is a good way to achieve this—and simmer for 2 hours. I don't like to simmer chicken stock for too long, as the flavor tends to flatten out after a lengthy simmer. This also has the added benefit of leaving you with chicken meat and ham hocks that still have some flavor—good for chicken salad, good for the dog, etc.

3. Fish out the chicken and larger pieces of meat from the stock, then strain the stock through a fine-mesh sieve into a container. Season with fish sauce and let cool, then store in the refrigerator for up to a week or in the freezer for up to 2 months.

Salt Cod: Available at Italian grocers as baccalà, and at some fishmongers and specialty markets, this is, as the name says, cod that's been cured with salt. Salt cod must be soaked in several changes of cold fresh water before it's cooked.

Salted Chili Condiment:
This condiment brings fresh, peppery heat and a little salinity to whatever it anoints—Sweet Potato Leaves with Kabocha Squash (page 264), Smashed Cucumbers (page 204), Chili-Pickled Long Beans (page 230), General Tso's Sauce (page 233). It's like sambal oelek, but without the secondary flavorings. It's just chiles, salt, and a little fermented twang.

MAKES ABOUT 1½ CUPS

1 pound red Fresno chiles or jalapeños, coarsely chopped
1 tablespoon kosher salt

1. Pulse the chiles and salt in a food processor until you have a consistency just shy of a puree. Transfer to a glass or plastic container with an airtight lid. Leave in a warm place for 2 days, or until the condiment has the consistency of a wet salsa and a slightly fermented flavor.

2. The condiment will keep in an airtight container—a glass pint jar works great—in the refrigerator for up to a month.

Sansho Pepper: The seedpods of Japanese prickly ash trees, sansho peppercorns are like the Japanese cousin of Sichuan peppercorns. They produce a similar numbing sensation, but with an intense, almost spicy citrus flavor. You can find sansho whole or ground in Japanese markets and online. It's traditionally used to season broiled eel or grilled chicken. If you can't find it, substitute Sichuan pepper.

Shaoxing Wine: Shaoxing is Chinese rice wine that is used for cooking and marinades—think cooking sherry. It's a little bit sweet, a little bit medicinal, not great to drink, and dirt cheap at most Chinese markets.

Shio Koji: *Shio koji* is rice that's been inoculated with *Aspergillus oryzae*—the mold responsible for such wonders as miso, soy sauce, *shochu* (Korean liquor), and sake—and mixed with salt and water. If left to bloom for a few weeks, the mold breaks down the proteins and starches in the rice into glutamic acid and sugar. The result is a chunky beige paste that's an ideal marinade—salty, sweet, and savory. You can buy *shio koji* ready-made, or as part of a kit for a homemade version, which is cheaper and a cinch to prepare if you've got the time. Look for packages in the refrigerated section of Japanese markets.

1 (20-ounce) package shio koji
  (the do-it-yourself kind)
Kosher salt

1. Follow the directions on the koji packaging, which will more or less tell you to add water and salt to the rice and wait. Let the koji ferment for 12 to 14 days in a container with enough space for gases to be released, stirring once a day. The koji will darken from white to light brown as it ages. It's ready to go when it's creamy and the rice grains have broken down quite a bit. It'll look like overcooked rice porridge and smell like sake or Korean makgeolli.

2. At this point, the koji makes an ideal marinade for chicken and for fish, especially heads and collars. Rub them with Ginger-Scallion Sauce (page 296) and koji, refrigerate overnight, and grill over charcoal. Again, the instructions will help you out, but to keep the koji working indefinitely, just add steamed rice or buckwheat to "feed" it.

Shiro Shoyu: This is a primarily wheat-based soy sauce that's sweeter, less salty, and fruitier than regular soy sauce, which is from a higher proportion of soybeans. Shiro shoyu is more expensive than regular soy, so we use it as a condiment or finishing touch, in the way you'd use balsamic vinegar.

Shiso: An herb with minty, vaguely medicinal, tender leaves that is occasionally labeled as perilla. You can find bunches of green or purple shiso in most good Asian markets, particularly Japanese ones. The leaves are arrow shaped, with jagged edges. We use shiso often as a garnish, but we never cook with it.

Sichuan Peppercorns: These generate the numbing half of the numbing-spicy flavor balance (*ma la*) that is the beating heart of Sichuan cuisine. Sichuan peppercorns are the dried berries of a tree in the citrus family, and for many years, there was a loosely enforced ban on importing them into the United

States because they could potentially harbor a canker harmful to other citrus trees. That ban has been lifted, but many Sichuan peppercorns are heat-treated to kill potential diseases, which weakens their potency, so finding strong, good-quality ones can still be a crapshoot. If you get a line on a good source—in Chinatown, online, or elsewhere—remember that lighter, unopened red peppercorns are better than darker ones that have been crushed or cracked open. The peppercorns should taste floral and create an intense tingly sensation, like you've put a battery to your tongue. Green peppercorns are fruitier and even harder to find. If you can't find them, try mixing in a small amount (10 percent) regular green peppercorns with red Sichuan peppercorns. Store Sichuan peppercorns in the freezer in a zip-top bag with the air pressed out.

Sichuan Peppercorn Oil (aka Tingly/Prickly Oil):

This is the numbing sensation of *ma*—a hallmark of Sichuan cuisine, generated by Sichuan peppercorns (see page 303)—concentrated into liquid form. It's possible to make it at home, but it won't be as strong as the commercial stuff. We prefer Youjia brand.

Smoked Cola BBQ Sauce:

This is barbecue sauce like I used to eat in Oklahoma. It's sweet, smoky, tart, and as hot as you want it to be. If you're a smoked-meat purist, there's no convincing you to sauce your meat, but if you're a philistine like most of the rest of us, feel free to slather this liberally onto ribs, brisket, hot links, or chicken.

MAKES ABOUT 3 CUPS

Special equipment: Smoker, 8 ounces hickory wood chips, and 2 ounces mesquite wood chips

1 (12-ounce) bottle cola
½ onion, coarsely chopped
1 cup smoker drippings from Smoked Beef Brisket (page 36)
¼ cup tomato paste
2 tablespoons ground toasted cumin seeds
1 tablespoon freshly ground black pepper
1 teaspoon minced garlic
1⅔ cups ketchup
3 tablespoons distilled white vinegar
1 tablespoon Worcestershire sauce
2 tablespoons dark brown sugar, plus more as needed
2 tablespoons Dijon mustard
About ¼ cup Chili Vinegar (page 291) or hot sauce of your choice
Kosher salt

1. Heat your smoker to 215°F, then load it with the hickory and mesquite chips. Obviously, if you're smoking cola, you should be smoking other things at the same time—a whole brisket (page 36), pastrami (page 222), pig trotters, whatever.

2. Combine the cola and onion in a heatproof container and slot it above or next to any meat you're smoking to prevent drippings from falling into it. (This makes

much more smoked cola than you'll need for one batch of BBQ sauce, but it's not worth smoking a smaller amount, and it keeps fine in the fridge.) Smoke the cola for as long as you're smoking the meat—at least 4 hours. Remove from the smoker, strain, and reserve.

3. Heat a medium saucepan over medium heat. Add a tablespoon of fat scooped off the top of your brisket drippings and swirl to coat the pan. Add the tomato paste and cook, stirring continuously, for about a minute, until the tomato paste takes on a rustier hue. Add the cumin and pepper and stir for another 20 seconds, then toss in the garlic. Cook and stir for 1 minute more.

4. Add the remaining smoker drippings to the pan, along with the ketchup, ¼ cup smoked cola, vinegar, Worcestershire, brown sugar, and mustard. Stir to combine and bring the sauce to a simmer, then reduce the heat to low and cook for 30 minutes. The sauce will bubble and spit, so keep the pan mostly covered to avoid a mess and stir regularly to prevent scorching the bottom. Allow the sauce to cool.

5. Stir in the chili vinegar, then season with salt and more brown sugar, if you so desire. Thin with a little bit of water, if necessary,

and stir well before serving. The sauce will keep in the refrigerator for up to a month.

Smoked Garlic Confit:

An accessory for Beijing Vinegar Peanuts (page 203), a good topping for toast or noodles, and a fine homemade Christmas gift. If you don't have smoked oil on hand, you can substitute vegetable oil to make regular garlic confit. (Alternatively, you can put the garlic cloves in an ovenproof pan, cover them with oil, and smoke them in an electric smoker for 4 hours at 180°F, thereby yielding both smoked garlic confit and smoked garlic oil.) This recipe calls for 30 cloves, but you can make as large a batch as you like. Smoked garlic (or any other confit) will last longest if kept completely covered in oil in the fridge.

MAKES 30 CLOVES

30 garlic cloves, peeled and ends trimmed slightly
2 cups Smoked Oil (page 306) or vegetable or peanut oil
1 teaspoon kosher salt

1. Preheat the oven to 180°F.

2. Put the garlic cloves in a small ovenproof saucepan and cover them completely with cold water. Bring to a simmer over medium heat, then remove from the heat and drain the garlic. Return the garlic to the pan and cover with

the oil. Add the salt. Lay a piece of parchment paper directly on top of the oil, then cover the pan tightly with aluminum foil. Slide into the oven and cook for 4 hours, or until the garlic is soft but not falling apart. Let cool before storing.

Smoked Oil: Any time you've gone through the trouble to set up a smoker for brisket or ribs, take the opportunity to replenish your smoked-goods pantry. Smoked oil adds a new dimension to confits, vinaigrettes, or stir-fries. We also use it to make a vegan version of thrice-cooked bacon. To make it, pour a few cups of vegetable, peanut, grapeseed, or other neutral oil into a baking pan (aluminum pie pans also work well). Slot it into the top shelf of your smoker (to avoid any drippings) and smoke at between 215° and 250°F for 3 to 5 hours. Sealed in an airtight container, it will keep in a cool, dark place for a couple of months.

Soft-Cooked and Soy-Cured Eggs:
Like a fancy watch or diamond earrings, a soft-cooked egg is a timeless accessory. On menus everywhere these days, served with noodle soup or rice porridge or other dishes, they are often cooked in temperature-controlled water baths. At home, the easiest thing to do is just boil your eggs for 5 to 7 minutes,

depending on how you like them. Our soft-cooked egg whites are fairly well set, while the yolks are creamy. A soak in a soy sauce bath will stain the eggs brown and give them a salty punch.

MAKES AS MANY EGGS AS YOU LIKE

Eggs, at room temperature
Kosher salt
Soy sauce
Dark soy sauce

1. Bring a large pot or saucepan of water to a boil. Have an ice bath ready. Put the eggs in a strainer basket, or use a slotted spoon, and gently lower them into a large pot or saucepan of unsalted boiling water. As you're lowering the eggs, sprinkle the surface of the water above the eggs with a couple tablespoons of salt. The water will foam up around the eggs, which, in my experience, seems to keep the shells from cracking. Don't push me on the science. Cook the eggs for 5½ minutes over high heat, then immediately plunge them into a bowl of ice water. Let cool completely, then peel. At this point, you've got soft-cooked eggs.

2. *To make soy-cured eggs,* submerge the peeled eggs in a bath of 2 parts soy sauce to 1 part dark soy sauce to 1 part water and refrigerate overnight.

3. Pull the eggs out of the soak and store in the fridge for up to 3 days. You can bring the soy sauce soak to a quick simmer, let cool, and store for reuse.

Sticky Rice: Sometimes referred to as "sweet" or "glutinous" rice (though it's not sweet and contains no gluten), sticky rice is a staple in dim sum (steamed in lotus leaves) and in Southeast Asian cuisine. When cooked, it comes out very tacky and chewy. To prepare sticky rice, soak it in cold water then steam it—don't boil it.

Tianjin Chiles: These medium-hot dried red peppers are used in Sichuan Province for any number of chili-heavy dishes: kung pao chicken, *la zi ji* (aka Chongqing Chicken Wings, page 135), water-cooked fish. I was thrilled when the chef Yu Bo introduced these to me in Chengdu, and frustrated when I returned to the States and couldn't find them. Several online outlets sell imported and domestic Tianjin (aka tien tsin) chiles, but I find chiles Japones—commonly found in Latin markets as well as online—to be a good substitute. Don't substitute chiles de árbol, even though they look very similar—they supposedly register lower on the Scoville scale, but I find them to be much hotter. You want a red chili with some heat,

but not something that will blow your ass off.

Ume Vinegar (aka *Ume Zu*): A by-product of pickled plums, this vinegar gets its red color from the red shiso leaves used in the pickling process. Its flavor is herbaceous, salty, tart, and unlike any other vinegar.

XO Sauce: XO sauce is named for the cognac designation, but it has nothing to do with the liquor. The moniker just implies that the sauce is special in a generally ritzy way. It's made with dried seafood (the source of its poshness), chiles, shallots, and garlic. Typically, Chinese cookbooks instruct you to soak the dried seafood overnight in water before chopping and mixing it with the remaining ingredients. But when I set out to make ours, I realized that soaking the seafood leaches out all the flavor. My friend and Chinese-food guru Brandon Jew suggested steaming the seafood instead, and it worked like a charm.

My first taste of XO came at the French-Japanese fine-dining restaurant where I worked as a fresh-faced cooking school graduate in New York. We would take jarred XO sauce and kick it up with minced shallots and cinnamon. Doctoring the XO was always on my prep list, so I ended up eating pounds of it. Even though I've tried dozens of different versions since then, that's always been my reference point for how XO should taste.

First and foremost, the sauce should taste like the ocean—briny and full of umami from the scallops and shrimp. It should be a little smoky from the bacon and finish with a little kick from the red pepper flakes. Play around with different dried seafood—squid, little anchovies, whatever you can scrounge up at the market.

MAKES ABOUT 2½ CUPS

½ cup dried shrimp
½ cup dried scallops
4 ounces bacon, cooked (or substitute country ham or prosciutto)
½ cup chopped lap cheong (Chinese sausage; about 2 links)
1½ cups canola oil
2 shallots, minced
¼ cup red pepper flakes
¼ cup thinly sliced garlic
1 (3-inch) piece fresh ginger, peeled and finely chopped
3 star anise
½ cinnamon stick
¼ cup soy sauce
½ cup store-bought fried shallots
¼ cup Fried Garlic (page 294)

1. Arrange the dried shrimp and scallops in a steamer and steam for about 30 minutes, until the seafood is somewhat reconstituted but still firm.

2. Drop the shrimp and scallops into the bowl of a food processor and pulse until finely chopped. Transfer to a bowl. Combine the bacon and Chinese sausage in the food processor bowl and pulse, aiming for more or less uniform size. Toss into the bowl with the shrimp and scallops and set aside.

3. In a large heavy-bottomed skillet, heat 1 cup of the oil over medium-high heat. Add the shallots and cook, stirring, until soft and translucent, about a minute. Add the red pepper flakes and cook for 1 minute more.

4. Add the garlic, ginger, star anise, and cinnamon and stir to combine. Raise the heat to high, add the seafood and meat, and stir for a minute. Add the remaining ½ cup oil, drop the heat as low as it goes, and simmer gently for 30 minutes, stirring often. Remove the sauce from the heat and let it cool.

5. Fish out the star anise and cinnamon, and mix in the soy sauce, fried shallots, and fried garlic. Transfer the sauce to an airtight container. Refrigerate for up to 1 month.

Yuzu Juice: If you have access to fresh yuzu—an Asian citrus fruit—by all means, use it. Otherwise, the bottled stuff from Asian markets is fine. In a pinch, a 50:50 mix of fresh

lemon and lime juice will work as a substitute.

———————————————

Yuzu Kosho: A fragrant Japanese paste of fermented pepper and citrus peel, yuzu kosho is spicy, sour, and salty. All the fancy chefs like it. A little goes a long way, so use it cautiously. If you can't find it, we've got a recipe for a similar condiment made from lemons on page 186.

Acknowledgments

Danny Bowien: This book owes everything to the people who have built, supported, represented, and worked super hard for the restaurants. To all of the team members who have put in shifts at Mission Chinese in San Francisco, and Mission Chinese and Mission Cantina in New York, THANK YOU!

Thank you to the people who believed strongly enough in what we do to bet on us: Andrew Yang, Roy Yang, Dan Bonoff, Huey Cheng, Scott Kasen, Ellen Myint, Karen Leibowitz, Dennis Kim, Wes Roberts, Van Robbins, Allen Yuen, Kristin Godburn, Matt Godburn, Mark Ibold, Todd Selby, and Eli Horowitz.

To the people who have helped shape me as a cook and eater, your lessons are constantly in my head: Stephen Lewandowski, Ritsu, Erin Rooney, Adachi Hiroyuki, Shin, Paolo Laboa, Mike Selvera, Brandon Jew, Chad Robertson, Jason Fox, Xelina Leyba, Amanda and Howard at Duc Loi, the Nguyens, Anh, Chaffee, Erick Gregory, Audrey and Lydia Taylor.

When we moved to New York, we were welcomed like family. And like family, some people stuck with us through the toughest times. They are: Daniel Boulud, Wylie Dufresne, Mario Batali, Brooks Headley, Kate Krader, Dana Cowin, Adam Rapaport, Christine Muhlke, Sue Chan, Mark Gravel, Geoff Rickly, Chris Conley, Arun Bali, Rodrigo Palma. Caroline Tepper Marlin, Sam Anderson, and Quynh Le, you guys keep the New York ship afloat. Thank you.

Thanks to TEAM LUNG SHAN for your faith and dedication: Shu Zhou Jian, Liang Zhou Pei, Grandma, and Tony. T Bone and Lo Lei (number one & number two!), David Cabello, Brooks Rogers, thanks for all of your talent and work.

Alanna Hale and Gabriele Stabile have shown an interest in documenting the insanity that is MCF since before anybody else was paying attention. Without them, this book would require you to use your imagination a lot more.

Andrew Rowat: Thanks for your sense of humor in indulging us and turning our ideas into amazing photographs.

Rene: Holy shit, chief. You are a bright light in the dark.

Frank Castronovo: You make this whole thing look easy. Your positivity and energy are inspiring. I truly look up to you.

Frank Falcinelli: What a ride. Thanks for your constant friendship through the highs and especially the lows. Mission-Frankies pop-up must return!

Christina Tosi: Thanks for helping us the whole way. ATL 2016/road trip?

Peter Meehan: I love you, man.

Dave Chang: Thanks for giving me the hard truth when I need it and the motivation to be the best. I'm lucky to count you as a friend.

Angela Dimayuga: Chef, I'm so proud of you. Thank you for enabling my reckless creativity. You are the change the game needs, and deserves.

Greg Wong: It's silly to think that you almost went to culinary school. You're too good for that. Thanks for always having my back.

Jesse Koide: I can still remember our first shift together and how excited I was to become a real cook. Thank you for teaching me.

Chris Ying: Thanks for never hesitating to put on an apron and cook (at Mission Street Food, Mission Chinese, and MAD). Thanks for waiting tables on opening night (and at Vietnamese breakfast!) and thanks for helping me wrangle all of this madness together into an awesome book. Next: ADHD.

Anthony Myint: How unbelievable is to see our little idea become something huge? Thank you for being a great partner and an incredible friend.

Youngs: None of this would have been possible without you. Thank you for making me believe in myself, for never letting me give up, for Mino, and for helping me realize my dreams. I love you more than anything in this world. Forever. (Seeks of the mareds)

And, Dad, I'm so proud to be your son. I love you.

Chris Ying: I would second all of Danny's thanks and add:

Anthony Bourdain, for putting his weight behind this book while also giving us free rein.

Dan Halpern, Libby Edelson, Suet Chong, Gabriella Doob, Allison Saltzman, Rachel Meyers, and Judith Sutton from our incredibly patient publishing team at Ecco.

Jon Heindemause, for speedily transcribing hundreds of hours of interviews. Anthony, Angela, Brooks, Jesse, Kristin, Karen, Eli, Russell Quinn, and Breville, for all manner of support. Our agent, Kim Witherspoon. Kim, we're just glad you're on our side.

My team at Lucky Peach, especially Pete and Dave, for roping me into this food-writing business and then having my back at every turn.

My sweet Walter Green, who designed this book and has been my creative accomplice for the better part of a decade.

Danny: This book is essentially our diary of the past three years. I wouldn't believe everything that's happened except that, well, it's all in here. Thanks for trusting me with your story, brother. Here's to doing whatever the hell we want to do next.

My family: my brother and sister and especially my Chinese parents, who came to America and worked so hard so that their son could have a better life, only to see me spend my career to writing about a Chinese restaurant. Love you, guys.

Huck: I still wish you could read.

Jami Witek, my darling wife, who tested a great many of the recipes in this book, and accepts full responsibility for anything that doesn't work. Thank you for humoring me, understanding me, propping me up, and keeping me alive. I more than love you.

Index

Note: Page references in *italics* indicate recipe photographs.